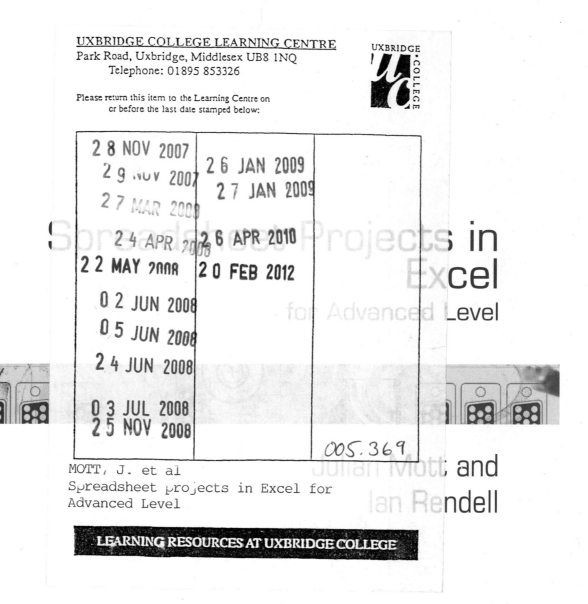

Spreadsheet Projects in Excel for Advanced Level

Julian Mott and Ian Rendell

Hodder & Stoughton

A MEMBER OF THE HODDER HEADLINE GROUP

Orders: please contact Bookpoint Ltd, 130 Milton Park, Abingdon, Oxon
OX14 4SB. Telephone: (44) 01235 827720. Fax: (44) 01235 400454. Lines are
open from 9.00–6.00, Monday to Saturday, with a 24 hour message answering
service.
You can also order through our website www.hodderheadline.co.uk.

British Library Cataloguing in Publication Data
A catalogue record for this title is available from The British Library

ISBN 0 340 81202 8

First published 2003
Impression number 10 9 8 7 6 5 4 3 2 1
Year 2009 2008 2007 2006 2005 2004 2003

Typeset by Tech-Set Ltd, Gateshead, Tyne & Wear.
Printed in Great Britain for Hodder & Stoughton Educational, a division of
Hodder Headline Plc, 338 Euston Road, London NW1 3BH by Martins The
Printers, Berwick upon Tweed.

CONTENTS

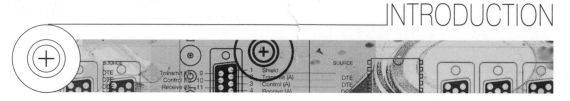

Introduction and project ideas

Aims

The book is aimed at a number of Advanced courses of study within the National Qualifications Framework currently available in schools and colleges, supported by AQA, OCR and Edexcel.

The book covers all the key software skills required in practical components of specifications where a study of spreadsheets using Microsoft Excel is required.

The materials in this book support the following courses of study:

○ The coursework components for students studying **A/S** and **A levels** in **ICT**.
○ The mandatory unit in Spreadsheet Design for students studying the **Advanced VCE** in **ICT**.
○ The Computing project component for students studying **A/S** and **A levels** in **Computing**.

The book also offers advice and support materials to assist students in documenting the systems they have developed. Students are taken through the process of analysing, designing, implementing, testing and evaluating solutions to problems using a software package.

The materials and approach used in the book might also be applicable to students on many courses in further and higher education where a study of spreadsheets through Microsoft Excel is necessary.

Teacher's resources

Julian Mott and Ian Rendell have written two coursework books:

○ Spreadsheet Projects in Excel for Advanced Level
○ Database Projects in Access for Advanced Level

Materials used in the books can be freely downloaded from the web site **www.hodderictcoursework.co.uk**

Advanced features in Excel

The following advice is intended only for guidance. Teachers should use this in conjunction with the Specification and Examiners Reports to ensure the correct features are being used appropriately.

Use of these features alone does not guarantee high marks. It is down to how the student uses some of them to solve and document an ICT problem. Students might use the following as a reference document to ensure their work takes into account some of the features available.

Students are expected to make use of features beyond the simple arithmetic of $+$, $-$, $\times$, $\div$ and simple formulas.

Solutions might include linked sheets and not a series of unrelated 'flat' sheets. Where appropriate, cells and cell ranges should be named to improve readability and aid development.

Students should be introduced to some of the mathematical and financial functions available in Excel. Functions such as IF, LOOKUP would certainly and routinely have a high priority.

Dialogue boxes, combo boxes, drop-down lists and UserForms are ways of aiding and automating input that students might be introduced to.

Pivot tables, solver, goal seek and multiple scenarios are other advanced features and are equally appropriate at this level.

Students would be expected to use macros to automate commonly used features and sort and process data appropriately.

Programming and the use of Visual Basic are not usually within the spirit of the specifications or the systems promoted in this book. The chosen software package should drive the solution and not Visual Basic code. However, students may enter the self-generating macro code and tinker with it to enhance their solution.

Students are encouraged to work towards the production of fully automated and customized solutions, thereby hiding the software from the user. Customizing menus and interfaces, removing toolbars and automating features are some of the options available that students might include.

Excel 2002/2000/97 issues

It is not necessary to have the latest software version. All the materials in this book are compatible with all three versions. If you are new to Excel 2002 and prefer the desktop feel of Excel 2000 you can right click on the desktop and change the Appearance properties to Windows Classic. All the screen images in this book have been produced in Excel 2002.

What's the difference between Excel 2000 and Excel 2002?

Excel 2002 (sometimes called Excel XP) has much the same look, feel and functions as its previous versions Excel 97 and Excel 2000. It is unlikely the many new features in Excel 2002 will affect the general user. Briefly Excel 2002 offers:

○ automatic repair of corrupt files;
○ background auditing when setting up formulas to try and identify errors;
○ you can now choose which areas to protect when setting cell protection;
○ it is possible to place graphics in header and footers.

Probably the biggest change is the introduction of the task pane (common to all Microsoft Office XP suite applications). The task pane (see Figure 0.1) appears on the right-hand side of the Excel application window when you use certain features in Excel. The task pane gives you quick access to your files.

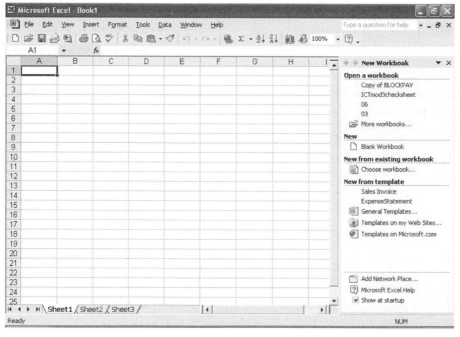

Figure 0.1

If you wish to turn the pane off click on **Tools, Options**. Select the **View** Tab and uncheck the **Show Startup Task Pane Option**.

How to use this book

The book assumes students have a working knowledge of Windows and Windows based software. Students will have been introduced to spreadsheets via the National Curriculum or the study of ICT at Key Stage 3 and Key Stage 4.

The book can be used as a formal teaching aid by lecturers or students can work independently through the self-study units in class or away from the classroom.

Part 1 takes the student through a series of self-study units which demonstrate the higher level features of Excel, together with exercises using these features. These can be worked through as stand-alone units but initially are probably best worked through in sequence.

It is not necessary to work through every unit as no project is likely to include them all. However, to get the highest marks project work is likely to cover a number of these features.

Part 2 takes the student through the implementation of a system using a range of Excel features. The system is fictitious and has been designed to incorporate as many features as is possible for demonstration purposes only. This section pulls together and builds on much of the work covered in Part 1.

Part 3 covers the major issues in documenting coursework projects and offers pointers, hints and examples of good practice.

Part 4 offers a range of useful tips to support the units and should provide interesting reading. These could be used as further activities for students. It is hoped that they can be the starting point for finding out even more about Excel.

A note to students and lecturers

It is important to note that the system used in the text is not being put forward for a particular grade at any level. The system is fictitious and is aimed at showing the student the potential of Microsoft Excel and how software features can be incorporated to produce a working ICT system.

All boards provide exemplar materials, support and training, and it is vital that students in conjunction with their tutors are guided by the specifications.

The documentation of ICT solutions at this level follows the systems life-cycle approach of analysis, design, implementation, testing and evaluation. Again though, different specifications and different solutions will have a different emphasis.

A word of real caution. Students must on no account copy materials in text books and submit them for examination. Moderators, examiners and the exam boards are very aware of published exemplar materials. You will be penalized severely.

Choosing a coursework project

Don't try to do everything. Using every single feature of Excel would almost certainly lead to a very contrived project. It is better to choose a problem that involves some of the advanced features rather than all of them in the solution.

Don't try to do too much. It is easy to be over-ambitious. Computerizing the payroll, income tax, national insurance and pension records of a county council or producing a stock control system for a multinational company is unrealistic at this level. It is best to stick to something that you know you can achieve.

Don't try to do too little. However, the opposite is also true. Your project must not be too simple at this level. It should go beyond simple arithmetic. If you can set the system up in a few lessons, it is likely the project chosen does not have enough scope.

Do try to find a real user. It is best to choose a real problem with a real end-user. You will find a real problem far more interesting and challenging. The user could be one of your parents or a friend or neighbour. They could be a member of staff in your school or college. The local painter, gardener, handyman, fancy cakemaker, plumber and mobile hairdresser often provide a source of ideas. Having a real user does make analysis, testing and evaluating your solution all the easier. *For some courses a real end-user is essential.*

Ideas for projects

TASK	INPUT DATA	PROCESSING REQUIREMENTS	OUTPUT INFORMATION
1. **Car insurance premiums**	Details of the car. Personal details of the driver, e.g. age and gender, their postcode and the number of years' no-claims bonus	Look up insurance group of car from a table. Look up costs of insurance for that group from a table. Calculate costs. Calculate discounts. Store the information for possible later use	The cost of insurance. Printed quotation with the date for future reference

TASK	INPUT DATA	PROCESSING REQUIREMENTS	OUTPUT INFORMATION
2. Personal computer price calculator	Details of the chosen computer (which could also be chosen from a list) such as processor speed, size of RAM, hard disc capacity, video card, monitor and modem	Look up the price of components from a table. Calculate the cost of the PC. Details of the price and the name of the potential buyer will be stored for possible later use	The cost of the computer including a printed quotation
3. Sports league table	Teams in the league. The scores of the matches in the league played so far. Possibly dates of matches	Calculate the result of each match and therefore the number of points gained and goal difference for each team. This information will be put into a league table and sorted into order	The league table. A full table of results. This might also include printed output, depending on the requirements of the user
4. Carpet cost calculator	Dimensions of room(s). Requirements (heavy duty, light use etc.). Material costs. Prices	Look up prices in a table. Calculate costs of carpet. Add on costs of fitting, VAT etc.	A printed invoice with full breakdown of costs. Scenarios could be set up of typical rooms in houses
5. Invoice production for a small printing company	Customer details. Work done. Number of documents printed. Size of documents. Type of paper used. The number of photographs included etc.	Look up the price of different items from a table. Calculate the cost of the order. Store the information so that a record can be kept of payment	An on-screen account and a printed invoice. Scenarios could be set up of typical print runs

TASK	INPUT DATA	PROCESSING REQUIREMENTS	OUTPUT INFORMATION
6. Heating costs calculator	The dimensions of a house. The number of rooms and the type of windows. Existence of cavity wall and loft insulation. The required temperature	Look up information in a table. Calculate how much it will cost to heat a house for a year. Store the information for future comparisons	The likely number of units used. The cost of heating. Scenarios could be set up of typical types of houses
7. Department accounts	Starting balance. Details of items ordered. Possible future purchases	Calculate running total of the balance. Predict likely year-end figures. Calculate carried forward totals	Current and predicted financial position day by day, possibly also in the form of a graph
8. Foreign exchange	Country to be visited (chosen from a list). Present currency (chosen from a list). The amount of currency required	Look up currency rates in a table. Calculate what you will get and what it will cost	Exact cost. Amount provided. Exchange rate including a printed version
9. Stocks and shares portfolio	Details of share portfolio. Latest share prices	Keep an up-to-date record of the value of shareholding. Calculate the profit and percentage profit made on each investment	Provide up-to-date information about shares, possibly in graphical form

TASK	INPUT DATA	PROCESSING REQUIREMENTS	OUTPUT INFORMATION
10. Dietary analysis	The age and gender of the person would need to be entered as this affects the recommended daily intake. Details of your daily diet including quantities of each foodstuff	Look up the food information from a table. Calculating the intake of calories, protein, fibre, fat etc. and compare with the recommended daily intake for someone of that age and gender. Information on different patients may be stored for comparison purposes	Report on daily intake and how this compares with their recommended daily intake. This information can be presented in the form of a graph
11. Car price calculator	Details of the chosen car and accessories such as alloy wheels, metallic paint, CD interchanger etc.	Look up the price of accessories from a table. Calculate the cost of the car. Details of the price and the name of the potential buyer will be stored for possible later use	The cost of the car including a printed quotation
12. Electronic attendance register	Student names. Attendance details. Records of notes received	Calculate total attendance figures. Calculate average attendance figures. Sort details into order of worst attendance	Print details of attendance. Print attendance statistics and graphs. Produce lists of those for whom no note has been received

TASK	INPUT DATA	PROCESSING REQUIREMENTS	OUTPUT INFORMATION
13. Electronic mark book	Student names. Student marks for various assignments, homework and tests	Calculate average marks. Compare individual results with the class average. Aggregate marks. Predict grades	Print out full student records. Print out predicted grades. Print out student report based on marks in the markbook
14. The fast food restaurant till and stock controller	The types of meal purchased (selected from a list or by a macro button)	Calculate the cost of a meal. Keep a record of sales for stock control purposes	Tell the customer the cost of the meal. Provide stock ordering information in printed form for the staff

Project timetable

A project timetable helps you ensure that the workload is spread evenly throughout the project period, allowing for other factors such as module tests in ICT and other subjects, holidays and half-terms, workloads in other subjects etc.

You should break your project up into sub-tasks and draw up the timetable at the start and try to stick to it. If you don't, you can end up with too much to do at the last minute. This means that deadlines cannot be met and the final sections are rushed and only get low marks.

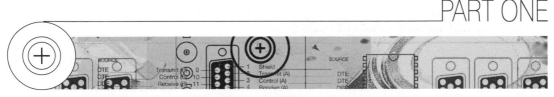

PART ONE

Practical introduction to Excel

⊕ Unit 1 Introduction to Excel

When working through this unit it is hoped that students will be familiar with the Windows environment and in particular the icons found on the Standard and Formatting toolbars. It is also assumed that students are familiar with the spreadsheet concepts of rows, columns and entering data into cells.

The Standard toolbar as shown in Figure 1.1 offers the usual Windows functions Save, Print, Print Preview, Cut, Copy and Paste etc. If it is not showing click on **View, Toolbars** and select **Standard**.

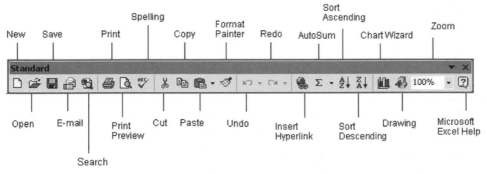

Figure 1.1

The Formatting toolbar as shown in Figure 1.2 offers ways of changing the appearance of your spreadsheet such as changing the font, font size, aligning text, borders and shading. There are some further options particular to Excel which you will meet in later units.

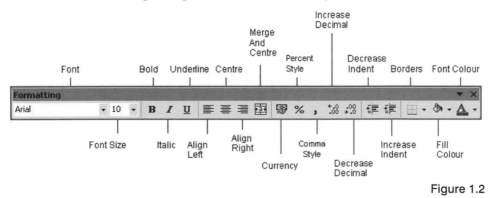

Figure 1.2

Practical introduction to Excel

In Unit 1 you will revise and review some of the basic spreadsheet features in Microsoft Excel by working through some example spreadsheets. You may feel that you wish to miss this section but you do need the spreadsheets for later work. The skills covered are:

- the general spreadsheet layout of rows, columns and cells;
- entering data into a spreadsheet;
- different data types such as currency, text, numbers and percentages;
- inserting and deleting rows and columns;
- highlighting cells and cell ranges;
- the general formatting of data, different fonts, font sizes, alignments, colours;
- entering simple formulas to carry out calculations;
- the Windows environment and the Excel Standard and Formatting toolbars;
- using copy and paste to speed up the entry of data and formulas;
- saving and printing work.

Worked example 1: Comparing mobile phone costs

You are going to set up a spreadsheet model which will work out the cheapest mobile phone network to use for different types of user. It will allow you to type in your typical usage and calculate the costs with each company. They will only be using pay as you go plans and they do not need to include the price of the phone. The price of a call depends on if it is made during peak or off-peak times of the day. Also some people use their phones to send text messages.

Typical rates for each company are shown below.

O₂

Peak per min	Off-peak per min	Text per message
35p	10p	10p

vodafone

Peak per min	Off-peak per min	Text per message
35p	2p	12p

T··Mobile···

Peak per min	Off-peak per min	Text per message
30p	30p	10p

orange

Peak per min	Off-peak per min	Text per message
35p	10p	12p

Entering the data

1   Open a new worksheet. Click on cell A2. Enter **Call charges (peak)**. The text is too long to fit in the cell, so highlight A2 again and click on **Format, Column, AutoFit selection**. Column A will be made wider to fit the text. Alternatively you can drag out the column divider to adjust the column width as required.

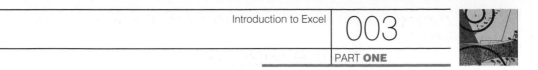

2   Enter the rest of the row and column headings as shown in Figure 1.3. Adjust the column widths as appropriate.

	A	B	C	D	E	F	G	H
1		O_2	Vodafone	T Mobile	Orange			
2	Call charges (peak)							
3	Call charges (off peak)							
4	Cost per text message							
5								

Sheet1 / Sheet2 / Sheet3 /

Figure 1.3

3   Enter the call charges taken from the call charge tables given. Don't worry about the £ sign or number of decimal places yet. See Figure 1.4.

	A	B	C	D	E	F	G	H
1		O_2	Vodafone	T Mobile	Orange			
2	Call charges (peak)	0.35	0.35	0.3	0.35			
3	Call charges (off peak)	0.1	0.02	0.3	0.1			
4	Cost per text message	0.1	0.12	0.1	0.12			
5								

Sheet1 / Sheet2 / Sheet3 /

Figure 1.4

4   Darren Stride is a student aged 16. He records his mobile phone use over a typical week. Complete the row and column headings as shown. Enter the data for Darren Stride. See Figure 1.5.

	A	B	C	D	E	F	G	H
1		O_2	Vodafone	T Mobile	Orange			
2	Call charges (peak)	0.35	0.35	0.3	0.35			
3	Call charges (off peak)	0.1	0.02	0.3	0.1			
4	Cost per text message	0.1	0.12	0.1	0.12			
5								
6	No.of minutes used (peak)	10						
7	No.of minutes used (off peak)	20						
8	No.of text messages	20						
9								
10	Total cost of calls (peak)							
11	Total cost of calls (off peak)							
12	Total cost of text messages							
13								
14	Total cost							
15								
16	User name	Stride						
17	Age	16						
18	Date	12/07/03						
19								

Sheet1 / Sheet2 / Sheet3 /

Figure 1.5

You will notice that the data needs to be formatted. Formatting data means changing the way it is displayed. Excel by default aligns text to the left and numbers to the right. The costs of the calls need formatting with a pound sign and set to 2 decimal places. You can control the data formats from the **Format Cells** dialogue box shown in Figure 1.6.

5 Highlight the cells B2 to E4 by starting at B2 and dragging across them with the mouse. Click on **Format, Cells** to display the Format Cells options.

6 The default format for all cells in a new worksheet is set to General. Select **Currency**, ensure **Decimal Places** is set to 2 and click **OK**. See Figure 1.6.

Note If you have formatted a cell to currency and you wish to convert it back to number format, click on the **Comma Style** icon on the Formatting toolbar.

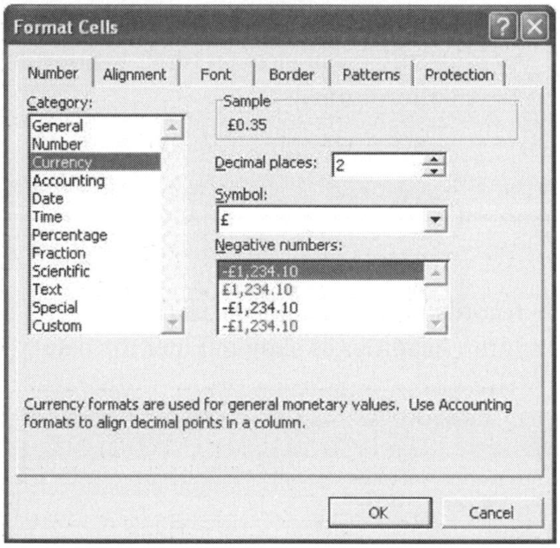

![Format Cells dialogue box showing the Number tab with Category list (General, Number, Currency highlighted, Accounting, Date, Time, Percentage, Fraction, Scientific, Text, Special, Custom), a Sample reading £0.35, Decimal places set to 2, Symbol set to £, and Negative numbers options.]

Figure 1.6

Your spreadsheet should appear as in Figure 1.7.

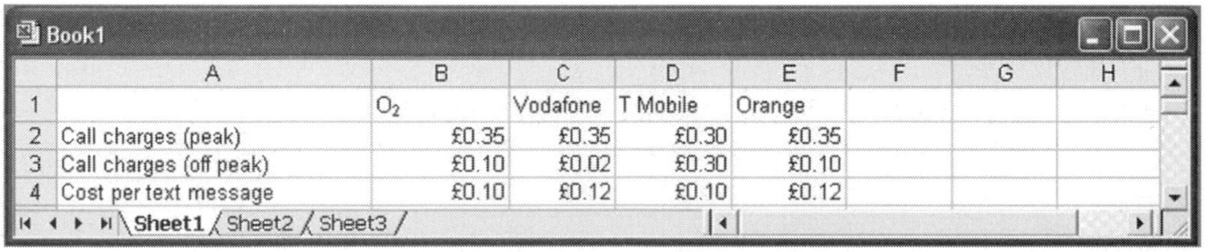

	A	B	C	D	E	F	G	H
1		O$_2$	Vodafone	T Mobile	Orange			
2	Call charges (peak)	£0.35	£0.35	£0.30	£0.35			
3	Call charges (off peak)	£0.10	£0.02	£0.30	£0.10			
4	Cost per text message	£0.10	£0.12	£0.10	£0.12			

Book1 — Sheet1 / Sheet2 / Sheet3

Figure 1.7

7 Highlight cell B18. Select **Format, Cells** and the **Date** category. From the **Type** list select **14/03/01** (this may be different depending on your version of Windows) and click **OK**. Try typing in 12/12/2002, you will see your date is automatically formatted to 12/12/02.

8   Save your file as **Mobile**.

Excel offers a range of different data formats. The more commonly used are listed below.

Try loading a blank worksheet and experimenting with the simple examples given. In each case enter the number into a cell and select **Format, Cells** to display the options.

NUMBER FORMAT	DESCRIPTION	EXAMPLE
General	Default format for all cells in a new worksheet. Leaves out leading zeros and extra zeros to the right of the decimal place	Type in the numbers 0345 and 12.340
Number	Allows you to set the number of decimal places, comma separators and options for the appearance of negative numbers	Type in the number 1234.40 and set decimal places to 1 and check the comma separator
Currency	Same as number options with the addition of the pound separator	See the previous example
Accounting	Same options as Currency but allows you to line up the currency symbols and decimal points in a column	Enter the numbers 12.45,12 and 1200 in adjacent vertical cells
Date	Allows you to set the way a date is displayed	Enter the date 12/12/02 and from the Type list choose 14.3.01
Percentage	Allows you to enter a number as a percentage and set the number of decimal places	Enter 0.786 Format as a percentage with no decimal places
Text	Treats the contents of a cell as text even if it is a number	Set the format to Text and enter the telephone number 01332 312768
Custom	Allows you to customize formatting to your own needs	Enter any whole number, e.g.12. Select the custom format and from the Type list select 0. After the zero enter the text 'mins'

Some of the more commonly used formatting options are readily available on the Formatting toolbar. Currency, percentage and increasing or decreasing the number of decimal places have icons. It is simply a case of entering the data and clicking on the icon to set its format.

Entering the formulas

1. With the file **Mobile** loaded, click on cell B10 and enter the formula **= B6*B2**. This will multiply the number of minutes used by the cost per minute for peak calls and put the result in B10.

2. In the same way click on cell B11 and enter the formula **= B7*B3**. Click on cell B12 and enter the formula **= B8*B4**.

3. The total in B14 is the sum of cells B10, B11 and B12. Click on B14 and type **= B10+B11+B12** or **=SUM(B10:B12)**. Alternatively you can click on the **AutoSum** icon on the Standard Toolbar which will put the formula in automatically.

The cost of O_2 to this user should equal £7.50. We now need to complete the rest of the spreadsheet for the other companies.

4. Click on cell C10 and enter the formula **= B6*C2**. This will multiply the number of minutes used by the cost per minute for peak calls with Vodafone and put the result in C10.

5. In the same way click on cell C11 and enter the formula **= B7*C3**. Click on cell C12 and enter the formula **= B8*C4**.

6. Using one of the three methods above, set up the formula in C14 to calculate the cost for Vodafone users. You will need to add up cells C10, C11 and C12.

7. Complete the spreadsheet for the other two companies. Your finished spreadsheet should appear as in Figure 1.8.

8. Save your file as **Mobile**.

	A	B	C	D	E	F	G	H
1		O_2	Vodafone	T Mobile	Orange			
2	Call charges (peak)	£0.35	£0.35	£0.30	£0.35			
3	Call charges (off peak)	£0.10	£0.02	£0.30	£0.10			
4	Cost per text message	£0.10	£0.12	£0.10	£0.12			
5								
6	No. of minutes used (peak)	10						
7	No. of minutes used (off peak)	20						
8	No. of text messages	20						
9								
10	Total cost of calls (peak)	£3.50	£3.50	£3.00	£3.50			
11	Total cost of calls (off peak)	£2.00	£0.40	£6.00	£2.00			
12	Total cost of text messages	£2.00	£2.40	£2.00	£2.40			
13								
14	Total cost	£7.50	£6.30	£11.00	£7.90			
15								
16	User name	Stride						
17	Age	16						
18	Date	12/07/03						
19								

Book1 — Sheet1 / Sheet2 / Sheet3

Figure 1.8

Presenting your spreadsheet

It is important to present your spreadsheet professionally with full attention to its appearance and general layout.

Excel offers a number of tools to change fonts, align data, add colour, shade areas and add borders to name a few. These options are available from the Format Cells dialogue box and the Formatting toolbar. The Format Cells dialogue box in Figure 1.9 shows for example some of the Border options available.

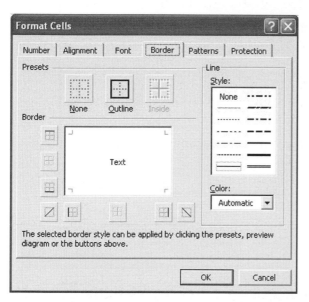

Figure 1.9

We will use the options from the **Formatting** toolbar (see Figure 1.2). If it is not showing click on **View, Toolbars** and select **Formatting**. It is assumed, as we have said earlier, that many of these options will be familiar to the reader through previous use of Windows software.

The next few simple steps take you through formatting the appearance of your spreadsheet. The finished sheet will appear as in Figure 1.10.

	A	B	C	D	E	F	G
1							
2							
3		Mobile Phone Cost Comparison Table					
4							
5			O_2	Vodafone	T Mobile	Orange	
6		Call charges (peak)	£0.35	£0.35	£0.30	£0.35	
7		Call charges (off peak)	£0.10	£0.02	£0.30	£0.10	
8		Cost per text message	£0.10	£0.12	£0.10	£0.12	
9							
10		No.of minutes used (peak)	10				
11		No.of minutes used (off peak)	20				
12		No.of text messages	20				
13							
14		Total cost of calls (peak)	£3.50	£3.50	£3.00	£3.50	
15		Total cost of calls (off peak)	£2.00	£0.40	£6.00	£2.00	
16		Total cost of text messages	£2.00	£2.40	£2.00	£2.40	
17							
18		Total cost	£7.50	£6.30	£11.00	£7.90	
19							
20		User name	Stride				
21		Age	16				
22		Date	12/07/03				

Figure 1.10

1   Load the file **Mobile**.

2   We will start by positioning the sheet central to the screen by inserting rows and columns. Drag down across row headers 1 to 4 and select **Insert, Rows**. This will insert 4 rows.

3   Click on column header A and select **Insert, Columns** to insert a column.

In the same way rows and columns can be deleted by selecting **Edit, Delete** from the menus. A number of formatting options are also available by highlighting the cell or cell ranges and right clicking the mouse button.

4   Highlight cell ranges B6 to B22 and C5 to F5 (hold down CTRL while selecting the second range) and click on **Bold** from the Formatting toolbar.

5   Highlight cells C5 to F22 and click on **Align Left** from the Formatting toolbar.

6   In cell B3 enter the text **Mobile Phone Cost Comparison Table**. Don't worry about column widths.

7   Drag across cells B3 to D3 to select them and click on the **Merge and Center** icon from the Formatting toolbar. Select again and alter the font size to 14 point.

8   The next step is to highlight key areas with colour. Select cells B3 to D3 and B5 to F5. From the Fill Color drop-down on the Formatting toolbar, select **Teal** (see Figure 1.11). Select the cells again and from the Font Color drop-down select **White** and then **Bold**.

Mobile							
	A	B	C	D	E	F	G
3		Mobile Phone Cost Comparison Table					
4							
5			O_2	Vodafone	T Mobile	Orange	
6		Call charges (peak)	£0.35	£0.35	£0.30	£0.35	
7		Call charges (off peak)	£0.10	£0.02	£0.30	£0.10	
8		Cost per text message	£0.10	£0.12	£0.10	£0.12	

Sheet1 / Sheet2 / Sheet3 /

Figure 1.11

9   Highlight cells B6 to F8 and change the Fill Color to **Light Green**. Repeat for cells B10 to F12 and B14 to F16.

10   Highlight cells B20 to F22 and change the Fill Color to **Gray-25%**.

11   Highlight cells B18 to F18. Click on the Borders drop-down on the Formatting toolbar and select **Top and Bottom Border**.

12   Save your file as **MobilePro**.

Your spreadsheet should appear as in Figure 1.10. You may wish to click **Tools, Options** and uncheck the **Gridlines** to remove the gridlines from your spreadsheet.

Printing your spreadsheet is covered in a later unit. When printing it is important to consider the way your work will fit on the page, the paper orientation (portrait or landscape) and the addition of headers and footers.

You may wish to refer to Unit 3 now. Print your work with a suitable header and footer (your name, date, title) with the page set to Portrait.

Worked example 2: Invoices

A common use of Excel is to set up and calculate invoices. A sportswear shop supplies kits to football clubs.

We are going to set up the spreadsheet to calculate and display the cost of kit and work out the total cost including VAT at 17.5 per cent. We will develop the spreadsheet to give it a more professional look.

Entering the data

1   In cell A1 type **Casey's Sportswear**. Drag across cells A1 and B1 and click on the **Merge and Center** icon.

2   In cell A3 enter **Address 1**. Highlight cells A3 to A5 and select **Edit, Fill, Series,** select **AutoFill** and click **OK**.

3   Enter the text **Post Code** and **Tel. No.** in cells A6 and A7.

4   In D5 enter the text **Customer Address**. **Merge and Center** across D5 and E5.

5   Highlight cells A3 to A7 and click on **Copy**. Move the cursor to D7 and click on **Paste**. Complete this step by pressing ESCAPE.

6   Continue to enter the column headings and data as shown in Figure 1.12. You may need to widen the column widths by dragging out the column dividers.

	A	B	C	D	E	F	G
1	Casey's Sportswear						
2				Invoice No	1		
3	Address 1			Date	12/11/03		
4	Address 2						
5	Address 3			Customer Address			
6	Post Code						
7	Tel. No.			Address 1			
8				Address 2			
9				Address 3			
10				Post Code			
11				Tel. No.			
12							
13	Quantity	Catalogue No	Item	Unit Price	Price		
14	13	1	Football shirts	13.5			
15	1	11	Goalkeeper shirts	15.5			
16	14	21	Shorts	8.5			
17	14	31	Pair socks	6.99			
18							
19				Sub Total			
20							
21				VAT			
22							
23				Total			

Sheet1 / Sheet2 / Sheet3 /

Figure 1.12

We now need to add the number formats to some of the cells.

7   Place the cursor in E2. The Invoice No will always be a whole number. Select **Format, Cells** and set the **Number** format to **0** decimal places.

8   In E3 set the **Date** format to **14/03/01**. (The date may be slightly different in previous versions of Excel.)

9   Select cells D14 to D17 and set the format to **Accounting** and **2** decimal places.

10 Save your file as **Invoice**.

Entering the formulas

1   Enter the formula **=A14*D14** into cell E14. It calculates £175.50.

2   Copy the formula in E14 into cells E15 to E17. There are various ways of doing this:
    - Highlight the cells E14 to E17 and click on Edit, Fill Down.
    - Click on E14. Click on **Edit, Copy** or the **Copy** icon. Highlight the cells E15 to E17 and click on **Edit, Paste** or the **Paste** icon.
    - Click on E14 and drag the formula down to E17 using the Drag Copy short cut method shown on page 250. Note that as the formula is copied it changes. In row 14 it is =A14*D14, in row 15 =A15*D15 and so on.

3   Click on E19 and click on the **AutoSum** icon and then press **Enter**. This will add up the costs of the items.

4   In cell E21 enter the formula **=E19*17.5%**. This will calculate the VAT.

5   In cell E23 enter the formula **=SUM(E19:E21)** to calculate the Total.

6   Format cells E14 to E23 to **Accounting** and **2** decimal places. Symbol = **£** sign.

7   Save your spreadsheet again as **Invoice**.

Your spreadsheet should now look like Figure 1.13.

	A	B	C	D	E	F	G
1	Casey's Sportswear						
2				Invoice No	1		
3	Address 1			Date	12/11/03		
4	Address 2						
5	Address 3			Customer Address			
6	Post Code						
7	Tel. No.			Address 1			
8				Address 2			
9				Address 3			
10				Post Code			
11				Tel. No.			
12							
13	Quantity	Catalogue No	Item	Unit Price	Price		
14	13	1	Football shirts	£ 13.50	£ 175.50		
15	1	11	Goalkeeper shirts	£ 15.50	£ 15.50		
16	14	21	Shorts	£ 8.50	£ 119.00		
17	14	31	Pair socks	£ 6.99	£ 97.86		
18							
19				Sub Total	£ 407.86		
20							
21				VAT	£ 71.38		
22							
23				Total	£ 479.24		

Invoice — Sheet1 / Sheet2 / Sheet3 /

Figure 1.13

Presenting your spreadsheet

We will now use the formatting tools to smarten the appearance of the invoice and give it a more professional feel.

With a few simple changes we can quickly turn the spreadsheet in Figure 1.13 to the one shown in Figure 1.14.

Casey's Sportswear   **Invoice**

Address 1   **Invoice No**   1
Address 2   **Date**   12/11/03
Address 3
Post Code   **Customer Address**
Tel. No.
                                          Address 1
                                          Address 2
                                          Address 3
                                          Post Code
                                          Tel. No.

Quantity	Catalogue No	Item	Unit Price	Price
13	1	Football shirts	£ 13.50	£ 175.50
1	11	Goalkeeper shirts	£ 15.50	£ 15.50
14	21	Shorts	£ 8.50	£ 119.00
14	31	Pair socks	£ 6.99	£ 97.86
			Sub Total	£ 407.86
			VAT	£ 71.38
			Total	£ 479.24

For Office Use Only

Figure 1.14

1   Highlight **Casey's Sportswear**, change the Font size to 16 and click on **Bold**. Select cells A1 to C1 and click the **Merge and Center** icon. Click on **Left Align**.

2   In cell D1 type **Invoice**. Change the Font size to 16 and click on **Bold**. You will need to select cells D1 and E1, click on the **Merge and Center** icon again and **Align Left**. Set the Colour Fill to **Light Gray** (Gray-25%).

3   Highlight cells A3 to A7 and click on **Bold**. Repeat for cells D3 to E11 and cells D19 to D23. You may have to widen the column a little by dragging out the column divider.

4   Highlight cells A13 to E13 and click on **Bold**. With cells highlighted set the fill colour to **Light Gray** from the Colour Fill drop-down.

5   Select cells A1 to E12. Select **Format, Cells** and click on the **Border Tab**. Select **Color White** and click on the Presets **Outline** and **Inside**.

6   Select cells A13 to E17 and D18 to E23 and click on **Format, Cells**. Click on the **Border** tab, select colour **Black**, a thicker line and click on **Outline** and **Inside**.

7   Change the Fill Colour of cells E14 to E23 to **Light Yellow**.

8   Shade an area at the foot of your spreadsheet to grey and title it **For Office Use Only**.

9   Turn off the gridlines by clicking on **Tools, Options** and unchecking the **Gridlines** box.

10   Your spreadsheet should appear as in Figure 1.14. Save your work as **InvoicePro**.

11   Print your spreadsheet in Portrait mode, without the spreadsheet gridlines and ensuring that the document is centred on the page. Refer to Unit 3 on printing for instructions.

Note   In reality your invoice would be designed to fill an A4 page and cater for more than four items by providing many more rows. A later unit shows you how to protect the invoice from errors.

Worked example 3: Block paving cost calculator

A contractor providing quotes for the cost of block paving a drive wants to print out a simple table showing how much it will cost to lay. At present he charges £25 for each square metre of block paving but this is liable to change shortly.

	A	B
1	Price	£25.00
2		
3	Area	Cost
4	2	£50.00
5	4	
6	6	
7	8	
8	10	
9	12	
10	14	
11	16	
12	18	
13	20	
14	22	
15	24	
16	26	
17	28	
18	30	
19	32	
20	34	
21	36	
22	38	
23	40	

Figure 1.15

1   Enter the data into cells A1, B1, A3 and B3 as shown in Figure 1.15.

2   Enter the data for different areas into cells A4 to A23 as shown. Enter 2 in A4, highlight cells A4 to A23 and click **Edit, Fill, Series**. Make sure **Linear** is selected and set the **Step value** to 2.

3   In cell B4 enter the formula **=A4*B1**. This will work out the cost of 2 sq metres of block paving. Format the cell to currency. (It should read £50.00.)

If you copy the formula in B4 down to B23, it does not work. Try it and see. The computer has changed the reference to **=A5*B2**, **=A6*B3**, which will not work.

This is because we want the formula to keep the reference to B1, e.g. **=A5*B1**, **=A6*B1**, etc.

There are two ways in which we can put this right.

(a) Absolute references

An absolute reference is one that does not change when it is copied. It is shown by using the $ sign, e.g. $A$1.

4   Edit the formula in cell B4 to read **=A4*$B$1**. The reference to A4 will change as this cell is copied but the reference to B1 will not change.

5   Copy the contents of this cell into all the cells down to B23.

(b) Naming cells

We can give a cell a name and use this name in formulas. Naming cells is good practice.

6   Click on cell B1. Click on **Insert, Name, Define**. Call the cell **Price**.

7   In cell B4 enter the formula **=A4*Price**. Copy this cell into all the cells down to B23.

As you change the price in cell B1, it will change the data in the table. Test it by changing the price to £35 per sq metre.

Save your file as **Block**.

Worked example 4: The school play

The school drama society wants to use a spreadsheet to store details of seat bookings and income from the sale of tickets and programmes.

The school hall has seats for 144 people. The seats are arranged in 4 blocks of 6 rows with 6 seats in each row.

The layout is shown in Figure 1.16.

Figure 1.16

The cells of the spreadsheet are used for the rows and columns of the seats. Each cell will represent one seat.

When a seat is booked a number 1 is entered in the cell as shown in Figure 1.16. Seats that are vacant are left blank.

The seats in the front two blocks are priced at £5.00 and the seats in the rear blocks at £3.00.

We will start by setting up the spreadsheet as shown. You will need to work in Landscape mode. Click on **File, Page Setup** and select **Landscape**.

1 Highlight columns B to O, and click on **Format, Column, Width** and set the column width to 5.

2 Enter **The Stage** into cell B2. Highlight cells B2 to O2 and click on the **Merge and Center** icon to merge the cells for the stage.

3 Change the title to font size 16 point.

4 Highlight each of the four blocks of seats in turn and click on **Format, Cells** and click on the **Borders** tab. Click on **Outline** and **Inside** to format the borders of each cell.

5 Similarly for each block click on **Format, Cells** and click on the **Patterns** tab. Select a suitable fill colour.

Practical introduction to Excel

You are going to design a spreadsheet model to store the number of seats sold in each row, the total number of seats sold and the total income from the sale of seats.

You may need to adjust the width of columns A, H, I and P to make your spreadsheet fit the screen.

6   In Q3 and R3 enter the headings **Seats Sold** and **Income** as shown in Figure 1.17.

7   In Q4 you will need to put a formula that adds up all the cells from B4 to O4. **Copy** and **Paste** this formula down to Q17.

8   In R4 you will need to put a formula which multiplies the contents of Q4 by 5. This will need **Copy** and **Pasting** to R9. This formula multiplies the number of seats sold by £5.00 which is the cost of each seat in these rows.

9   You will need to repeat step 8 for cells R12 to R17 but remember the price in these rows is £3.00.

10   In cell R19 set up a formula to add the contents of cells R4 to R17. In cell Q19 set up the formula to add the contents of cells Q4 to Q17.

11   Extend your spreadsheet to store details of income from programmes sold. Programmes sell at £1.00. Assume that you sell one programme for every two people in the audience.

12   In cell R23 set up a formula to add the contents of cells R19 to R21.

13   Test your model so that as a seat is sold, the total number of seats sold increases by 1 and the income increases accordingly. Use your formatting skills to try and present your spreadsheet professionally (see Figure 1.17). Save your file as **Play**.

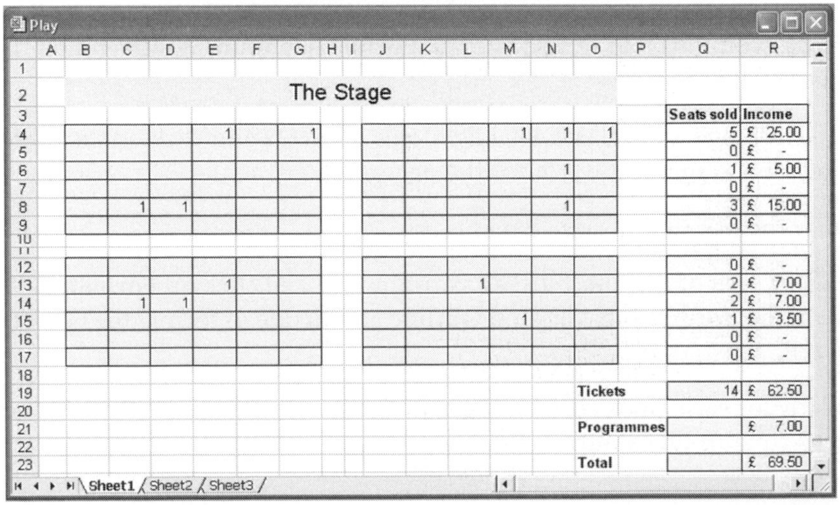

(Spreadsheet screenshot titled "Play" — "The Stage")

Row	Seats sold	Income
3	Seats sold	Income
4	5	£ 25.00
5	0	£ -
6	1	£ 5.00
7	0	£ -
8	3	£ 15.00
9	0	£ -
12	0	£ -
13	2	£ 7.00
14	2	£ 7.00
15	1	£ 3.50
16	0	£ -
17	0	£ -
19 Tickets	14	£ 62.50
21 Programmes		£ 7.00
23 Total		£ 69.50

Figure 1.17

Conditional formatting

You can use conditional formatting to make cells stand out if they meet certain criteria.

For example, in the school play spreadsheet we can colour seats that are sold with a red background.

1 Open the file **Play**.

2 Highlight all the seats in one block by dragging across cells B4 to G9. Hold the CTRL key down and highlight another block. Repeat this until all four blocks are highlighted.

3 Click on **Format, Conditional Formatting**.

4 Choose **equal to** from the drop-down list and set the value to **1** (see Figure 1.18).

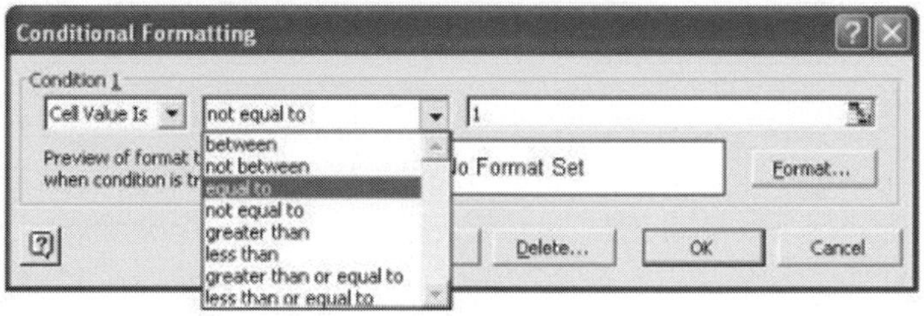

Figure 1.18

5 Click on **Format** and click on the Patterns tab to set the Cell shading to red (see Figure 1.19).

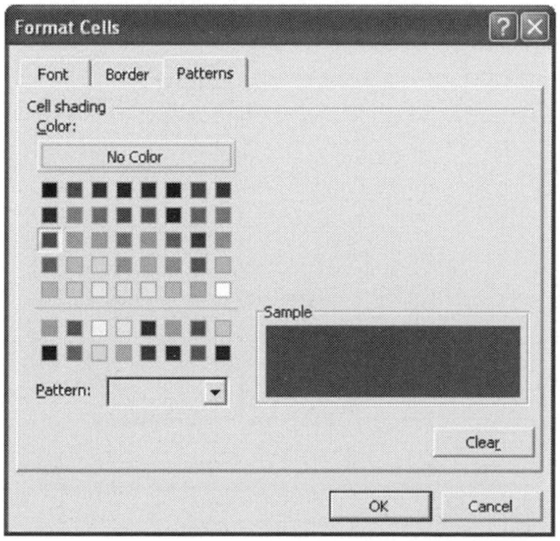

Figure 1.19

You can now easily see where seats are sold as shown in Figure 1.20.

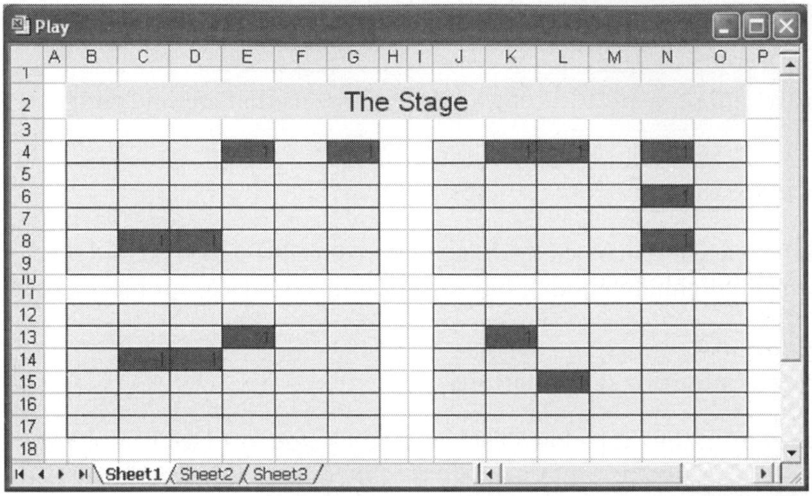

Figure 1.20

6   Save your file.

Note

Sometimes it is hard to tell where you have applied conditional formatting.

Click on **Edit**, **GoTo**, **Special** and check **Conditional formats**. Click on OK.

The cells with conditional formatting will be highlighted.

⊕ Unit 2 Workbooks and multiple worksheets

In this unit you will cover the following features of Excel:

○ multiple worksheets;
○ copying data between worksheets;
○ linking worksheets;
○ viewing multiple worksheets;
○ custom views;
○ grouping worksheets.

Working with worksheets

When you start Excel a blank workbook opens with the default title **Book1** (Figure 2.1).

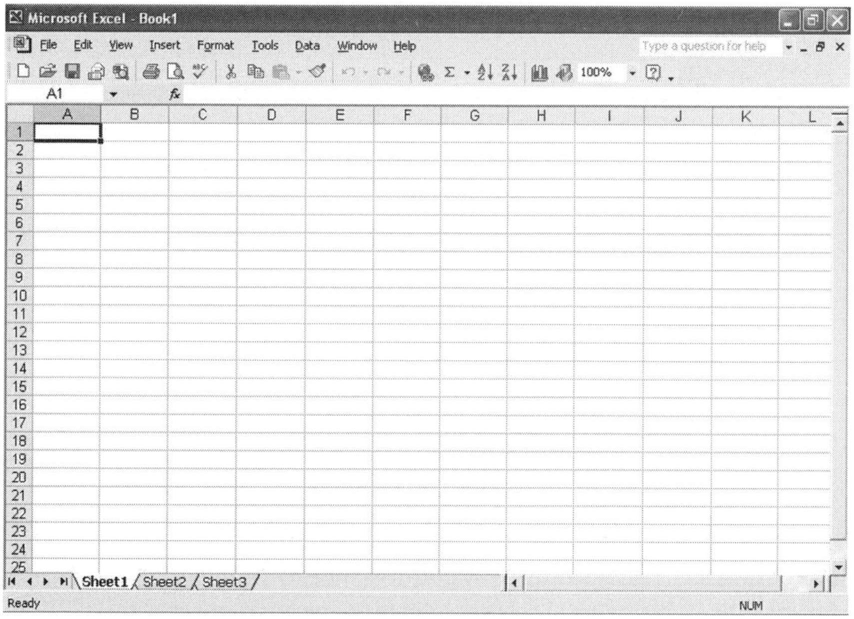

Figure 2.1

A worksheet is a 'page' in Excel.

A workbook is an Excel file and is much like a folder containing several worksheets.

It is possible to link these worksheets together to store, share and exchange information.

A typical use might be departmental, financial and numeric data combined to form an overall summary.

Basic worksheet operations

When you open a workbook Sheet1 is the active sheet. At the bottom left are the **Sheet tabs** labelled Sheet1, Sheet2 and Sheet3. You can move to another by clicking on the sheet tab.

By default an Excel workbook has three worksheets Sheet1, Sheet2 and Sheet3. This can easily be changed by clicking on **Tools**, **Options**, clicking on the **General** tab and increasing the number of **Sheets in new workbook** option.

Right clicking on a sheet tab brings up a short cut menu from which it is easy to rename, delete, add and insert sheets (see Figure 2.2). You can also change the Tab Colour.

Figure 2.2

As ever there are many alternative ways of achieving the same operation.

○ To change the name of a sheet, double click the sheet tab and type in the new name.
○ You can insert a new sheet by pressing SHIFT + F11.
○ You can change the order of the sheets by simply dragging the sheet tab to its new position.

Worked example: The school play

The school play is running on three nights, Thursday, Friday and Saturday.

We will use a different worksheet sheet for each performance to store details of ticket sales and a fourth sheet to store the total sales for the three performances.

1   Open the file from Unit 1 called **Play**.

2   Rename Sheet1 by double clicking on the Sheet tab and typing in **Thursday**.

3   Rename Sheet2 as **Friday** and Sheet3 as **Saturday**.

4   Click on **Insert, Worksheet** to add another sheet and name it **Total** (see Figure 2.3). You will need to move it to a new position by holding the mouse button down and dragging.

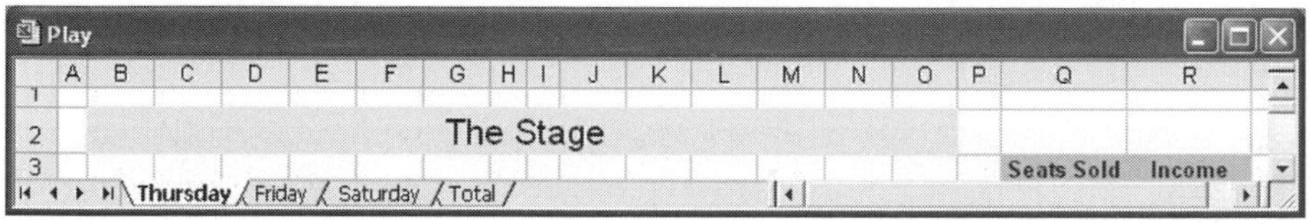

Figure 2.3

The next step is to copy all the detail on the Thursday worksheet including formulas, colours and formatting to both Friday and Saturday worksheets.

5   Go to the Thursday worksheet by clicking on the Sheet tab.

6   Select the whole sheet by clicking on the Select All button (see Figure 2.4).

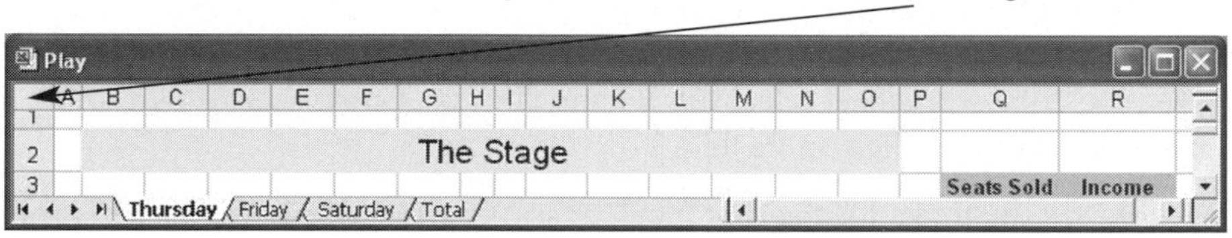

Figure 2.4

7   Click on **Edit, Copy**.

8   Switch to the Friday sheet. Ensure the cursor is in A1 and click on **Edit, Paste**.

9   Go to the Saturday sheet and click on **Edit, Paste** again.

Your worksheet should be copied across and you now have a sales record for each day's performance.

Setting up the Total worksheet

1   Go to the Thursday worksheet, select the whole sheet by clicking on the Select All button as before (see Figure 2.4).

2   Click on **Edit, Copy**.

3   Switch to the Total worksheet, select cell A1 and click on **Edit, Paste**.

We now need to add formulas to the Total worksheet that will sum across the worksheets Thursday to Friday and Saturday.

4   In cell B4 of the Total worksheet enter
     =Thursday!B4+Friday!B4+Saturday!B4.

Alternatively in cell B4 of the Total worksheet you can type = then switch to the Thursday worksheet and click on B4, then enter +.

Switch to the Friday worksheet and click on B4 and enter + again. Switch to the Saturday worksheet, click on B4 and press ENTER. The formula builds as you go (see Figure 2.5).

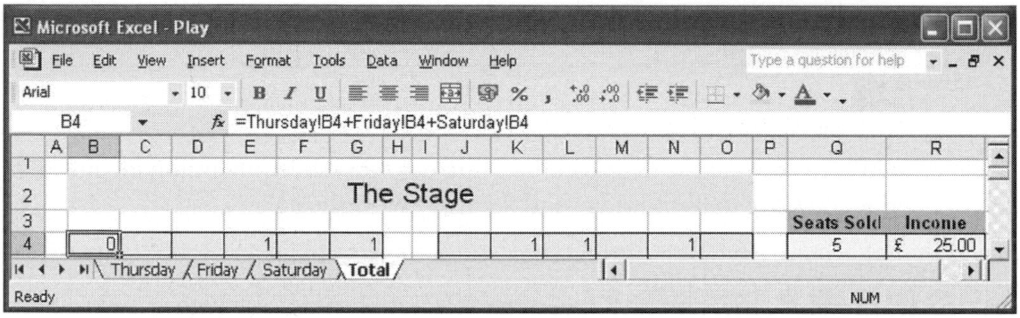

Figure 2.5

5   On the Total worksheet select cell B4 and click on **Copy**. Drag down to B9, then across to G9 and click on **Paste**.

You should see the totals for the first block of seats (see Figure 2.6). You will probably lose your colour formatting but you can set that back later.

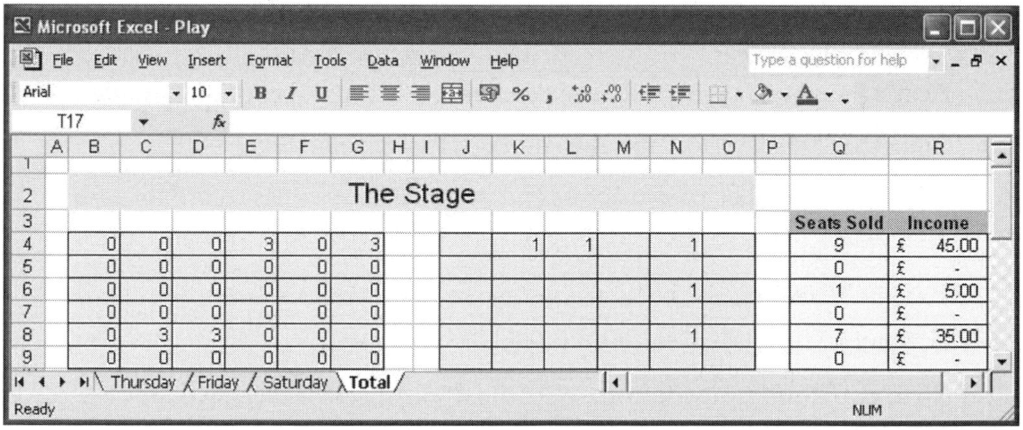

Figure 2.6

We now need to copy across to the other three blocks.

6   Highlight cells B4 to G9 and click on **Copy**.

7   Select in turn B12, J12 and J4 and click on **Paste**.

8   The spreadsheet will now show you how many times each seat has been sold as in Figure 2.7. See Unit 3 to find out how to print multiple worksheets.

Play

	A	B	C	D	E	F	G	H	I	J	K	L	M	N	O	P	Q	R
1																		
2						The Stage												
3																	Seats Sold	Income
4		0	0	0	3	0	3			0	3	3	0	3	0		15	£ 75.00
5		0	0	0	0	0	0			0	0	0	0	0	0		0	£ -
6		0	0	0	0	0	0			0	0	0	0	3	0		3	£ 15.00
7		0	0	0	0	0	0			0	0	0	0	0	0		0	£ -
8		0	3	3	0	0	0			0	0	0	0	3	0		9	£ 45.00
9		0	0	0	0	0	0			0	0	0	0	0	0		0	£ -
10																		
11																		
12		0	0	0	0	0	0			0	0	0	0	0	0		0	£ -
13		0	0	0	3	0	0			0	3	0	0	0	0		6	£ 18.00
14		0	3	3	0	0	0			0	0	0	0	0	0		6	£ 18.00
15		0	0	0	0	0	0			0	0	3	0	0	0		3	£ 9.00
16		0	0	0	0	0	0			0	0	0	0	0	0		0	£ -
17		0	0	0	0	0	0			0	0	0	0	0	0		0	£ -
18																		
19																Tickets	42	£ 180.00
20																		
21																Programs		£ 21.00
22																		
23																Total		£ 201.00
24																		

Thursday / Friday / Saturday \ **Total** /

Figure 2.7

9   Save your file as **PlaySummary**.

Viewing multiple sheets

To view more than one sheet from the same workbook at a time, open a new window for each sheet you wish to view.

1   Load the file **PlaySummary**.

2   Click on **Window, New Window**. Nothing appears to happen yet but it has created another window with your file in.

3   Click on the **Friday** tab.

4   Click on **Window, New Window** again and click on the **Saturday** tab.

5   Click on **Window, New Window** again and click on the **Total** tab.

Four windows are now open, each showing a different sheet.

6   Click on **Window, Arrange** to display the dialogue box (see Figure 2.8).

Figure 2.8

7   Choose the way you wish to view your worksheets. Figure 2.9 is tiled.

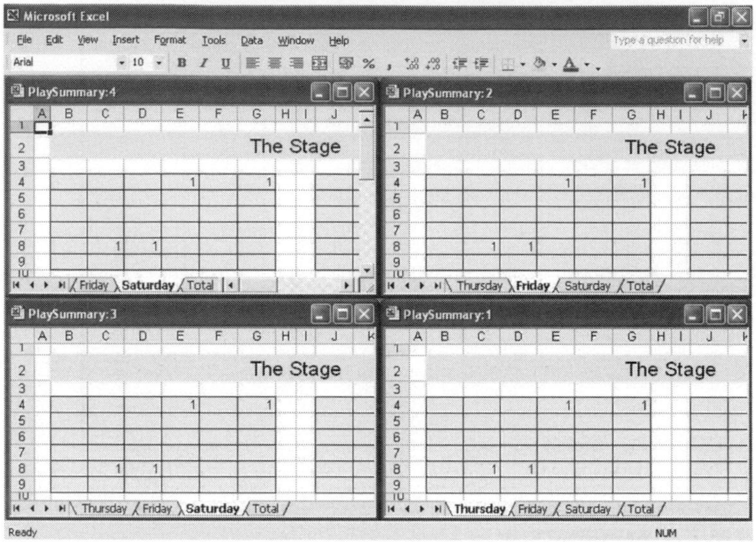

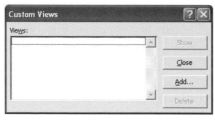

Figure 2.9

Using custom views

You may wish to return regularly and quickly to the tiled view previously used.

1   Click on **View, Custom Views** (see Figure 2.10).

Figure 2.10

2   Click on **Add** and call the view **Overview** (see Figure 2.11).

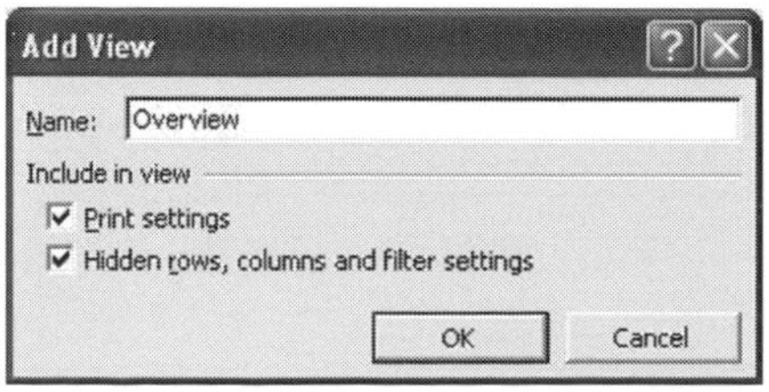

Figure 2.11

Whenever you wish to return to the custom view, from the menu click on **View, Custom Views** and choose **Overview**.

Grouping sheets

If a number of sheets are going to contain the same headings, data and format it might be quicker to work with grouped sheets.

Every operation carried out on the active sheet is copied across to the sheets in the selected group.

Select adjacent sheets by clicking on the tab of the leftmost sheet, hold down SHIFT and click on the tab of the rightmost sheet.

To include non-adjacent sheets hold down CTRL while clicking the sheet tab of the sheets you wish to include.

Grouping is shown by the word **Group** in the caption bar at the top of the screen (see Figure 2.12).

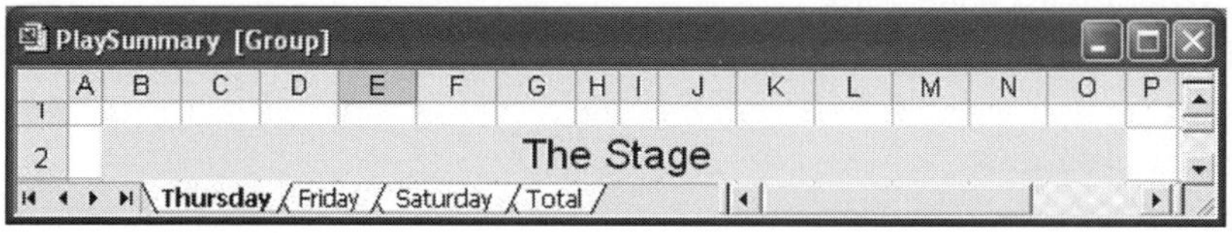

Figure 2.12

You can turn off sheet grouping by right clicking the sheet tab of the sheet you wish to become active and select ungroup sheet from the shortcut menu.

⊕ Unit 3 Printing in Excel

Most users just click on the print icon without realizing that it is possible to customize printing to suit your needs. In this unit you will cover the following features:

○ printing a single worksheet;
○ printing multiple worksheets;
○ adding a header and footer to your printouts;
○ printing the gridlines and row and column headings;
○ draft quality and black and white printing;
○ reusing the row and column headings on subsequent pages;
○ adjusting the size of your page to fit;
○ landscape and portrait printing;
○ scaling the page;
○ adjusting the print margins;
○ setting the print area;
○ inserting a page break.

Printing a single worksheet

1   Click on **File, Print** to call up the standard printing dialogue box (see Figure 3.1).

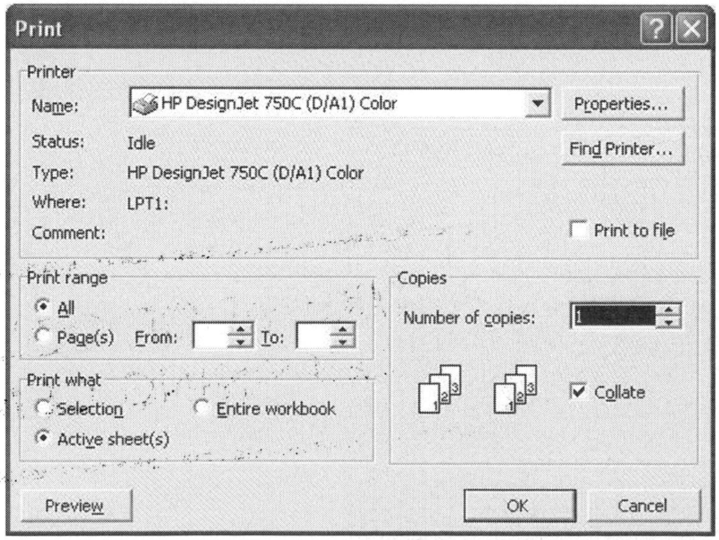

Figure 3.1

2   Choose your number of copies by incrementing the **Number of copies** control.

3   Choose your page range by either selecting **All** the pages or choosing a **Print range** by adjusting the **From** and **To** controls.

Hint

Using **File, Print Preview** before printing can save a lot of wasted paper.

Printing multiple worksheets

1   Click on **File, Print** as before.

2   Check **Entire workbook** to print out every sheet in the workbook which contains data. Blank sheets are not included.

3   Check **Active sheet(s)** to print only selected sheets. Hold down CTRL and click on the sheet tabs you wish to print.

Adding a header and footer to your printouts

The header and footer will appear on every page of your printout. Use the header and footer to print important information, such as your name, the title of the project and the page number.

Customize the header and footer as follows:

1   Click on **View, Header and Footer** (see Figure 3.2).

Figure 3.2

Practical introduction to Excel

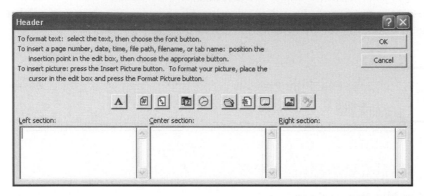

Figure 3.3

The header is in three sections, Left, Centre and Right. You can use whichever you think is suitable.

○ Add text by typing in any of the sections.
○ To add a page number, click on the second (#) icon. It appears on screen as **&[Page]**.
○ To add the date, click on the fourth (calendar) icon. It appears on screen as **&[Date]**.
○ To add the time, click on the fifth (clock) icon. It appears on screen as **&[Time]**.

Note

○ You can use the built-in drop-down list to choose a header.
○ It is common to number pages in the footer and to put a title and your name in the header.
○ Use **Custom Footer…** to set up the footer in the same way.

Printing the gridlines and row and column headings

1   Click on **File, Page Setup** to call up the standard **Page Setup** dialogue box.

2   Click on the **Sheet** tab (see Figure 3.4).

Note

If you want some gridlines to print and not others, you will need to place a border around your cells. Click **Format**, **Cells** and click the **Border** tab to give a range of types, styles and colours.

To remove simply click **No Border**.

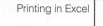

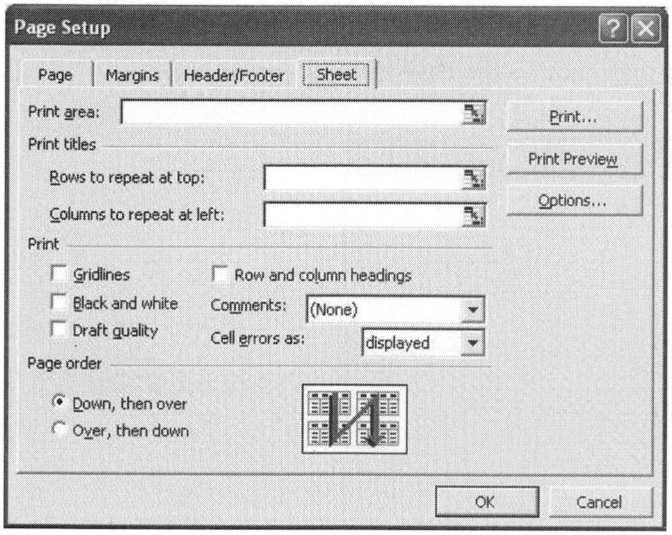

Figure 3.4

Other options available from the Page Setup, Sheet dialogue box

Check **Draft Quality** to speed up the printing of graphics. Worksheets with lots of graphic images can slow printing down, if you are prepared to lose a little quality you can gain in speed.

Check **Black and White**. If you have done a lot of graph/chart work with colours and have a black and white printer it is better to print as a black and white image. Excel substitutes the colours with a range of grey tones and gives you a crisper image.

Repeating the row and column headings on subsequent pages

If your spreadsheet carries on to another page then you can lock the headings to appear on the next page.

With the **Sheet** tab clicked on the **Page Setup** dialogue box:

1   Click in the **Rows to repeat at top** box.

2   Click on the row number you wish to be the header and click **OK**.

Adjusting the size of your page to fit

Click on **File, Page Setup** and then click on the **Page** tab (see Figure 3.5).

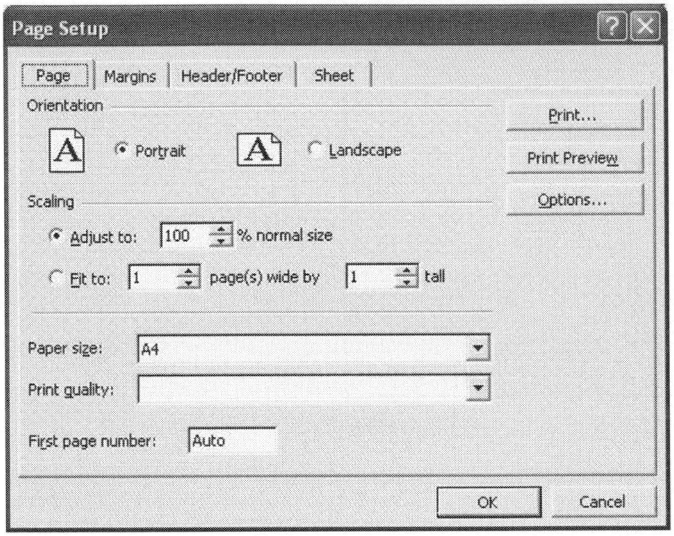

Figure 3.5

Landscape and portrait printing

Printing in landscape mode is often more suitable as it reflects the shape of the screen. Set the **Orientation** to either **Portrait** or **Landscape**.

Scaling the page

Click the **Adjust to** option to reduce your worksheet to a specific percentage. For example if you set it at 85% then every item on the worksheet would be reduced to 85% of its original size.

Alternatively if you set the **Fit to** option 1 wide by 1 tall Excel will reduce the worksheet by whatever percentage is needed to fit everything to the page.

Adjusting the print margins

1   Click on **File, Page Setup** to call up the standard **Page Setup** dialogue box.

2   Click on the **Margins** tab (see Figure 3.6).

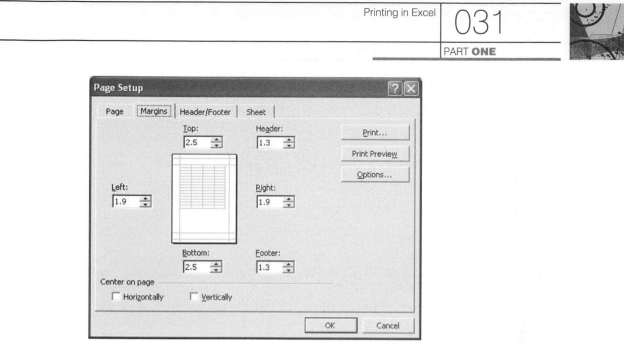

Figure 3.6

3   Click on the margin controls to reduce the white space around the edge of your spreadsheet.

4   Check the Horizontal and Vertical control boxes to position as required.

Setting the print area

If you don't want to print the whole worksheet area but just a part of it then:

1   Highlight the area to be printed.

2   Click **File, Print Area, Set Print Area**.

Only the selected area will be printed. A dashed line should appear around your print area. To clear click **File, Print Area, Clear Print Area**.

Inserting a page break

The position of page breaks can be viewed by clicking **Tools, Options**, selecting the **View** tab and checking **Page Breaks**.

To force a page break where you want it:

1   Place the cursor in Column A below the row you wish to insert the page break.

2   Click **Insert, Page Break**.

A horizontal dashed line will appear across the worksheet.

To remove the page break place the cursor in the row below the page break and click **Insert, Remove Page Break**.

⊕ Unit 4 Using the IF function

In this unit you will cover the following features of Excel:

○ the **IF** function;
○ nested **IFs**.

Introduction

The **IF** function tests the value in a cell and does one thing if the test is true and another if the test is false.

The function has three arguments: the test, the action to carry out if true and the action to carry out if false.

The format is **IF(logical test, action if true, action if false)**.

Load Excel and try this:

1   Enter 7 in cell A1.

2   Select Cell B4 and enter the following: **=IF(A1=0, "TRUE", "FALSE")**
     (see Figure 4.1).

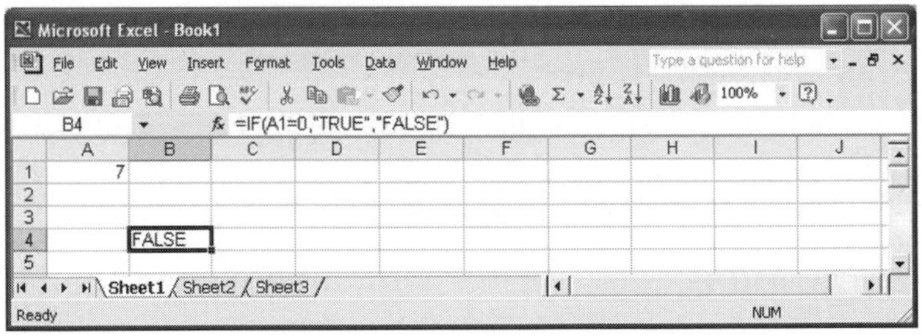

Figure 4.1

Excel looks at A1 and checks its value. A1 is not zero so it ignores the first action and returns FALSE in B4.

3   Enter 0 in A1 and Excel will return the first action TRUE in B4.

Further examples of using IF

(a) **Cell D5** contains a formula to calculate departmental expenditure

=IF(D5>=1000, "over budget","")

The function will return over budget if D5 is greater than or equal to 1000 and a blank if not.

(b) **Cell C10** is named MARK and stores the exam mark for a student.

=IF(MARK<50,"fail","pass")

The function will return fail if MARK is less than 50 and pass if it is greater than or equal to 50.

The format of the **IF** function can be quite complex involving functions and formulas:

=IF(A10>1000, SUM(C5:C10), "")

=IF(B2>100,B2,B3-B2)

Worked example 1: Football results

Set up the spreadsheet as below with the results as shown (see Figure 4.2).

Book1						
	A	B	C	D	E	F
1						
2		Home	For	Away	Against	Result
3						
4		Arsenal	3	Barcelona	2	
5		Lazio	2	AC Milan	1	
6		Celtic	0	Bruges	1	
7						

Sheet1 / Sheet2 / Sheet3 /

Figure 4.2

We are going to use the **IF** function to display whether the result was a home win, an away win or a draw. We will use the **Function Wizard** although if you prefer formulas can be entered manually.

We need to compare cells C4 and E4, if C4 is greater than E4 then clearly the result is a home win. The formula needed is: =IF(C4>E4,"Home","Away").

1 Position the cursor in cell F4.

2 From the **Insert** menu, select **Function**.

3   Select **IF** from the functions displayed (see Figure 4.3).

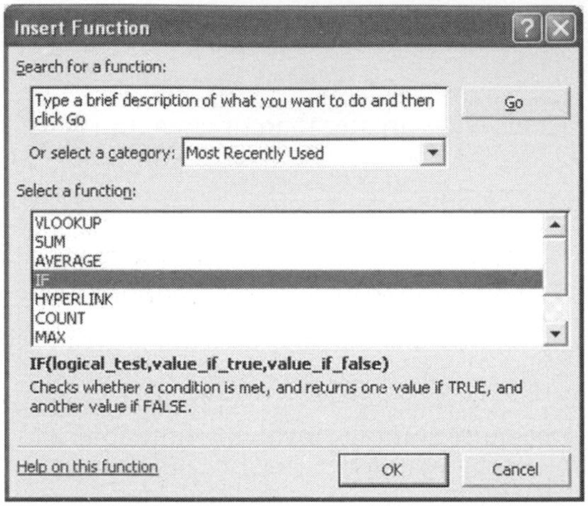

Figure 4.3

4   Enter the details as shown (see Figure 4.4). The speech marks are inserted automatically for text but are not needed for numbers. Click on **OK**.

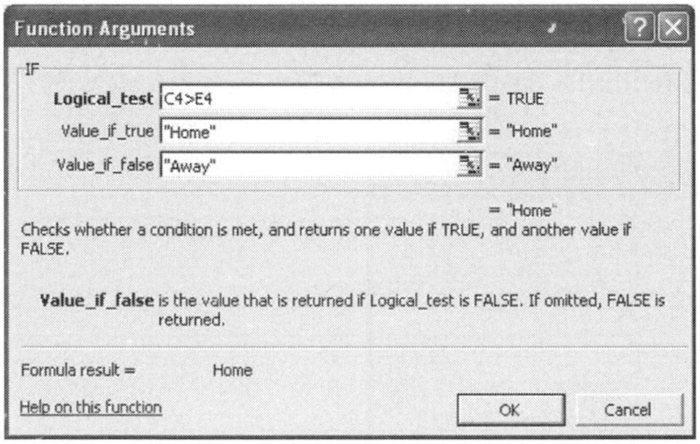

Figure 4.4

5   Copy and paste the formula to cells F5 and F6 to produce the spreadsheet seen in Figure 4.5. Save your file as **Football**.

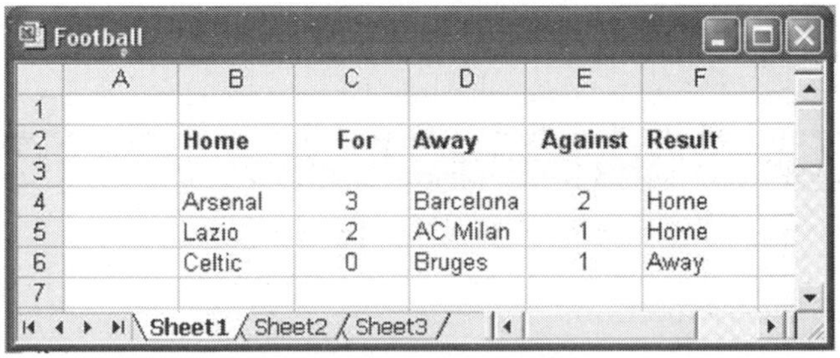

Figure 4.5

Further development

The **IF** function so far has operated on only two outcomes, clearly in a football match there can be a draw.

To solve this we use a **nested IF** statement.

The logic is a little more complex.

We compare cells C4 and E4. If C4>E4 then it is a Home win. If it is not we use another **IF** statement to decide if C4 =E4. If it is, the result is a Draw. If not the remaining action must be an Away win.

The formula needed is: **=IF(C4>E4,"Home",IF(C4=E4,"Draw","Away"))**.

Enter the formula in cell F4 and copy and paste to F5 and F6.

6   Test by changing the score of the Celtic game to 1-1. Check that the result is a draw as shown in Figure 4.6.

Football

	A	B	C	D	E	F
1						
2		Home	For	Away	Against	Result
3						
4		Arsenal	3	Barcelona	2	Home
5		Lazio	2	AC Milan	1	Home
6		Celtic	1	Bruges	1	Draw
7						

Sheet1 / Sheet2 / Sheet3 /

Figure 4.6

7   Save your file.

Worked example 2: A mobile phone bill

A mobile phone company has two tariffs for their contract customers called tariff A and B. The rates are shown below.

TARIFF	PEAK RATE	OFF-PEAK RATE	LINE RENTAL
A	30p	5p	£15.00
B	10p	2p	£20.00

A customer also pays line rental according to the tariff used.

Practical introduction to Excel

	A	B	C	D	E	F	G
1							
2	**Mobile Phone Account**						
3							
4		Minutes	Price per minute	Cost			
5	Call charges (peak)	147					
6	Call charges (off peak)	94					
7	Line rental						
8	Total						
9	VAT						
10	Total with VAT						
11							
12	Tariff						
13	A						

Figure 4.7

Set up the spreadsheet as shown in Figure 4.7.

In cells C5 and C6 we need an IF statement to enter the correct price dependent on the tariff used in A13.

1   In C5 enter **=IF(A13="A",0.30,0.10)**.

2   In C6 enter **=IF(A13="A",0.05,0.02)**.

In D7 we need an IF statement to enter the line rental charge dependent on the tariff used in A13.

3   In D7 enter **=IF(A13="A",15.00,20.00)**.

Set up the formulas to complete the spreadsheet as shown in Figure 4.8. VAT is charged at 17.5%.

	A	B	C	D	E	F	G
1							
2	**Mobile Phone Account**						
3							
4		Minutes	Price per minute	Cost			
5	Call charges (peak)	147	£0.30	£44.10			
6	Call charges (off peak)	94	£0.05	£ 4.70			
7	Line rental			£15.00			
8	Total			£63.80			
9	VAT			£11.17			
10	Total with VAT			£74.97			
11							
12	Tariff						
13	A						

Figure 4.8

4   Save your file as **PhoneBill**.

Further development

The company has announced a new tariff, tariff C.

TARIFF	PEAK RATE	OFF-PEAK RATE	LINE RENTAL
C	9p	free	£30

This means there are now three tariffs and we need to use a nested IF statement. We must alter the formula in C5 that is currently **=IF(A13="A", 0.30,0.10)** to the following:

=IF(A13="C",0.09,IF(A13="A",0.30,0.10))

The logic is as follows. Excel looks at A13, if it is tariff C then it returns 9p, if it is not it tests to see if it is Tariff A. If it is, it returns 30p else it must be Tariff B in which case 10p is returned.

Complete the nested IFs for cells C6 and D7. The spreadsheet should appear as in Figure 4.9.

	A	B	C	D	E	F
1						
2	**Mobile Phone Account**					
3						
4		Minutes	Price per minute	Cost		
5	Call charges (peak)	147	£0.09	£13.23		
6	Call charges (off peak)	94	£0.00	£ -		
7	Line rental			£30.00		
8	Total			£43.23		
9	VAT			£ 7.57		
10	Total with VAT			£50.80		
11						
12	Tariff					
13	C					

Figure 4.9

Save your file.

Exercise

The grade boundaries for coursework submissions are given in the table below.

GRADE BOUNDARY	GRADE
65–90	Merit
42–64	Pass
0–41	Fail

The spreadsheet below shows a section of a teacher's markbook. Use nested IFs to calculate the grades from the marks shown in Figure 4.10.

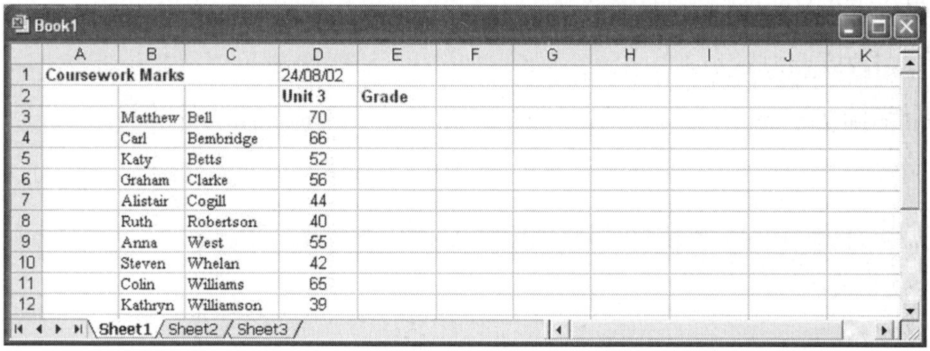

	A	B	C	D	E	F	G	H	I	J	K
1	Coursework Marks			24/08/02							
2				Unit 3	Grade						
3		Matthew	Bell	70							
4		Carl	Bembridge	66							
5		Katy	Betts	52							
6		Graham	Clarke	56							
7		Alistair	Cogill	44							
8		Ruth	Robertson	40							
9		Anna	West	55							
10		Steven	Whelan	42							
11		Colin	Williams	65							
12		Kathryn	Williamson	39							

Book1 — Sheet1 / Sheet2 / Sheet3

Figure 4.10

⊕ Unit 5 Excel functions

Excel comes with many built-in mathematical, statistical and financial functions. The range of functions available is easily viewed from the Insert Function Dialogue Box.

Click on **Insert, Function** to display the Dialogue Box (see Figure 5.1).

Insert Function

Search for a function:

Type a brief description of what you want to do and then click Go | Go

Or select a category: Most Recently Used

Most Recently Used
All
Financial
Date & Time
Math & Trig
Statistical
Lookup & Reference
Database
Text
Logical
Information

Select a function:

IF
VLOOKUP
SUM
AVERAGE
HYPERLINK
COUNT
MAX

IF(logical_test,value
Checks whether a condition is met, and returns one value if TRUE, and another value if FALSE.

Help on this function | OK | Cancel

Figure 5.1

The range of functions is extensive and it may be worthwhile browsing them. If you type worksheet functions into the Excel Help you will get a detailed description of each one.

The table below shows some of the more commonly used functions and ones we will be working through in this unit.

MAX	Finds the number with the highest value in a given range
MIN	Finds the number with the lowest value in a given range
AVERAGE	Finds the average of numbers in a given range
SUMIF	Adds the cells that meet certain criteria
COUNT	Finds the number of cells containing numbers in a given range
COUNTA	Finds the number of cells containing text or numbers in a given range
COUNTIF	Counts the number of cells in a range that meet certain criteria
COUNTBLANK	Counts the empty cells in a given range
RAND	Returns a random number between 0 and 1
INT	Rounds a number down to the nearest integer

Working with random numbers

It is easy to generate random numbers using the **RAND** and **INT** functions in Excel. This has many uses in statistics, simulations and in situations where you want to generate data quickly.

1 Open a new worksheet, select cell A1 and enter **=RAND()** (see Figure 5.2).

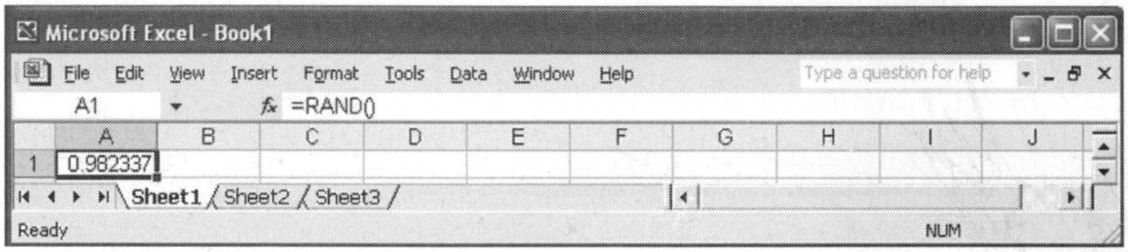

Figure 5.2

2 A randomly generated decimal should appear in the cell. Press F9 to recalculate the spreadsheet. You should notice the function generates numbers in the range 0 to 1.

3 Edit the formula to **=RAND()*10** (see Figure 5.3). Press F9 to recalculate the spreadsheet. You should notice the function now generates decimal numbers in the range 0 to 10.

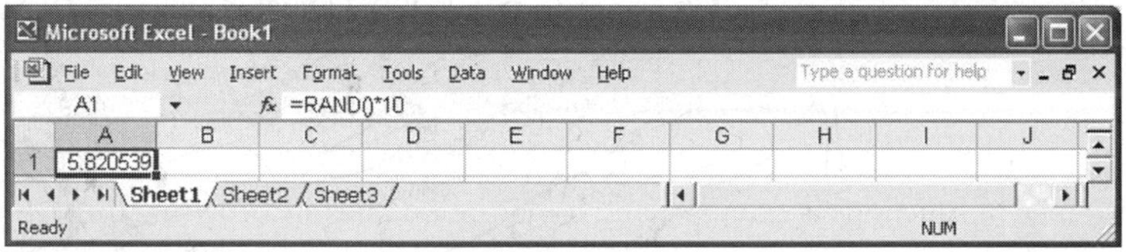

Figure 5.3

We wish to generate whole numbers. The **INT** function rounds a number down to the nearest integer.

4 Edit the formula to **=INT(RAND()*10)** (see Figure 5.4). Press F9 to recalculate the spreadsheet.

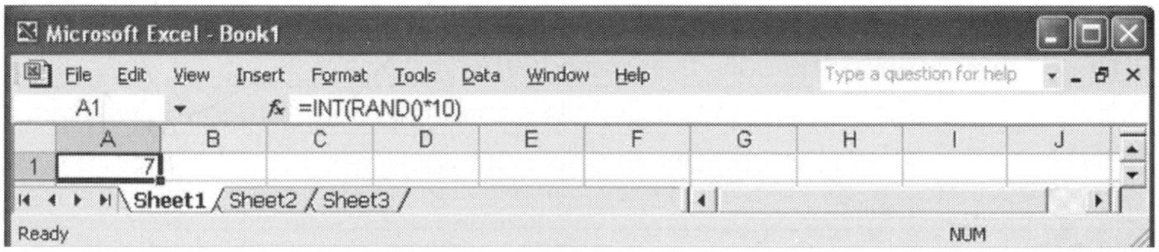

Figure 5.4

Clever use of mathematics can generate any range of numbers. For example **=10+90*RAND()** would generate numbers between 10 and 100.

Worked example 1: Lottery numbers

1 Open a new worksheet. Enter a suitable heading and type **Ball 1** in B3. Use **Edit, Fill, Series, AutoFill** to place ball numbers from B3 to G3.

2 In B5 enter **=INT(RAND()*49)+1**.

3 Select **B5** and click on **Copy**. Highlight cells B5 to G5 and click on **Paste**.

4 Pressing F9 should generate random sets of numbers between 1 and 49 (see Figure 5.5). N.B. It doesn't check for repeat numbers. You may be able to solve that!

	A	B	C	D	E	F	G	H
1	Lottery Number Generator							
2								
3		Ball 1	Ball 2	Ball 3	Ball 4	Ball 5	Ball 6	
4								
5		41	9	42	7	48	37	

Figure 5.5

Worked example 2: A teacher's markbook

A teacher stores unit test scores in her markbook as shown. Students sit 3 unit tests a year which are marked out of 100. We are going to randomly generate the markbook scores.

1 Set up the column headings and names as shown in Figure 5.6. Do not enter any marks.

	A	B	C	D	E	F	G	H	I	J
1	Unit Test Scores									
2				Unit 1	Unit 2	Unit 3	Average			
3										
4	James	Ballantyne	M							
5	Laura	Beasley	F							
6	Matthew	Bell	M							
7	Carl	Bembridge	M							
8	Katy	Betts	F							
9	Amanda	Brown	F							
10	Graham	Clarke	M							
11	Alistair	Cogill	M							
12	Wayne	Goslin	M							
13	Sarah	Hayford	F							
14	Robert	Head	M							
15	Michael	Norledge	M							
16	Ruth	Robertson	F							

Figure 5.6

2   Position the cursor in D4 and enter **=INT(RAND()*100)**.

3   **Copy** and **Paste** this formula from D4 to F16.

4   Delete the scores for Amanda Brown by highlighting D9 to F9 and clicking **Edit, Clear, All**. We will assume she didn't enter.

5   Position the cursor in G4 and click **Insert, Function, Statistical**.

6   Scrolling through you will see a range of Statistical functions, click **Average** (see Figure 5.7).

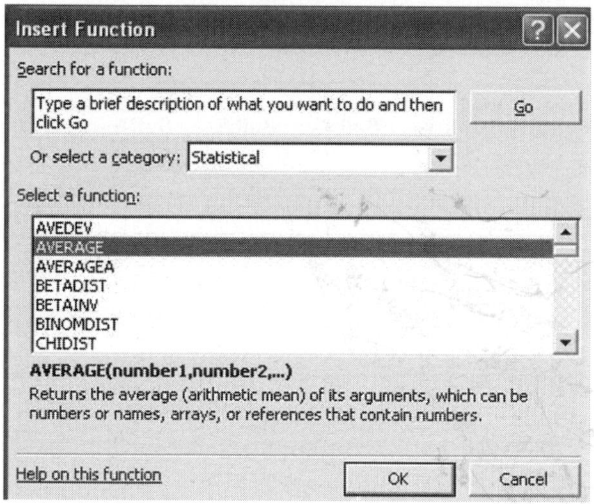

Figure 5.7

7   This displays the **Function Arguments box**. Enter D4:F4 or simply highlight the cells. N.B. You can of course just enter the formula **=AVERAGE(D4:F4)** in cell G4.

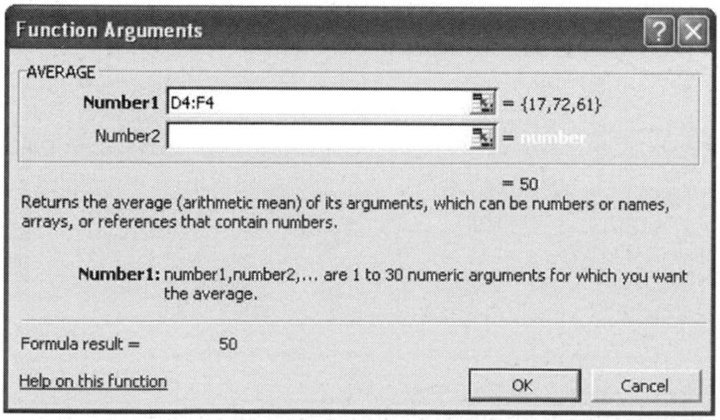

Figure 5.8

8   This formula will calculate the average and place the result in G4. Use **Copy** and **Paste** to calculate the average in cells G4 to G16.

9   Highlight the cells G4 to G16 and click the **Decrease Decimal** icon on the Formatting toolbar or Format to 0 decimal places.

The completed markbook should look something like Figure 5.9. You will need to clear G9. The next stage is to use Excel functions to provide an analysis of the results.

Book1

	A	B	C	D	E	F	G
1	Unit Test Scores						
2				Unit 1	Unit 2	Unit 3	Average
3							
4	James	Ballantyne	M	94	11	59	55
5	Laura	Beasley	F	97	36	63	65
6	Matthew	Bell	M	90	67	70	76
7	Carl	Bembridge	M	88	26	57	57
8	Katy	Betts	F	51	96	89	79
9	Amanda	Brown	F				
10	Graham	Clarke	M	91	7	64	54
11	Alistair	Cogill	M	26	33	24	28
12	Wayne	Goslin	M	4	25	34	21
13	Sarah	Hayford	F	87	39	43	56
14	Robert	Head	M	43	35	76	51
15	Michael	Norledge	M	35	49	40	41
16	Ruth	Robertson	F	59	13	54	42

Sheet1 / Sheet2 / Sheet3 /

Figure 5.9

10   Move to column H and set up the analysis as shown in Figure 5.10. Save your file as **Markbook**.

Book1

	H	J	K	L
1				
2	Analysis			
3				
4	No of students	=COUNTA(A4:A16)		
5	No of entries	=COUNT(D4:D16)		
6	No of non-entries	=COUNTBLANK(D4:D16)		
7	Highest Mark	=MAX(G4:G16)		
8	Lowest Mark	=MIN(G4:G16)		
9	Average Mark	=AVERAGE(G4:G8,G10:G16)		
10	No of Males	=COUNTIF(C4:C16,"M")		
11	No of Females	=COUNTIF(C4:C16,"F")		

Sheet1 / Sheet2 / Sheet3 /

Figure 5.10

Exercise

1   A teacher keeps a register in her markbook (see Figure 5.11).

Use the statistical functions available to produce an attendance report for the teacher. If this file is not available to you set up the register by generating randomly 0's and 1's.

	A	B	C	D	E	F	G	H	I	J	K	L	M	N	O	P	Q	R	S	T	U
1	Attendance Register																				
2	GCE Advanced ICT Group12A																				
3		5-Sep	6-Sep	7-Sep	8-Sep	9-Sep	12-Sep	13-Sep	14-Sep	15-Sep	16-Sep	19-Sep	20-Sep	21-Sep	22-Sep	23-Sep	26-Sep	27-Sep	28-Sep	29-Sep	
4	Daniel Shone	1	0	1	1	1	1	1	1	1	1	1	1	1	1	1	1	1	0	1	
5	Phillip Webster	1	1	1	1	1	0	1	1	0	1	1	1	0	1	1	0	1	1	0	
6	Tom Millington	1	1	0	1	1	1	1	1	1	1	1	1	1	1	1	1	1	1	0	
7	Amy Jackson	1	1	1	1	1	1	1	1	1	1	1	1	1	1	1	1	1	1	1	
8	Bryan Land	1	1	1	1	1	1	1	1	1	1	1	1	1	1	1	1	1	1	1	
9	Gemma Pegg	1	1	1	0	1	0	1	1	1	1	0	1	0	1	1	1	1	1	1	
10	Kevin Fisher	0	1	1	1	1	1	1	1	1	1	1	1	1	1	1	1	0	1	0	
11	Edward Short	1	1	1	1	1	1	1	1	1	1	1	1	1	1	1	1	1	1	1	
12	Peter Adams	1	1	1	1	1	1	1	1	1	1	1	1	1	1	1	1	1	1	0	
13	David Taylor	1	1	1	1	1	1	1	1	1	1	1	1	1	1	1	1	1	1	1	
14	Robert White	1	1	1	1	1	1	1	0	1	0	1	1	1	1	0	1	1	1	1	
15	Susan Welch	1	1	1	1	1	1	1	1	1	1	1	1	1	1	1	1	1	1	1	

Book1 — Sheet1 / Sheet2 / Sheet4 / Sheet3

Figure 5.11

Hints

Percentage attendance	Best/worst absence records
Best/worst attendance figures	Absence patterns
Number of absences	Projected figures
Figures given individually or for the group	

Note

You can download this file from **www.hodderictcoursework.co.uk**

2   The Geography Department run a school weather station and take daily readings as shown below. The results are keyed into a spreadsheet. Use the statistical functions available to produce a weekly weather report for the area.

Weather readings for week ending 21/10/02

	Mon	Tue	Wed	Thur	Fri	Sat	Sun
Temperature (C°)	12	13	15	12	12	12	11
Rainfall (mm)	0	0	4	3	2	0	0
Pressure (Mb)	996	1000	1000	888	992	946	1004
Sunshine (hrs)	1	2	2	1	1	2	2

⊕ Unit 6 Data validation and cell protection

Data validation

In this section we will look at how to use **Data Validation** to ensure that only reasonable and sensible data is entered into a cell.

To view the **Data Validation** option click **Data, Validation** and ensure the **Settings** tab is clicked (see Figure 6.1).

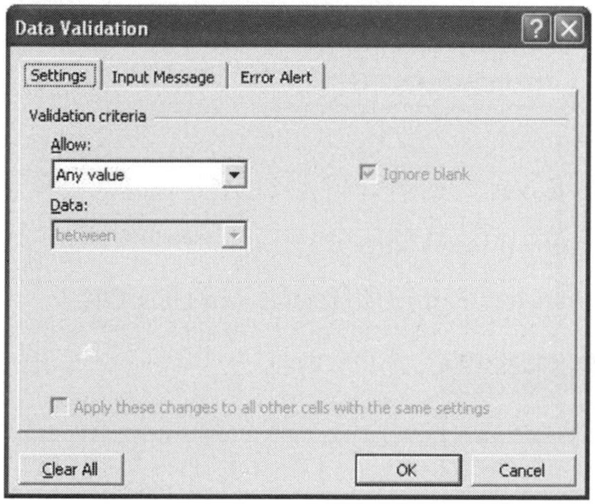

Figure 6.1

Click on the **Allow** drop-down to view the options.

○ Numbers can be restricted to whole numbers or decimals. Click on the **Data** drop-down to view the criteria and limit options.
○ Dates and times can be controlled in the same way.
○ Text entry can be restricted to a number of characters.
○ Valid entries can also be selected from a list.
○ You can custom build controls based on functions and formulas.

Worked example 1: Student details

Set up the spreadsheet as shown in Figure 6.2 to enter student details.

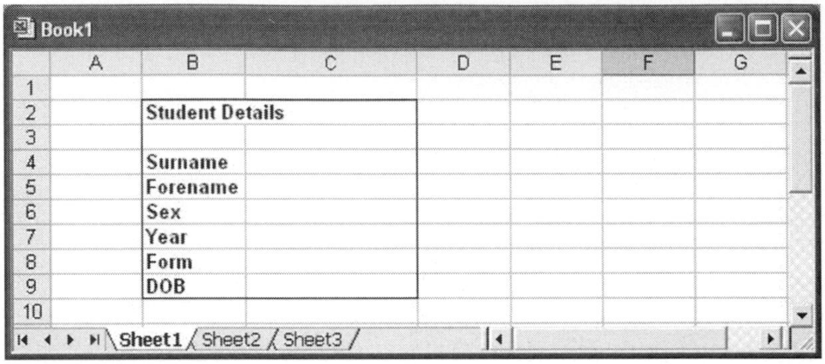

Figure 6.2

Validating the surname

1   Select C4 and click **Data,Validation**.

2   Click **Text length** in the **Allow** drop-down.

3   Select **between** from the **Data** drop-down (see Figure 6.3).

4   Enter **Maximum** and **Minimum** values to 16 and 1 character and click **OK**.

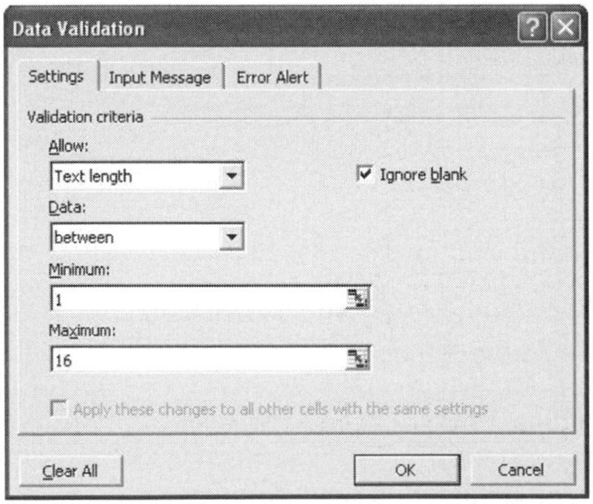

Figure 6.3

5   Click the **Input Message** tab and enter the details as shown in Figure 6.4.

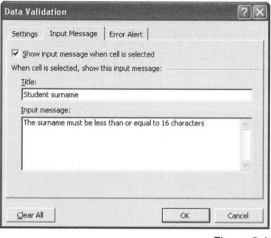

Figure 6.4

6   Click the **Error Alert** tab and enter the details as shown in Figure 6.5.

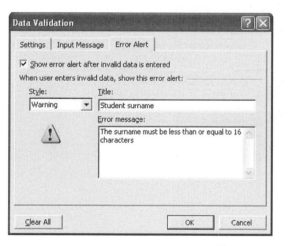

Figure 6.5

7   Test the validation check by entering a name over 16 characters in C4.

Validating the form

1   Select C8 and click **Data, Validation**.

2   Click **List** in the **Allow** drop-down (see Figure 6.6).

3   Enter the forms in the **Source** box as shown below.

4   Set up a suitable **Input Message** and **Error Alert,** click **OK**.

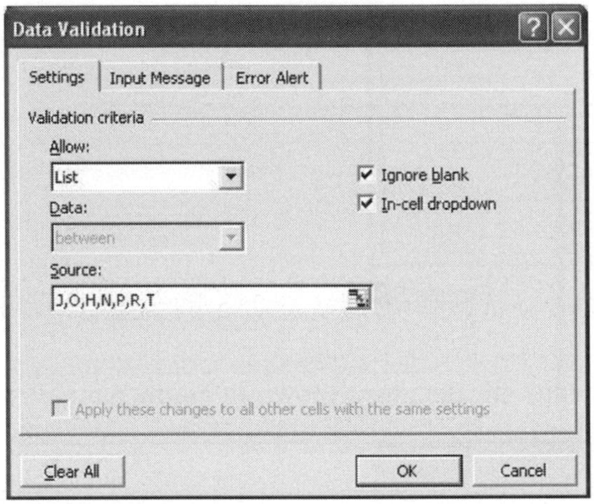

Figure 6.6

A drop-down appears from which you can enter the form (see Figure 6.7).

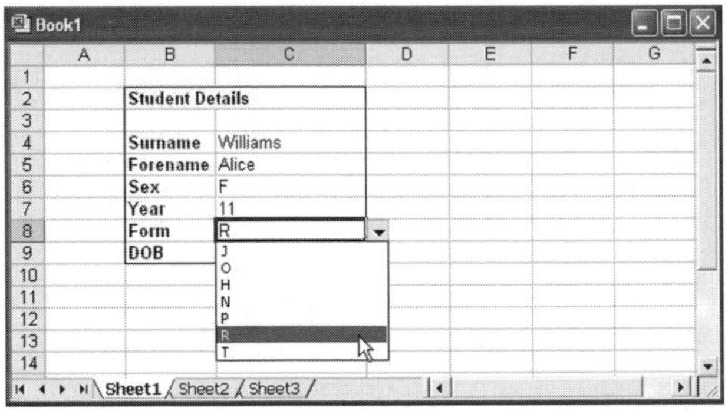

Figure 6.7

Note

The list option is very powerful. If the list is long or likely to change then enter the list range on another part of the sheet and name the range. When setting up the validation check enter the name in the **Source** box. You will cover cell naming in greater detail later.

Exercise 1

1   Complete suitable validation checks for all data in the above example.

2   In Unit 1 we set up the worksheet called **Play**. Design validation controls so the user can only enter a 1 when a seat is booked or a zero if it is not booked. Is it possible to copy and paste validation controls?

3   In Unit 1 we set up the worksheet called **Mobile** (see Figure 6.8). Set up suitable validation checks as follows
   - no. of minutes used to less than 100;
   - no. of text messages to less than 100;
   - surname to less than 20 characters;
   - age between 7 and 110;
   - date after the current date.

	A	B	C	D	E	F	G	H
1		O_2	Vodafone	T Mobile	Orange			
2	Call charges (peak)	£0.35	£0.35	£0.30	£0.35			
3	Call charges (off peak)	£0.10	£0.02	£0.30	£0.10			
4	Cost per text message	£0.10	£0.12	£0.10	£0.12			
5								
6	No. of minutes used (peak)	10						
7	No. of minutes used (off peak)	20						
8	No. of text messages	20						
9								
10	Total cost of calls (peak)	£3.50	£3.50	£3.00	£3.50			
11	Total cost of calls (off peak)	£2.00	£0.40	£6.00	£2.00			
12	Total cost of text messages	£2.00	£2.40	£2.00	£2.40			
13								
14	Total cost	£7.50	£6.30	£11.00	£7.90			
15								
16	User name	Stride						
17	Age	16						
18	Date	12/07/03						
19								

Book1

Sheet1 / Sheet2 / Sheet3 /

Figure 6.8

Note

Whenever we add validation, we must test that it works. You will need to test it with data that is valid and with data that is invalid.

For example when checking the **No. of minutes used** you will need to test that numbers bigger than 100 are rejected – test it with 99, 100 and 101.

Cell protection

In this section we will see how **cell protection** can prevent cells being changed, either accidentally or mischievously, by the user.

You can protect selected cells or a whole worksheet. It is also possible to set up cell protection so that it can only be changed if you know a password.

Protecting a whole worksheet

1   Load Excel and click on **Tools, Protection, Protect Sheet**. The box that appears depends on the version of Excel you are using. Excel XP users will see the box in Figure 6.9.

Figure 6.9

Excel 2000 or 97 users will see the box in Figure 6.10.

Figure 6.10

2   Enter a password here if required, but it is probably not a good idea – you may forget it. You will be asked to re-enter it as verification.

3   If you are using Excel XP you can decide how much protection you want and how much you want to allow the user to be able to do. It is best to allow the user only to select unlocked cells as shown in Figure 6.9.

4   If you now try to enter data into any cell, this message box (Figure 6.11) appears.

Figure 6.11

To turn off protection, click on **Tools Protection, Unprotect Sheet…** If you have used a password, you will be prompted to type it in now.

Worked example 2: Protecting part of a worksheet

You will need to load the file called **Play** used in Unit 1.

Play																Seats Sold	Income
	A	B	C	D	E	F	G H I	J	K	L	M	N	O P	Q	R		
2						**The Stage**											
3														Seats Sold	Income		
4				1		1		1	1		1			5	£ 25.00		
5														0	£ -		
6											1			1	£ 5.00		
7														0	£ -		
8		1	1								1			3	£ 15.00		
9														0	£ -		
12														0	£ -		
13				1				1						2	£ 6.00		
14		1	1											2	£ 6.00		
15									1					1	£ 3.00		
16														0	£ -		
17														0	£ -		
19								Tickets			14	£ 60.00					
21								Programs				£ 7.00					
23								Total				£ 67.00					

Sheet1 / Sheet2 / Sheet3 /

Figure 6.12

If you only want to protect some cells on a worksheet, you must first decide which cells you do **NOT** want to protect. Clearly in this case it is the cells containing the seat bookings.

The formulas on the right-hand side will stay the same. The seats can change (from 0 to 1 if a seat is sold).

N.B. Ignore passwords in this exercise.

1   Highlight all the cells that you want to allow to be changed. Highlight B4 to G9, J4 to O9, B12 to G17 and J12 to O17. (Hint: hold down the CTRL key.)

2   Click on **Format, Cells**.

3   Click on the **Protection** tab (see Figure 6.13).

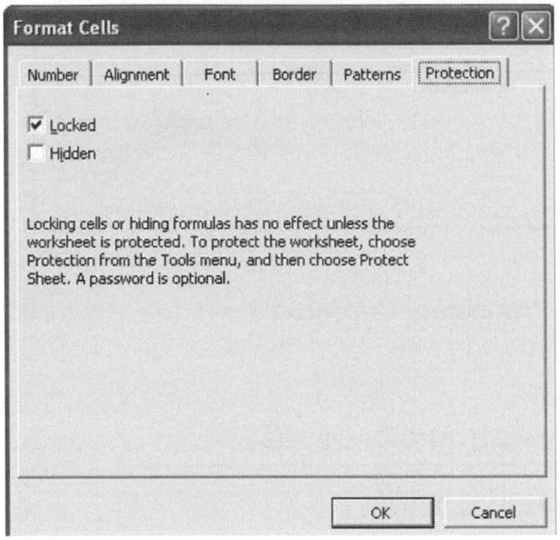

Figure 6.13

4   Remove the tick from the **Locked** box and click on **OK**.

5   Protect the worksheet in the normal way with **Tools, Protection**, **Protect Sheet**.

6   Test that the seats can still be sold but the formulas cannot be altered.

Exercise 2

Load the **InvoicePro** you set up in Unit 1 (see Figure 6.14).

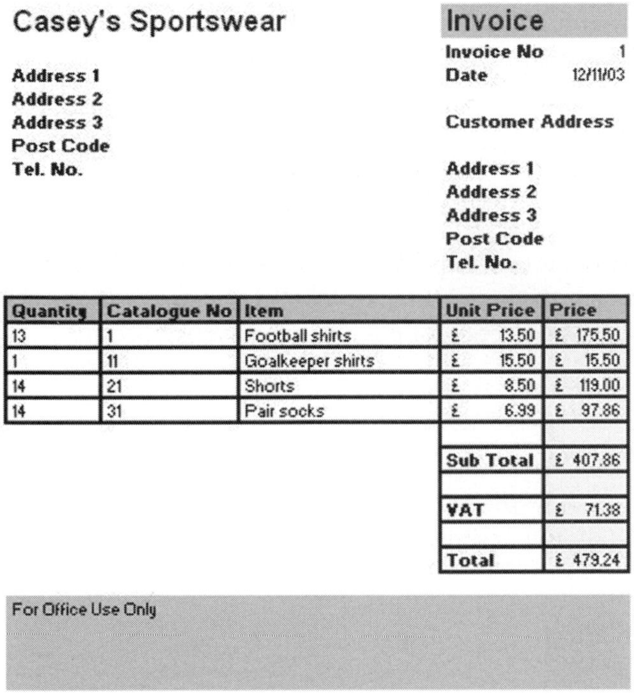

Casey's Sportswear

Address 1
Address 2
Address 3
Post Code
Tel. No.

Invoice

Invoice No	1
Date	12/11/03

Customer Address

Address 1
Address 2
Address 3
Post Code
Tel. No.

Quantity	Catalogue No	Item	Unit Price	Price
13	1	Football shirts	£ 13.50	£ 175.50
1	11	Goalkeeper shirts	£ 15.50	£ 15.50
14	21	Shorts	£ 8.50	£ 119.00
14	31	Pair socks	£ 6.99	£ 97.86
			Sub Total	£ 407.86
			VAT	£ 71.38
			Total	£ 479.24

For Office Use Only

Figure 6.14

Invoices are often processed by online keyboard operators. Decide on the areas of the invoice you want to protect from error and the areas which are edited regularly.

(a) Set up suitable cell protection for the invoice.

(b) Further protect the invoice from errors by setting suitable validation controls; e.g. ensure Quantity > 0, Unit Price < £50 etc.

⊕ Unit 7 Presenting information

In this unit you will cover how information can be presented using some of Excel's graphing tools and some of the features on the Drawing toolbar.

Excel graphs

One way of presenting information is to set up graphs. Excel calls them *Charts*. Setting up a graph in Excel is relatively easy as there is a Chart Wizard that does most of the work for you and Excel offers a large selection of possible chart types.

Worked example 1: Column graphs

Column graphs are often used to show the results of a survey. Once the information has been gathered, enter the details into a spreadsheet including column headings, as shown in Figure 7.1.

	A	B	C
1	Channel	Viewers	
2	BBC1	8	
3	BBC2	3	
4	ITV	9	
5	Channel 4	4	
6	Channel 5	1	
7	Satellite/cable	5	
8			

Figure 7.1

To set up a graph:

1   Highlight all the data *including column headings*.

2   Click on the **Chart Wizard** icon on the Standard toolbar (Figure 7.2) or click on **Insert, Chart**.

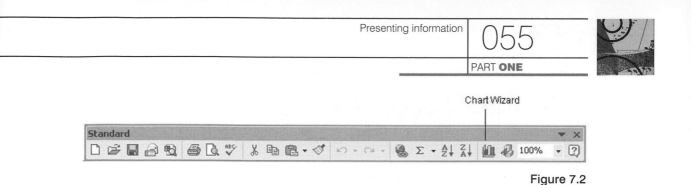

Chart Wizard

Figure 7.2

3   Select the chosen graph type – column graph is the default choice. There are seven different versions of column graph to choose from as shown in Figure 7.3. Select the first one on the second row. (If you click on the **Press and Hold to View Sample** button you get a preview of the graph.)

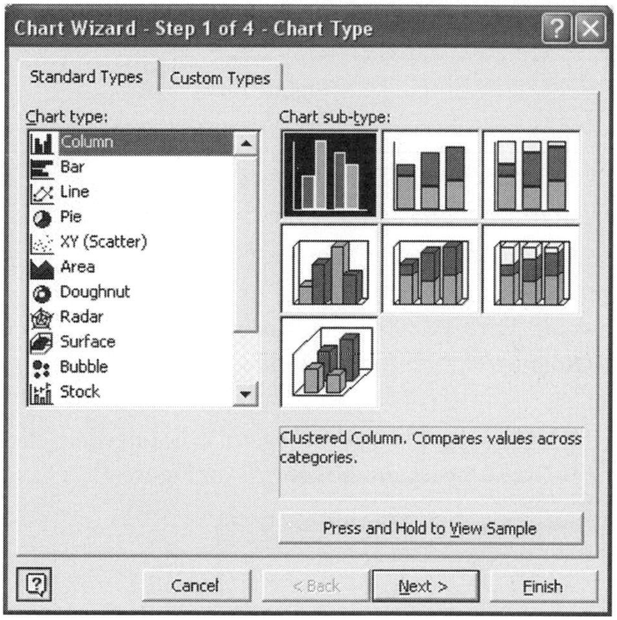

Figure 7.3

4   Click on **Next.** The next stage allows you to select the data if you have forgotten to highlight it.

5   Click on **Next.** Step 3 of the Chart Wizard allows you to add a title to the graph and the axes. Enter the titles and labels as shown in Figure 7.4.

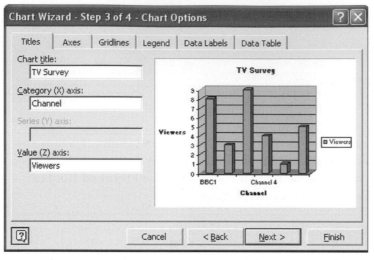

Figure 7.4

Note

Graphs should always have a title and the axes should always be labelled.

Note

The horizontal axis is called the **X-axis**. For three-dimensional graphs, the vertical axis is called the **Z-axis**. For two-dimensional graphs, the vertical axis is called the **Y-axis**.

6 In Excel the key is called the **legend**. In this case the legend is not needed, click on the **Legend** tab and uncheck the **Show legend** box shown in Figure 7.5. Click **Next**.

Figure 7.5

7   At Step 4 of the Chart Wizard you can choose whether to include the graph in a worksheet or to have it on a separate sheet as shown in Figure 7.6. Click on **As object in** and then click on **Finish**.

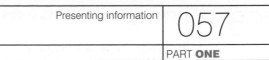

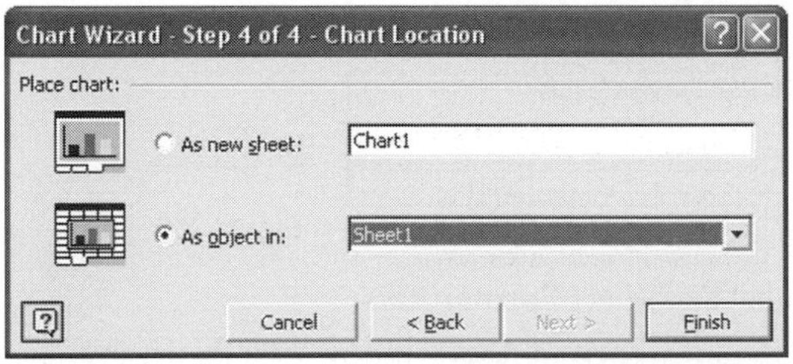

Figure 7.6

The graph appears on the worksheet as shown in Figure 7.7. It can be moved and resized in the usual way.

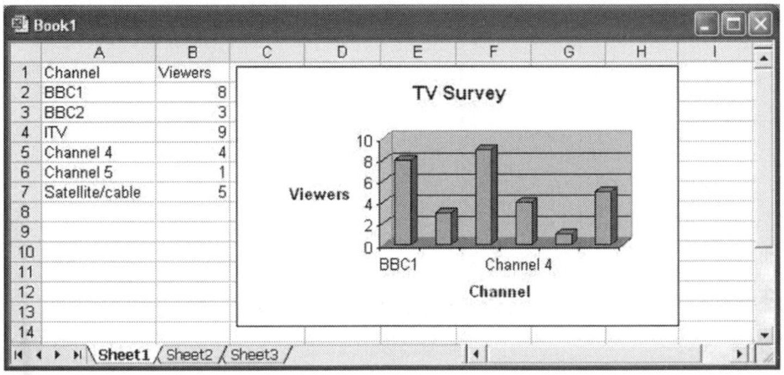

Figure 7.7

Note

If you edit the data used for the graph, the graph will automatically change.

Problems with the X-axis labels

Excel does not always produce all the headings for each column as can be seen in Figure 7.8. In this example, BBC1 and Channel 4 are displayed but not the others. This is fine if the labels go 2, 4, 6, 8 or January, March, May because the missing labels are obvious. But what can we do here to show all the labels?

The obvious way is to make the graph bigger. But this may not always work. The best method is to adjust the orientation and font size of the labels.

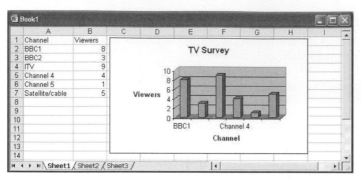

Figure 7.8

1   Right click on an X-axis label and select **Format Axis**.

2   Click on the **Alignment** tab in the **Format Axis** window (see Figure 7.9).

Figure 7.9

3   Set the Orientation to **90** degrees.

4   Click on the **Font** tab in the **Format Axis** window.

5   Select a small font (size 8 or 10) and click on **OK**. You will probably still need to adjust the size and shape of the graph. See Figure 7.10. Save your file as **TV Survey**.

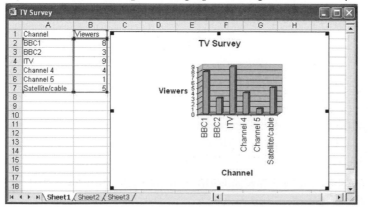

Figure 7.10

Printing the graph

If you wish to print the graph on a separate page, select the graph and click on the **Print** icon. If you wish to print the worksheet and the graph, click on the worksheet and then click on the **Print** icon. It is a good idea always to use Print Preview first.

Changing the type of graph

In this example, a pie chart would also be suitable. To change the graph to a pie chart:

1 Right click on the graph and choose **Chart type**.

2 Select **Pie** from the list. Select the required Pie chart version and choose **OK**.

3 Right click on the white space around the graph. Click on **Chart Options**.

4 Click on the **Legend** tab and check the **Show legend** box.

You can edit the titles and position the legend using Chart Options. Right clicking on the legend allows you to change the format.

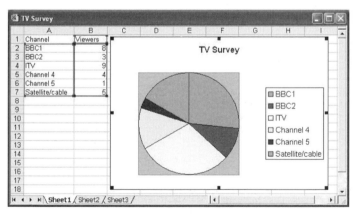

Figure 7.11

Changing the colour of a graph

It is easy to change the colour of a 'slice' of the pie.

1 Click on the top of the slice chosen. Only this slice is highlighted.

2 Double click on the slice. The **Format Data Point** dialogue box shown in Figure 7.12 appears.

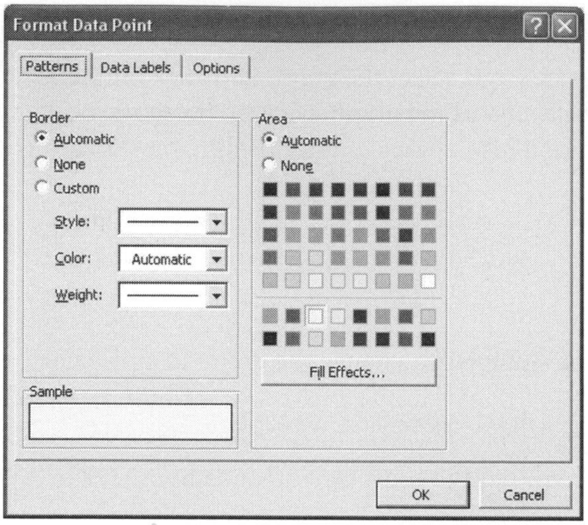

Figure 7.12

3   Select the area colour and click on **OK**. Use this method to change border colours and styles.

Worked example 2: Graphing one column against another

It is often necessary to graph two columns of data against one another in a line graph. See, for example, Figure 7.13.

	A	B
1	Price	£25.00
2		
3	Area	Cost
4	2	£50.00
5	4	£100.00
6	6	£150.00
7	8	£200.00
8	10	£250.00
9	12	£300.00
10	14	£350.00
11	16	£400.00
12	18	£450.00
13	20	£500.00
14	22	£550.00
15	24	£600.00
16	26	£650.00
17	28	£700.00
18	30	£750.00
19	32	£800.00
20	34	£850.00
21	36	£900.00
22	38	£950.00
23	40	£1,000.00

Figure 7.13

In Figure 7.13, we want column A to be the X-axis and column B to be the (vertical) Y-axis.

1   Load the file **Block** used in Unit 1 with the data shown in Figure 7.13.

2   Highlight cells A3 to B23 and click on the **Chart Wizard** icon.

3   Select **Line**, choose the first type of line graph and click on **Next**. Step 2 of the Chart Wizard gives you a preview of the graph. It has two lines and is not the graph we require.

4   Click on the **Series** tab as shown in Figure 7.14.

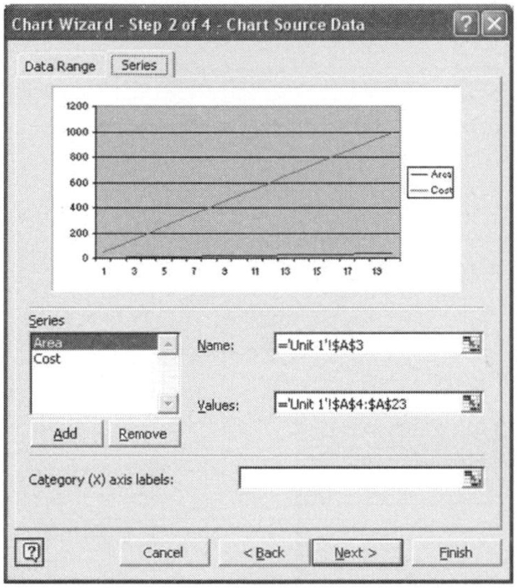

Figure 7.14

5   The preview shows two lines, one for Area and one for Cost. They are not graphed against each other. We do not want the Area line. As it is already selected click on **Remove**.

6   In the **Category (X) axis labels** box enter **=Sheet1!A4:A23** (the labels of the X-axis are stored in these cells). See Figure 7.15. Click on **Next**.

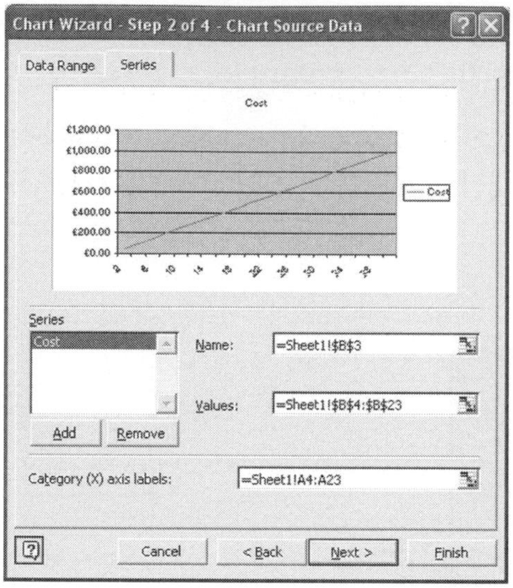

Figure 7.15

7   At Step 3 of the Chart Wizard continue as before, adding the titles and deleting the legend. The graph will look like Figure 7.16.

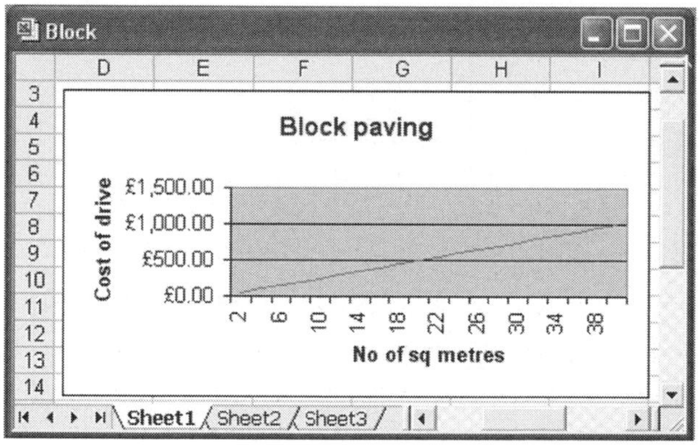

Figure 7.16

Customizing your graph

You can customize your graph in many ways to suit your presentation needs. Among the changes you may consider are:

1   resizing the graph as before;

2   formatting the X-axis labels as before;

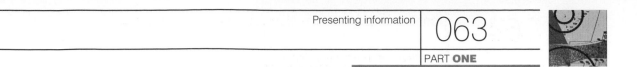

3   formatting the Y-axis labels to no decimal places;

4   making the title bigger – right click on the title and select **Format Chart Title**;

5   removing the grey box behind the graph – double click on the grey area and click on **Area, None**;

6   removing the horizontal grid – click on a horizontal line and press the DELETE key;

7   removing the rectangle around the graph in the same way;

8   changing the colour and thickness of the line – double click on the line and change the colour and the weight.

These changes are shown in Figure 7.17.

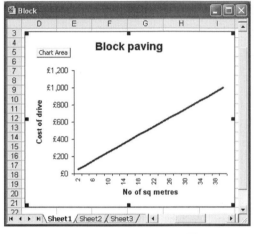

Figure 7.17

Taking your graph into Microsoft Word

You can take your graph into Microsoft Word simply by selecting the graph and clicking on **Edit, Copy**. Switch to Word and use **Edit, Paste**. This is very useful in reports.

You can get your graph to update automatically in Word; that is any changes in the data in the spreadsheet will change the graph in Word. Use **Edit, Paste Special, Paste Link** in Word instead when moving the graph into Word. This is an example of OLE (Object Linking and Embedding). If you double click on the linked graph in Word, the Excel file with the graph in it will open.

Using the Drawing toolbar

The Drawing toolbar contains many useful features that can help improve the presentation of your spreadsheet. See Figure 7.18.

Turn on the Drawing toolbar by clicking on **Forms, Toolbars, Drawing**.

Unlike the other toolbars, the Drawing toolbar appears at the bottom of the screen.

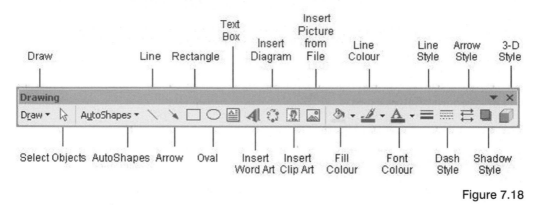

Figure 7.18

Features of the Drawing toolbar

The icons on the Drawing toolbar enable you to move objects, rotate them, align them with other objects, space them evenly and format the colour of text, background and borders. You can also add shapes such as lines, arrows, rectangles and circles. It is far more fun to explore the many options yourself!

AutoShapes and 3D

The AutoShapes enable you to add other shapes such as arrows, stars and speech bubbles (called Callouts). These shapes can be made to look three-dimensional using the 3-D icon. To insert a 3-D shape:

1 Turn on the Drawing toolbar.

2 Click on **AutoShapes** and choose a shape.

3 Click on the **3-D Style** icon and choose a 3D shape.

4 If you right click on your shape, you can use **Format AutoShape** to choose a colour or **Add Text** to enter text.

Examples of shapes are shown in Figure 7.19.

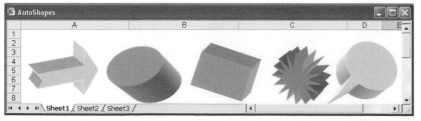

Figure 7.19

Formatting cells can really improve your output, make important information stand out, make it easier to read and make it look more professional as shown in Figure 7.20. A star AutoShape has been used. See if you can re-create this advert.

Hatfield Travel

	A	B	C	D	E
1		**Hatfield Travel**			
2	**DESTINATION**	**STANDARD RETURN**	**FIRST CLASS RETURN**		
3	Paris	£85	£160		
4	Dijon, Angers	£90	£170		**NEW!**
5	Lyon, Bordeaux	£110	£190		
6	Avignon, Montpellier, Nice, Marseille, Toulouse	£120	£200		
7					

Sheet1 / Sheet2 / Sheet3 /

Figure 7.20

Exercise

1   Set up the advertisement shown in Figure 7.21.

Quickprint

	A	B	C	D	E	F	G	H
1	great value			**Quickprint**				
2			**PRINT SIZE**	**24 EXP**	**NUMBER**	**36 EXP**	**NUMBER**	**TOTAL**
3			Regular	£1.99		£2.99		£0.00
4			50% bigger	£2.49		£3.49		£0.00
5			30% bigger	£2.99		£3.99		£0.00
6			Postage per film			£0.70	0	£0.00
7								
8			Extra sets of prints	£1.99		£2.99		£0.00
9								
10				**NEW FILMS**		**PRICE**	**QTY**	**AMOUNT**
11				35 mm 24 exp		£1.99		£0.00
12		Quickprint		35 mm 36 exp		£2.32		£0.00
13								
14								£0.00
15								
16								

Sheet1 / Sheet2 / Sheet3 /

Figure 7.21

Hint

o   Use formulas in column H to calculate the totals when the number of films is entered.

o   Use WordArt for the writing on the box.

o   Use **Format**, **Cells**, **Alignment** to slant the title text.

2   A Gantt chart like this is a common way of presenting project timetables. Set up a Gantt chart similar to this.

	A	B	C	D	E	F	G	H	I
					Jennifer Roberts				
1					A level ICT project - Gantt chart				
2		Task \ Week beginning	05-Oct-03	12-Oct-03	19-Oct-03	26-Oct-03	02-Nov-03	09-Nov-03	16-No
3		Decide on project.							
4	ANALYSIS	Draw up project timetable/Gantt chart				H			
5		Write a brief description of the problem.				A			
6		Make rough notes of the requirements				L			
7		Document full specification				F			
8		Describe hardware and software available				o			
9		Describe evaluation criteria				T			
10	DESIGN	Draw rough plans of sheets and front end				E			
11		Improve designs so that a third party could use				R			
12		Draw up test plan.				M			
13		Define test data, expected results							
14		Define validation							
15		Define any macros needed.							
16	IMPL	Start implementation. Set up sheet with cars and groups							
17		Set up quotation worksheet							

I will need to talk to my user at half term.

Figure 7.22

3   Find some information about your local weather in a newspaper or from the internet (use www.bbc.co.uk) *or* use the weather readings for the week ending 21/10/02 we used in Unit 5.

	Mon	Tue	Wed	Thur	Fri	Sat	Sun
Temperature (C°)	12	13	15	12	12	12	11
Rainfall (mm)	0	0	4	3	2	0	0
Pressure (Mb)	996	1000	1000	888	992	946	1004
Sunshine (hrs)	1	2	2	1	1	2	2

Present the information graphically with a range of graphs. Present your graphs in Word and ensure they update automatically such that any changes in the data in the spreadsheet will update the graphs in Word.

⊕ Unit 8 The LOOKUP function and combo boxes

In this unit, you will learn how to take data from a table and insert it in your spreadsheet using:

- ○ naming cells;
- ○ LOOKUP functions;
- ○ combo boxes.

Naming cells

As we saw in Unit 1, we can give a name to any cell or range of cells. This can make it much easier to find required data.

1   In a new workbook, enter the data shown in Figure 8.1 giving the cost of sending a small packet abroad.

	A	B	C	D	E	F
1	No	Max weight (g)	Europe	World Zone 1	World Zone 2	
2	1	100	£0.87	£1.15	£1.15	
3	2	120	£0.96	£1.32	£1.34	
4	3	140	£1.05	£1.49	£1.53	
5	4	160	£1.14	£1.66	£1.72	
6	5	180	£1.23	£1.83	£1.91	
7	6	200	£1.32	£2.00	£2.10	
8						

Book1 — Sheet1 / Sheet2 / Sheet3 /

Figure 8.1

Note

The numbers in column A are important as we shall see later.

2   Highlight the cells from A2 to E7 and click on **Insert, Name, Define**. Enter the name **weight** and click **OK**.

3   On Sheet2 set up the table in Figure 8.2 defining which countries are in which zone for postage.

Practical introduction to Excel

	A	B	C	D
1	No	Country	Zone	
2	1	Australia	World Zone 2	
3	2	Canada	World Zone 1	
4	3	France	Europe	
5	4	Germany	Europe	
6	5	Israel	World Zone 1	
7	6	Italy	Europe	
8	7	Japan	World Zone 2	
9	8	New Zealand	World Zone 2	
10	9	Spain	Europe	
11	10	USA	World Zone 1	

Figure 8.2

4   Highlight the cells from A2 to C11 and click on **Insert, Name, Define**. Enter the name **zone** and click **OK**.

5   Save the workbook as **Postage**.

One reason for naming cells is that if you click on the **Name Box** drop-down arrow, a list of all the named ranges appears as shown in Figure 8.3. Click on **weight** to go to the weight table.

		C	D
weight			
zone	y	Zone	
2	1 Australia	World Zone 2	
3	2 Canada	World Zone 1	
4	3 France	Europe	
5	4 Germany	Europe	
6	5 Israel	World Zone 1	
7	6 Italy	Europe	
8	7 Japan	World Zone 2	
9	8 New Zealand	World Zone 2	
10	9 Spain	Europe	
11	10 USA	World Zone 1	
12			

Figure 8.3

The LOOKUP function

The LOOKUP function looks up data in a table or list.

There are three lookup functions, **LOOKUP, VLOOKUP** and **HLOOKUP**. We will concentrate on the most commonly used function, VLOOKUP (vertical lookup).

HLOOKUP and LOOKUP are very similar and may be worth investigating further later.

	A	B	C	D
1	No	Country	Zone	
2	1	Australia	World Zone 2	
3	2	Canada	World Zone 1	
4	3	France	Europe	
5	4	Germany	Europe	
6	5	Israel	World Zone 1	
7	6	Italy	Europe	
8	7	Japan	World Zone 2	
9	8	New Zealand	World Zone 2	
10	9	Spain	Europe	
11	10	USA	World Zone 1	

Postage — Sheet1 \ **Sheet2** / Sheet...

Figure 8.4

An example of the LOOKUP function is **=VLOOKUP(7,A2:C11,2)**.
Referring to the table in Figure 8.4:

7 is the value to be looked up which the function finds in cell A8.
A2:C11 is the range where the lookup takes place.
2 points to the data in the 2nd column.
The function **=VLOOKUP(7,A2:C11,2)** would return **Japan** in the above example.

Examples of the LOOKUP function

1   Enter **=VLOOKUP(2,A2:C11,3)** into cell F10 of Sheet2.

It looks in the table between cell A2 and cell C11, going to the first column of the table shown in Figure 8.4 until it finds the row with **2** in it.

It then finds the data in this row which is in column **3** of the table.

Check that it returns the value **World Zone 1**.

2   You can use named ranges of cells in a LOOKUP function.

Enter **=VLOOKUP(3,zone,3)** into cell F12 of Sheet2.

Check that it returns the value **Europe**.

3   Switch back to Sheet1. Enter **=VLOOKUP(4,weight,5)** into cell G2. Check that the value is **1.72**.

4   Highlight the cells you have just used in this exercise and click **Edit, Clear, All**.

Note   The first column of the table must be in **alphabetical or numerical order** for LOOKUP to work.

Combo boxes

A **Combo Box** (sometimes called a Drop-Down Box) is a list of items from which you can choose one item of data.

To set up a combo box:

1 Load the workbook **Postage** and switch to Sheet2.

2 Display the Forms toolbar by clicking on **View, Toolbars, Forms** (see Figure 8.5).

Figure 8.5

3 Click on the Combo Box icon and drag out a box on the screen near cells E4 and F4 (see Figure 8.6).

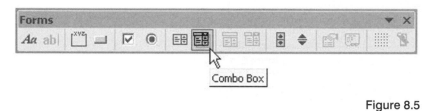

Figure 8.6

Note   If you hold the ALT key down, you will align the combo box with the cell gridlines. The smallest height for a combo box is slightly more than the default height for a cell.

---

4 Right click on the box and click on **Format Control**. The **Format Control** dialogue box seen in Figure 8.7 appears.

5 In the Input Range box enter **B2:B11**.

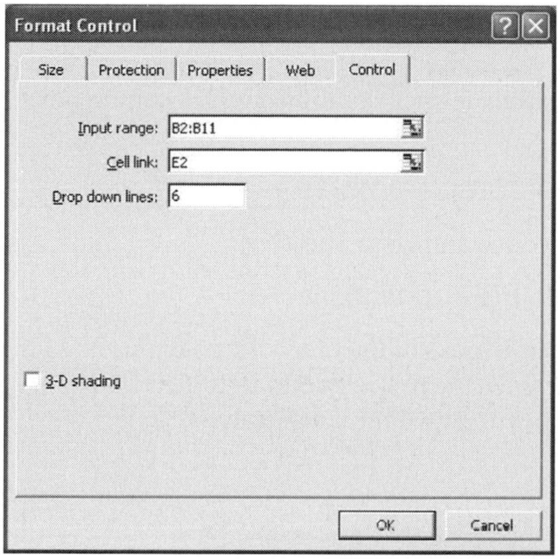

Format Control

| Size | Protection | Properties | Web | Control |

Input range: B2:B11

Cell link: E2

Drop down lines: 6

☐ 3-D shading

OK   Cancel

Figure 8.7

6   In the Cell link box type in the cell which will store the data from the Combo Box, **E2**.

7   Change the **Drop down lines** to **6**. Click on **OK** and save your work.

If you click on the arrow on your combo box, you get six lines of different choices. If you choose the fourth item on the list (Germany) cell E2 changes to 4 (see Figure 8.8).

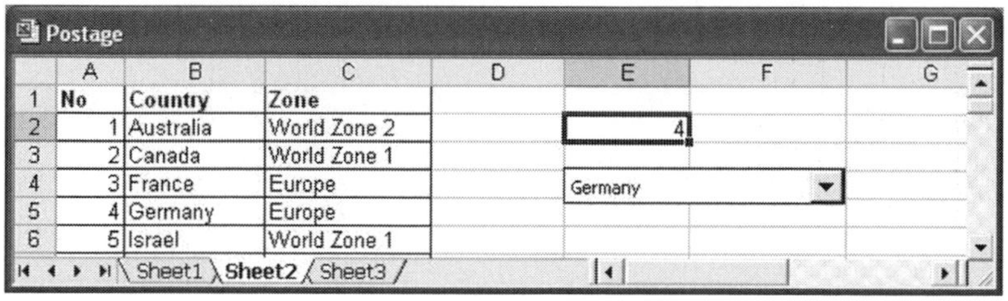

Postage

	A	B	C	D	E	F	G
1	No	Country	Zone				
2	1	Australia	World Zone 2		4		
3	2	Canada	World Zone 1				
4	3	France	Europe		Germany ▼		
5	4	Germany	Europe				
6	5	Israel	World Zone 1				

Sheet1 \ **Sheet2** / Sheet3 /

Figure 8.8

Remember

When you choose an item in a combo box list, the linked cell stores the number of that item, not the item itself. In this case, E2 stores 4.

LOOKUP and combo boxes

> The LOOKUP function becomes more powerful when combined with a combo box.

Worked example 1: LOOKUP and combo box

1   Load the file **Postage** if not already loaded and go to Sheet2.

2   Enter **6** into cell **E2**. Enter **=VLOOKUP(E2,zone,2)** into cell F2.

This looks in **E2** and finds the value **6**. Then it looks in the first column (column A) in the **zone** table shown in Figure 8.9 until it finds the row with **6** in it. It then finds the data in this row in column **2** of the table. It will return the value **Italy**.

3   Check it returns the value **Italy**.

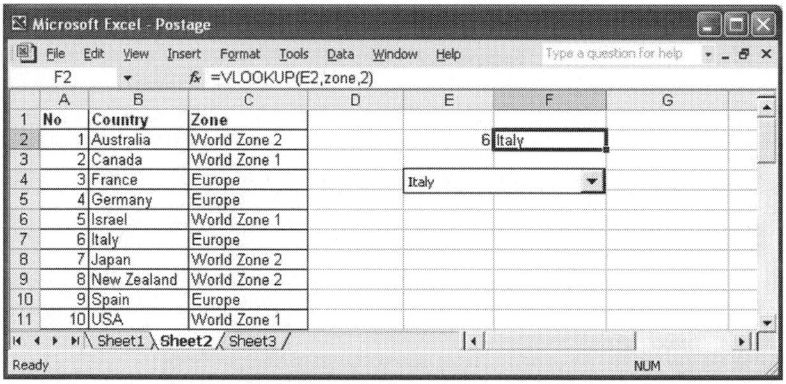

	A	B	C	D	E	F	G
1	No	Country	Zone				
2	1	Australia	World Zone 2		6	Italy	
3	2	Canada	World Zone 1				
4	3	France	Europe		Italy		
5	4	Germany	Europe				
6	5	Israel	World Zone 1				
7	6	Italy	Europe				
8	7	Japan	World Zone 2				
9	8	New Zealand	World Zone 2				
10	9	Spain	Europe				
11	10	USA	World Zone 1				

F2   =VLOOKUP(E2,zone,2)

Figure 8.9

4   Change the value of E2 to **9**. Check that **Spain** appears in cell F2.

5   Using the combo box click on **New Zealand.** Check that New Zealand appears in F2.

6   Enter **=VLOOKUP(E2,zone,3)** into cell **G2**.

7   Save your file.

8 Test that as you select a country using the combo box, the zone for that country appears in G2. Figure 8.10 shows USA as the selected country.

	A	B	C	D	E	F	G
1	No	Country	Zone				
2	1	Australia	World Zone 2		10	USA	World Zone 1
3	2	Canada	World Zone 1				
4	3	France	Europe		USA ▼		
5	4	Germany	Europe				
6	5	Israel	World Zone 1				
7	6	Italy	Europe				
8	7	Japan	World Zone 2				
9	8	New Zealand	World Zone 2				
10	9	Spain	Europe				
11	10	USA	World Zone 1				

Sheet1 \ **Sheet2** / Sheet3 /

Figure 8.10

Worked example 2: Automating an invoice

1 Load the file called **Invoice** set up in Unit 1 and shown in Figure 8.11.

	A	B	C	D	E	F	G
1	Casey's Sportswear						
2				Invoice No	1		
3	Address 1			Date	12/11/03		
4	Address 2						
5	Address 3			Customer Address			
6	Post Code						
7	Tel. No.			Address 1			
8				Address 2			
9				Address 3			
10				Post Code			
11				Tel. No.			
12							
13	Quantity	Catalogue No	Item	Unit Price	Price		
14	13	1	Football shirts	£ 13.50	£ 175.50		
15	1	11	Goalkeeper shirts	£ 15.50	£ 15.50		
16	14	21	Shorts	£ 8.50	£ 119.00		
17	14	31	Pair socks	£ 6.99	£ 97.86		
18							
19				Sub Total	£ 407.86		
20							
21				VAT	£ 71.38		
22							
23				Total	£ 479.24		

Sheet1 / Sheet2 / Sheet3 /

Figure 8.11

Casey's Sportswear sell three different makes of football kit, all at different prices.

We want to set up the spreadsheet so that when the catalogue number is typed into column B, the item name and unit price automatically appear in columns C and D. Column C may need widening a little.

2   On Sheet2 enter the details of the items and prices as shown in Figure 8.12. Define the area from A2 to C14 as **items**. Row 2 is necessary for the LOOKUP function to work.

	A	B	C	D	E
1	Catalogue No	Item	Unit price		
2	0	-	£-		
3	1	Football shirts (Jarvis & Co)	£ 13.50		
4	2	Football shirts (Skinner Bros)	£ 14.00		
5	3	Football shirts (BCW)	£ 16.00		
6	11	Goalkeeper shirts (Jarvis & Co)	£ 15.50		
7	12	Goalkeeper shirts (Skinner Bros)	£ 17.50		
8	13	Goalkeeper shirts (BCW)	£ 20.00		
9	21	Shorts (Jarvis & Co)	£ 8.99		
10	22	Shorts (Skinner Bros)	£ 8.50		
11	23	Shorts (BCW)	£ 10.00		
12	31	Pair socks (Jarvis & Co)	£ 6.99		
13	32	Pair socks (Skinner Bros)	£ 7.50		
14	33	Pair socks (BCW)	£ 8.00		
15					

Sheet1 \ **Sheet2** / Sheet3 /

Figure 8.12

> **Note**   You can download this file from **www.hodderictcoursework.co.uk**

3   Switch back to Sheet1. In cell C14 enter the formula **=VLOOKUP(B14,items,2)**.

This picks up the Catalogue No in B14, finds that number in column A of the named area **items** and returns what is in the 2nd column on that row.

4   In cell D14 enter the formula **=VLOOKUP(B14,items,3)**

This looks up the Unit Price for the Catalogue No returned in B14.

5   **Copy** and **Paste** these two formulas down as far as cells C17 and D17. Check that if you enter a catalogue number in column B, the right information appears in columns C and D.

6   Test that the lookups work. Investigate what happens if you type in a false product number in this workbook.

(a) Try one that is too big such as 35.

(b) Try one that is too small such as -5.

(c) Try one that doesn't exist such as 7.

7   To avoid such errors we can use validation. Click on B14. Use Data Validation so that only 1, 2 or 3 can be entered into this cell. Similarly only 11, 12 or 13 can be entered into B15; 21, 22 or 23 into B16 and 31, 32 or 33 in B17.

8   To use the spreadsheet enter the catalogue number in column B and the quantity in column A. If a line is not being used, leave column B blank.

9   Check the lookups work for all possible values. Save your work.

Exercise 1

1 Reopen the **Postage** workbook and switch to Sheet1. Set up a combo box linked to cell B13 as shown in Figure 8.13. Use VLOOKUP in cells C13, D13 and E13 to find the price of postage to each zone.

	A	B	C	D	E	F
1	No	Max weight (g)	Europe	World Zone 1	World Zone 2	
2	1	100	£0.87	£1.15	£1.15	
3	2	120	£0.96	£1.32	£1.34	
4	3	140	£1.05	£1.49	£1.53	
5	4	160	£1.14	£1.66	£1.72	
6	5	180	£1.23	£1.83	£1.91	
7	6	200	£1.32	£2.00	£2.10	
8						
9						
10		Weight	180 ▼			
11						
12			Europe	World Zone 1	World Zone 2	
13		5	£1.23	£1.83	£1.91	

Sheet1 / Sheet2 / Sheet3 /

Figure 8.13

Hint

The formula in cell C13 will be =**VLOOKUP(B13,weight,3)**.

2 Using VLOOKUP, set up two combo boxes to choose the weight and the zone so that the cost of postage appears in a cell as shown in Figure 8.14.

	A	B	C	D	E
17			180 ▼		
18	1	Europe			
19	2	World Zone 1			
20	3	World Zone 2			
21					
22		Weight	100 ▼	World Zone 1 ▼	
23					
24		1	2	£1.15	

Sheet1 / Sheet2 / Sheet3 /

Figure 8.14

Hints

○ You will need to set up a new table first as shown.
○ Link the combo boxes to cells B24 and C24.
○ The formula in D24 is =**VLOOKUP(B24,weight, C24+2)**.

Exercise 2

1   Load the file **PhoneBill** used in Unit 4.

2   The phone company has brought out a tariff D. Add the table shown in Figure 8.15 to the right of the sheet.

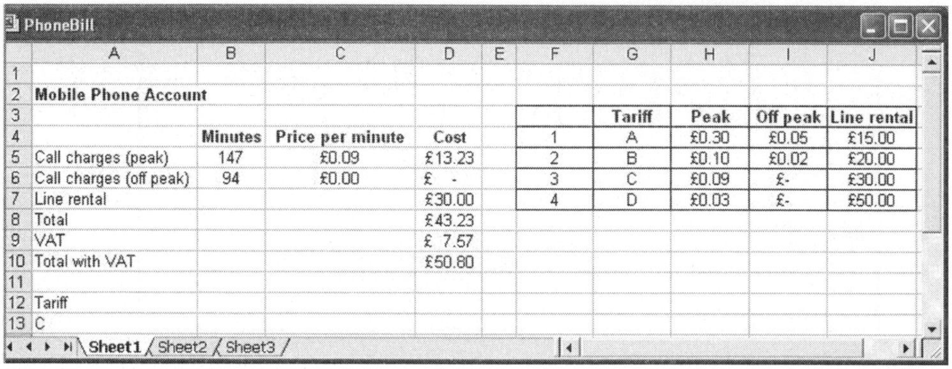

	A	B	C	D	E	F	G	H	I	J
1										
2	**Mobile Phone Account**									
3							Tariff	Peak	Off peak	Line rental
4		Minutes	Price per minute	Cost		1	A	£0.30	£0.05	£15.00
5	Call charges (peak)	147	£0.09	£13.23		2	B	£0.10	£0.02	£20.00
6	Call charges (off peak)	94	£0.00	£ -		3	C	£0.09	£-	£30.00
7	Line rental			£30.00		4	D	£0.03	£-	£50.00
8	Total			£43.23						
9	VAT			£ 7.57						
10	Total with VAT			£50.80						
11										
12	Tariff									
13	C									

Sheet1 / Sheet2 / Sheet3 /

Figure 8.15

3   Edit cells C5, C6 and D7 so that they use VLOOKUP and the tariff chosen in cell A13 to display the correct amounts.

4   Extend your spreadsheet to include a combo box to select the tariff.

5   Save your file.

Exercise 3

1   The phone company has a file of its customers and their phone use, part of which is shown in Figure 8.16.

2   Still using the file **PhoneBill**, switch to Sheet2 and enter the customer details.

3   Use **Insert, Name, Define** to give the data a name.

	A	B	C	D	E	F	G	H	I	J
1	Cust no	Forename	Surname	Address1	Address2	Address3	Tariff	Peak	Offpeak	
2	1251	Bill	Brown	21 Milton Avenue	Burton upon Trent	DE15 8PP	A	27	20	
3	1252	Eileen	Sands	32 Milton Avenue	Burton upon Trent	DE15 8PP	B	53	25	
4	1253	Elizabeth	Bird	80 Milton Avenue	Burton upon Trent	DE15 8PP	C	102	44	
5	1254	Charles	Bryant	104 Milton Avenue	Burton upon Trent	DE15 8PP	A	71	149	
6	1255	Darren	Foreman	14 Hartshorn Road	Burton upon Trent	DE15 8QP	A	71	64	
7	1256	Olive	Hassent	17 Hartshorn Road	Burton upon Trent	DE15 8QP	A	172	186	
8	1257	Katie	Johnson	21 Hartshorn Road	Burton upon Trent	DE15 8QP	D	190	93	
9	1258	Quinton	Harris	29 Hartshorn Road	Burton upon Trent	DE15 8QP	A	20	90	
10										

Sheet1 \ **Sheet2** / Sheet3 /

Figure 8.16

4   On Sheet1 set up lookups so that if the customer number is typed in cell B1, the customer's name, address, tariff, peak units and off-peak units used appear as in Figure 8.17.

	A	B	C	D	E	F	G	H	I	J
1	Customer number:	1252								
2	**Mobile Phone Account**									
3							Tariff	Peak	Off peak	Line rental
4		Minutes	Price per minute	Cost		1	A	£0.30	£0.05	£15.00
5	Call charges (peak)	53	£ 0.30	£ 15.90		2	B	£0.10	£0.02	£20.00
6	Call charges (off peak)	25	£ 0.05	£ 1.25		3	C	£0.09	£-	£30.00
7	Line rental			£ 15.00		4	D	£0.03	£-	£50.00
8	Total			£ 32.15						
9	VAT			£ 5.63						
10	Total with VAT			£ 37.78						
11										
12	Tariff									
13	A									
14										
15	Eileen Sands									
16	32 Milton Avenue									
17	Burton upon Trent									
18	DE15 8PP									
19										

Sheet1 / Sheet2 \ **Sheet3** /

Figure 8.17

5   Check it works for at least four different customer numbers.

6   Save your file.

⊕ Unit 9 Option buttons and check boxes

In this unit you will learn how to set up and use Option Buttons and Check Boxes.

Option buttons

Option buttons allow you to select one from a group of options. Option buttons are used when only one of several possibilities is allowed.

Worked example 1: How to set up an Option Button

1 Turn on the Forms toolbar: **View, Toolbars, Forms** (see Figure 9.1).

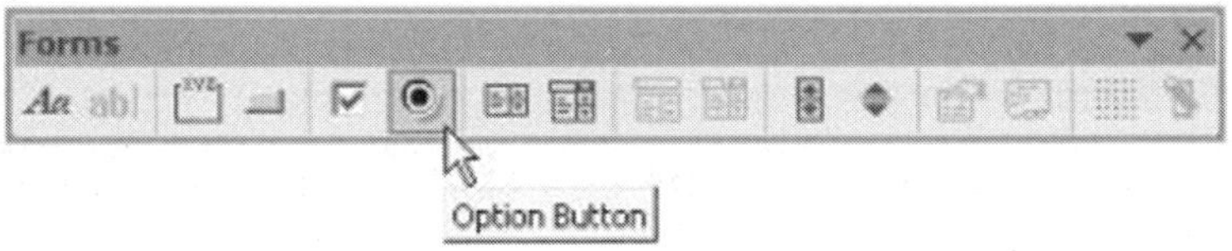

Figure 9.1

2 Click on the **Option Button** icon and drag out a rectangle on the worksheet (see Figure 9.2).

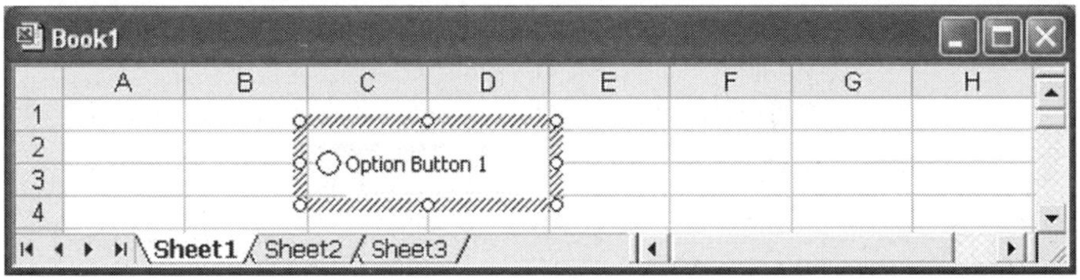

Figure 9.2

3 Highlight the text next to the button and enter the text Luxury (see Figure 9.3).

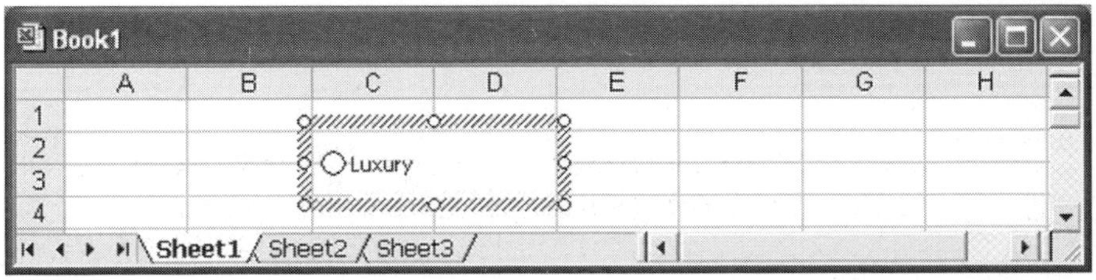

Figure 9.3

4   Right click on the control and use **Format Control** to set a cell link to A5 (see Figure 9.4).

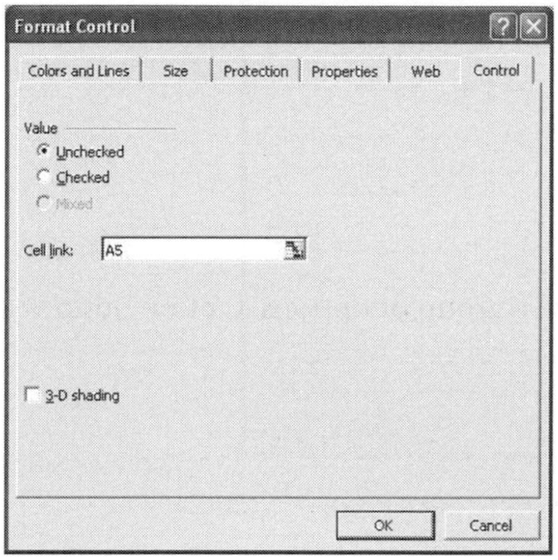

Figure 9.4

5   Add three more option buttons in the same way. You will notice that they all are linked to the same cell (see Figure 9.5).

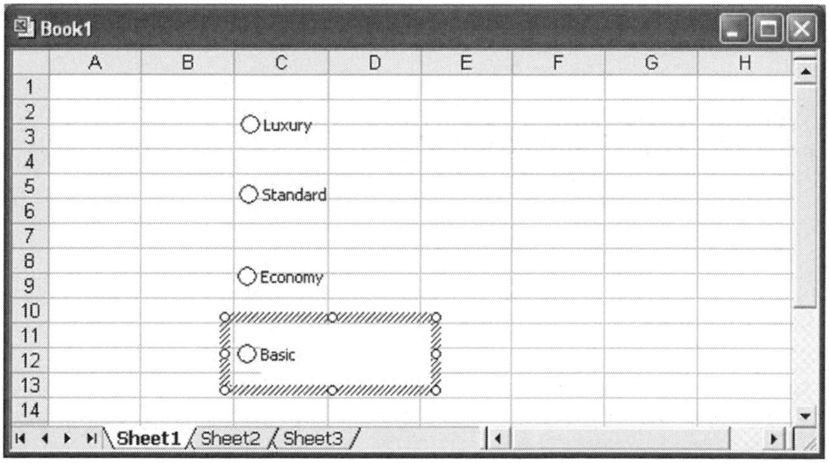

Figure 9.5

Hint

To get all the buttons exactly in line, turn on the **Drawing** toolbar. Click on the **Select Objects** pointer tool and drag across all four option button boxes. Then click on **Draw, Align or Distribute, Align Left**. Remember to deselect the pointer tool.

When you click on a button, it changes the value in the linked cell (see Figure 9.6).

Figure 9.6

Note

You can only select one option button at a time. If you want more than one group of option buttons on a worksheet, you will need to group them with a Group Box (see Figure 9.7).

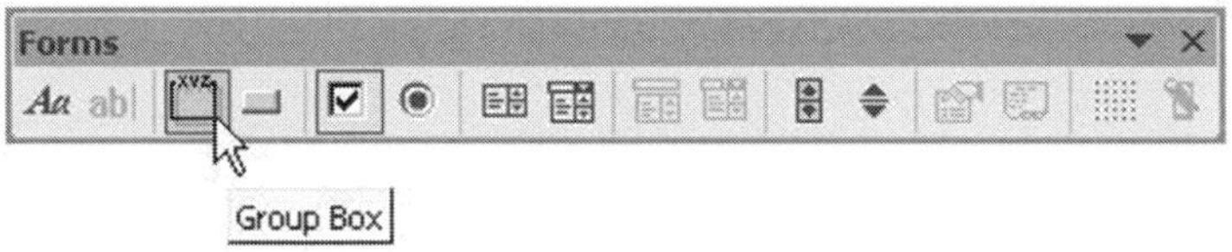

Group Box

Figure 9.7

A carpet shop offers different quality carpets at different prices as shown in Figure 9.8.

6 On Sheet2 enter the following prices (see Figure 9.8). Highlight the cells from A2 to C5 and name them **prices** with **Insert, Name, Define**.

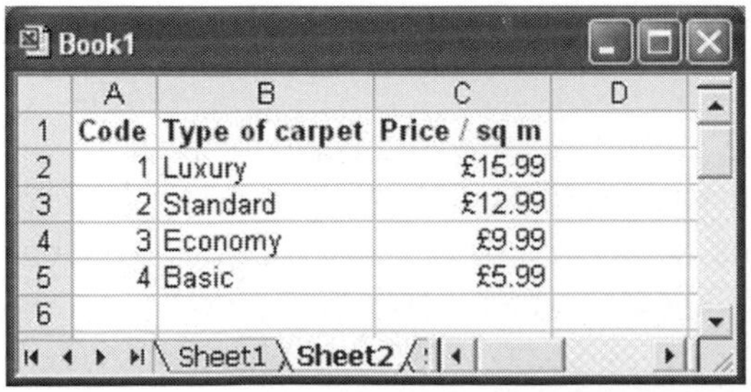

	A	B	C	D
1	Code	Type of carpet	Price / sq m	
2	1	Luxury	£15.99	
3	2	Standard	£12.99	
4	3	Economy	£9.99	
5	4	Basic	£5.99	
6				

Figure 9.8

7 Go back to Sheet1 and in cell E4 type in **=VLOOKUP(A5,prices,3)**.

8 Format cell E4 to currency.

9 Check that as you click on a different option button the price in cell E4 changes. You will also notice that cell A5 returns a different number depending on which option is chosen.

10 Change the colour of the font in A5 to white so that it does not show.

11 Set up the spreadsheet to have a cell for the number of square metres and another cell to calculate the cost of the carpet as shown in Figure 9.9.

Book1

	A	B	C	D	E	F
1						
2						
3			⦿ Luxury			
4				Price / sq m	£ 15.99	
5						
6			○ Standard			
7				Sq Metres	12	
8						
9			○ Economy			
10				Cost	£ 191.88	
11						
12			○ Basic			
13						

Sheet1 / Sheet2 / Sheet3 /

Figure 9.9

12 Check it works for all four types of carpet.

13 Save your file as **Carpet**.

Worked example 2: Using an option button to make decisions

1 Load the file **Invoice** used in the last unit. Football shirts are available in two types; plain or striped. Striped shirts cost an extra £1.00 per shirt.

2 Add 2 option buttons to the bottom left of the spreadsheet. Link the buttons to cell A19.

If the user clicks **Plain shirts** A19 returns a 1, if **Striped shirts** are selected A19 returns a 2. If A19 contains a 2, we want the spreadsheet to add the cost of striped shirts to the invoice.

3 Use the **IF** function in cell E18, so that if A19 is equal to 2, this cell (E18) is equal to A14, i.e. the quantity of shirts required which are a pound extra. The formula required in E18 is **=IF(A19=2,A14,0)**.

4   Make sure that the formula in E19 is **=SUM(E14:E18)**.

5   Save the file.

Your spreadsheet should appear as in Figure 9.10.

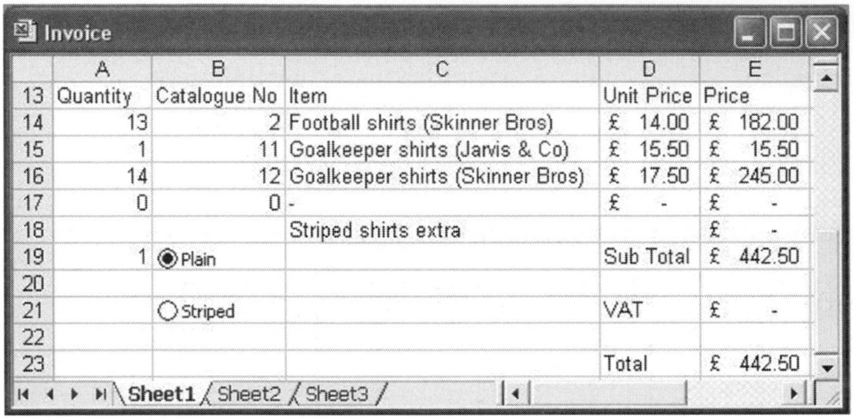

	A	B	C	D	E
13	Quantity	Catalogue No	Item	Unit Price	Price
14	13	2	Football shirts (Skinner Bros)	£ 14.00	£ 182.00
15	1	11	Goalkeeper shirts (Jarvis & Co)	£ 15.50	£ 15.50
16	14	12	Goalkeeper shirts (Skinner Bros)	£ 17.50	£ 245.00
17	0	0	-	£ -	£ -
18			Striped shirts extra		£ -
19	1	● Plain		Sub Total	£ 442.50
20					
21		○ Striped		VAT	£ -
22					
23				Total	£ 442.50

Sheet1 / Sheet2 / Sheet3 /

Figure 9.10

Check boxes

A **check box** allows you turn an option on or off.

Worked example 3: How to set up a check box

We will use a check box to show whether the customer wishes to pay for fitting the carpet or not using the spreadsheet set up earlier in the unit.

1   Load the spreadsheet **Carpet**.

2   Turn on the Forms toolbar: **View, Toolbars, Forms** (see Figure 9.11).

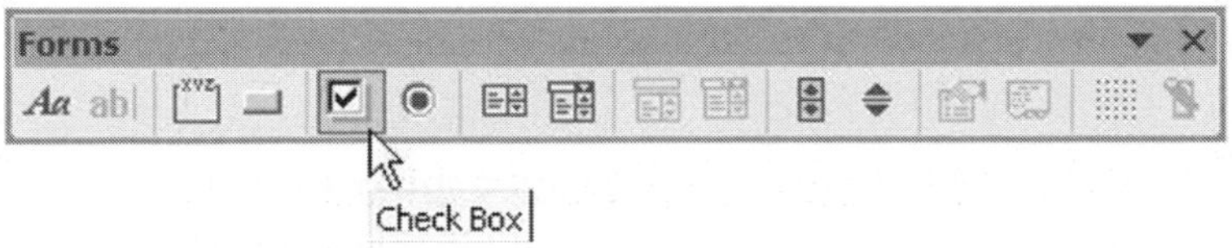

Check Box

Figure 9.11

3   Click on the **Check Box** icon.

4   Drag out a rectangle on the worksheet near cell C14 (see Figure 9.12).

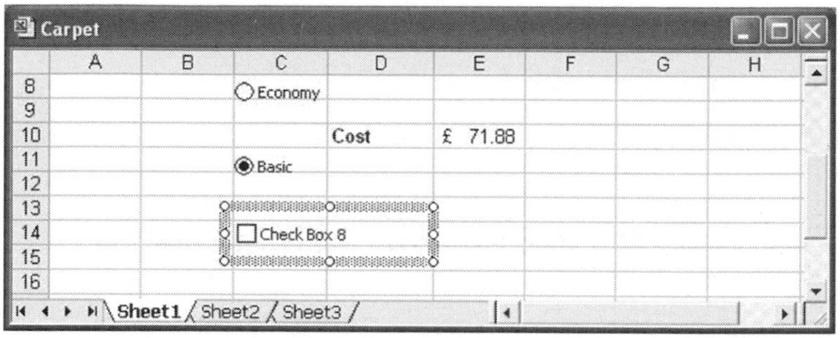

Figure 9.12

5   Highlight the text next to the box and enter the text **Fitting** (see Figure 9.13).

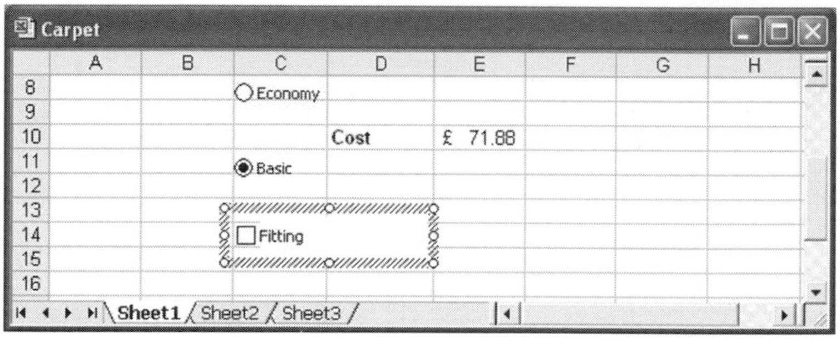

Figure 9.13

6   Right click on the control and use **Format Control** to set a cell link to A14.

7   As you tick the check box the linked cell changes from TRUE to FALSE (see Figure 9.14).

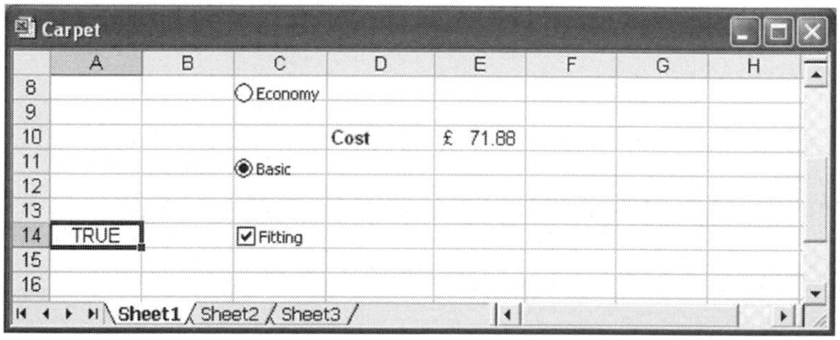

Figure 9.14

8   Fitting costs £25. We will use the value in A14 to decide if fitting costs need to be added to the bill. In cell E14 type in **=IF(A14=FALSE,0,25)**. In other words if the check box is not clicked the contents of E14 will be zero, if it is E14 will equal 25.

9   Test it works and format the cell to currency.

10 Add the contents of cells E10 and E14 in cell E17.

11 We don't want the words TRUE and FALSE to show, so change the colour of their text to white.

The worksheet should now appear as in Figure 9.15. As you check and uncheck the boxes, the amounts will change.

	A	B	C	D	E	F	G	H
2			○ Luxury					
3								
4				Price/sq m	£ 5.99			
5			○ Standard					
6								
7				Sq Metres	12			
8			○ Economy					
9								
10				Cost	£ 71.88			
11			● Basic					
12								
13								
14			☑ Fitting		£ 25.00			
15								
16								
17				Total	£ 96.88			

Carpet — Sheet1 / Sheet2 / Sheet3

Figure 9.15

12 Remove the gridlines, add a company name and present the spreadsheet professionally. Save your file.

Exercise

Load the file **Invoice** used in this unit. There is no VAT on children's football kits.

Add a check box to the invoice linked to cell A23 so that if the box is checked VAT is added on. If it is not checked, VAT is not added.

⊕ Unit 10 Spinners and scroll bars

In this unit you will learn how to set up and use spinner controls and scroll bars.

Spinners

A **spinner** or spin button is a button that enables you to increase or decrease the value of a number in a cell by clicking on the control.

How to add a Spinner

1   Turn on the Forms toolbar: **View, Toolbars, Forms** (see Figure 10.1).

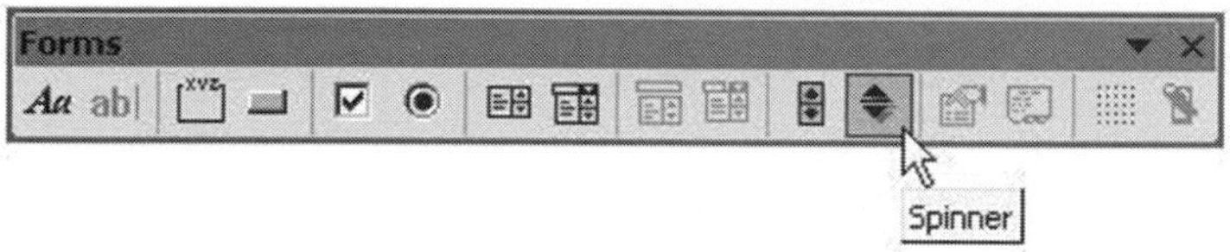

Spinner

Figure 10.1

2   Click on the **Spinner** icon.

3   Drag out a rectangle in a cell on the worksheet. If you hold down the ALT key it will lock the control to the gridlines.

4   Right click and use **Format Control** to link the control to a cell (see Figure 10.2).

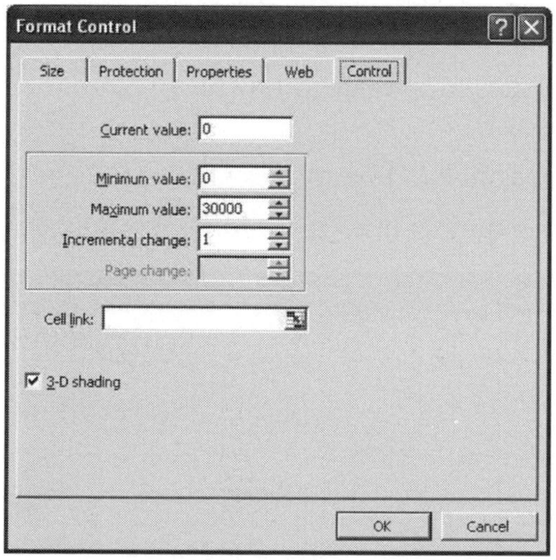

Figure 10.2

When you link the spinner to a cell, you have to specify maximum and minimum values and the incremental change every time you click on the spinner.

○ All the values must be whole numbers.
○ The minimum value cannot be negative.
○ The maximum value cannot be more than 30000.

Worked example 1: Using a spinner

The following steps show you how to add a spinner to the **Carpet** spreadsheet set up in Unit 9.

1   Load the file **Carpet**. We will use a spinner to edit the area of the carpet.

2   Turn on the Forms toolbar **View, Toolbars, Forms**.

3   Click on the spinner icon and drag out a box near G6, G7 and G8.

4   Right click on the control and click on **Format Control** (see Figure 10.3).

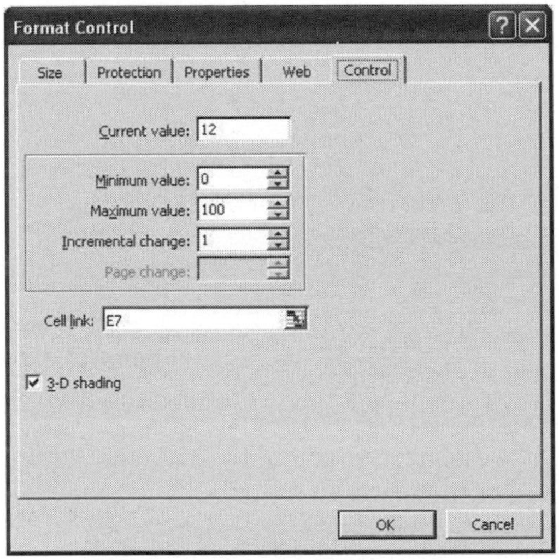

Figure 10.3

5   Set the maximum value to 100, the minimum value to 0 and the incremental change to 1.

6   Set the cell link to E7 and click **OK**.

7   Test your spinner (see Figure 10.4). It should change the value in E7.

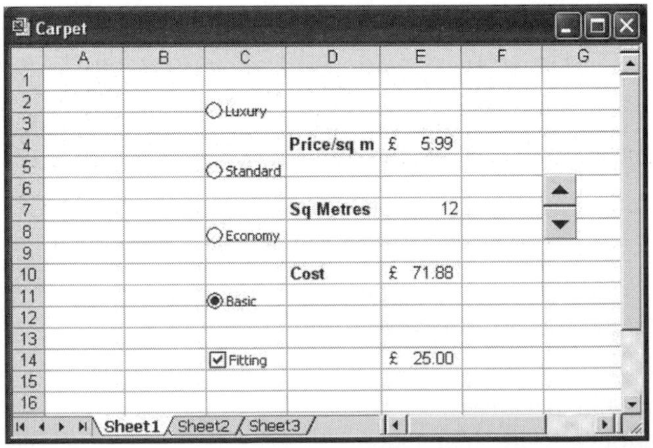

Figure 10.4

Incrementing by a decimal amount

Excel only lets a spinner increase or decrease a value by a whole number. We might want the system to use decimals. For example the area of the carpet may be 12.7 sq metres.

We can get around this as follows:

8 Right click on the spinner. Choose **Format Control**. Change the maximum value to 1000 and the cell link to H7.

9 In E7 enter the formula **=H7/10**.

10 Test that the spinner now increments 0.1 at a time.

11 Hide the contents of cell H7 by formatting the text to white.

12 Save your file.

Note
Even when a cell has a spinner attached, you can still type a value into the cell.

Exercise

Load the file **PhoneBill** from Unit 8. Add a spinner to increase or decrease the customer number by 1 so that you can cycle through all the records in the file.

	A	B	C	D	E	F	G	H	I	J
1	Customer number	1252								
2	**Mobile Phone Account**									
3							Tariff	Peak	Off peak	Line rental
4		Minutes	Price per minute	Cost		1	A	£0.30	£ 0.05	£15.00
5	Call charges (peak)	53	£ 0.30	£ 15.90		2	B	£0.10	£ 0.02	£20.00
6	Call charges (off peak)	25	£ 0.05	£ 1.25		3	C	£0.09	£ -	£30.00
7	Line rental			£ 15.00		4	D	£0.03	£ -	£50.00

Figure 10.5

Scroll bars

A **scroll bar** enables you to increase or decrease the value in a cell by clicking the control or dragging the slide bar.

How to add a scroll bar

1   Turn on the Forms toolbar: **View, Toolbars, Forms** (see Figure 10.6).

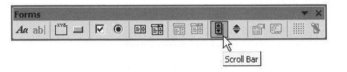

Figure 10.6

2   Click on the **Scroll Bar** icon.

3   Drag out a rectangle in a cell on the worksheet.

4   Right click and use **Format Control** to link the control to a cell (see Figure 10.7).

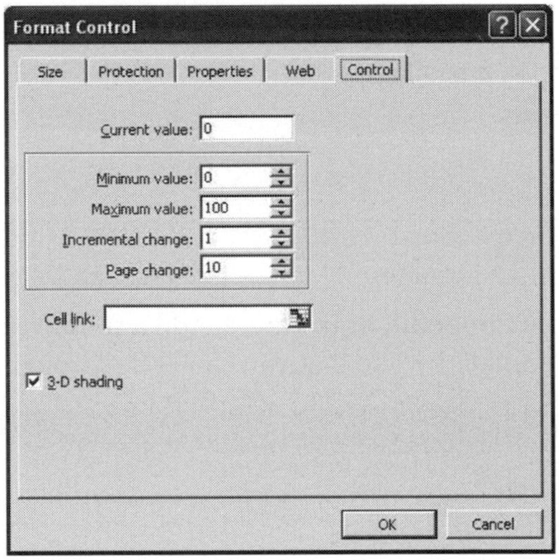

Figure 10.7

When you link the scroll bar to a cell, you have to specify maximum and minimum values and the incremental change every time you click on the scroll bar.

○ All the values must be whole numbers.
○ The minimum value cannot be negative.
○ The maximum value cannot be more than 30000.
○ You can choose whether or not to print spinners and scroll bars by right clicking on the control, clicking on **Format Control** and then clicking on the **Properties** tab. Check the **Print object** box.
○ The page change refers to the size of the change if you click on the scroll bar itself rather than on one of the arrows.

Worked example 2: A loan repayment calculator

1   Enter the row headings and data as shown in Figure 10.8.

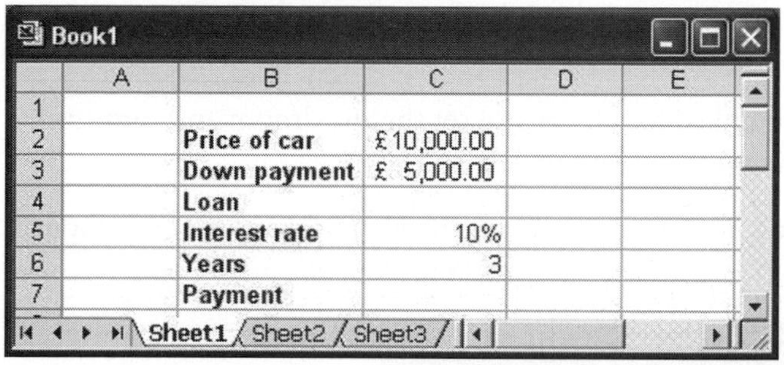

	A	B	C	D	E
1					
2		**Price of car**	£ 10,000.00		
3		**Down payment**	£ 5,000.00		
4		**Loan**			
5		**Interest rate**	10%		
6		**Years**	3		
7		**Payment**			

Book1 · Sheet1 / Sheet2 / Sheet3

Figure 10.8

2   In C4 enter the formula **=C2–C3**.

3   In C7 enter the formula **=PMT(C5/12,C6*12,C4)**.

This function works out the monthly repayments for a loan given the interest rate, the term of the loan and the amount of the loan. For more details on this function, see later in this unit.

4   Turn on the Forms toolbar **View, Toolbars, Forms**.

5   Click on the **Scroll Bar** icon and drag out a rectangle in D3.

6   Right click on the control and click **Format Control** (see Figure 10.9).

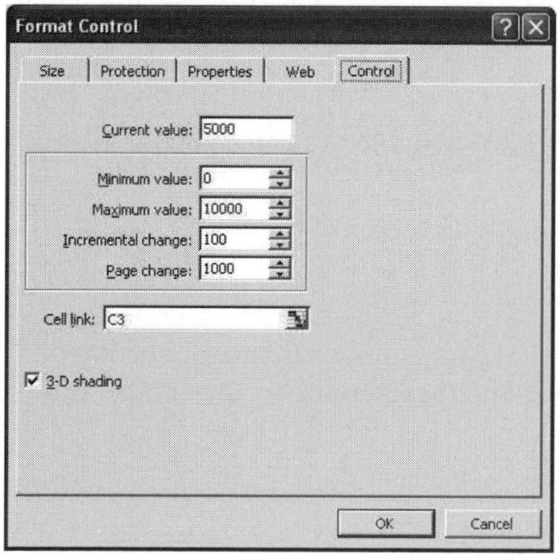

Format Control

Size | Protection | Properties | Web | Control

Current value: 5000

Minimum value: 0
Maximum value: 10000
Incremental change: 100
Page change: 1000

Cell link: C3

☑ 3-D shading

OK | Cancel

Figure 10.9

1.   Set the maximum and minimum values to 10000 and 0 with the increment at 100.

2.   Link the **Scroll bar** to cell C3.

3.   Set the page change to 1000.

4.   Put a scroll bar in D6 linked to cell C6 and set the maximum and minimum values to 5 and 1 with an increment of 1.

5.   Save your file as **loans**. Your finished spreadsheet should appear as in Figure 10.10.

	A	B	C	D	E
1					
2		Price of car	£10,000.00		
3		Down payment	£ 5,000.00	◄ ▶	
4		Loan	£ 5,000.00		
5		Interest rate	10%		
6		Years	3	◄ ▶	
7		Payment	-£161.34		

Figure 10.10

Further development

We have seen that spinners and scroll bars only increment in whole numbers and you have also seen a way around it.

Interest rates usually increment by one decimal place and down payments are often quoted as a percentage.

1. Add scroll bars for the interest rate.

2. Edit the scroll bar for the down payment to quote as a percentage of the car price.

Financial functions

Excel has many built-in functions. The **PMT** function is a financial function that calculates the repayments for a loan based on the interest rate, the number of payments and the amount borrowed.

There are many other financial functions available in Excel. Use Help to investigate further.

The **Future Value** and **Rate** functions are two of the more commonly used.

The Future Value (FV) function

This function returns the **future value** of an investment assuming constant periodic payments and a constant interest rate.

Suppose you invest £100 per month for 2 years at 5% interest per annum.

The formula to calculate the value of your money after 2 years is: **=FV(5%/12,24,-100)**
○ 5% is the interest rate;
○ 24 is the number of payments;
○ -100 means a monthly payment of £100. It is negative because it is a payment.

The Rate function

The **Rate** function works out the interest rate given the amount borrowed, the number of payments and the amount of each payment.

The formula **=RATE(24,-230,5000)** works out the interest rate for a loan of £5000, repaid at £230 a month for 24 months.

The result is **0.81%.**

(If your computer gives this as 1%, click on the **Increase decimal** icon.)

However, this is the monthly interest rate. Multiply by 12 for the annual interest rate.

The formula would be **=RATE(24,-230,5000)*12**.

The result is **9.7%.**

Developing systems

> The following example aims to build on the many Excel features covered so far and lead the student into combining them into solving a more complex problem. Units 12 and 13 offer similar extended problems. It is hoped the student can explore each problem further and add their own ideas and extensions to each solution. These ideas will hopefully encourage and enable the student to use Excel to develop usable systems.

Problem statement

The *Denton Gazette* is a weekly newspaper that sells advertising space to local businesses. An advertisement across one column costs £4.94 per centimetre, across two columns costs £9.88 per centimetre, across three columns costs £14.82 per centimetre and across four columns costs £19.76 per centimetre.

Advertisements in colour cost 50% extra. For an extra £5.10 the advertiser gets a guaranteed position on the page.

The *Denton Gazette* would like an automated computer system to calculate the cost of an advertisement and to store costs for each customer.

1 Load Excel. Go to Sheet2 and rename it **Prices**. Rename Sheet3 **Quotes** and rename Sheet1 **Calculator**.

2 On the Prices sheet enter the data as shown in Figure 10.11.

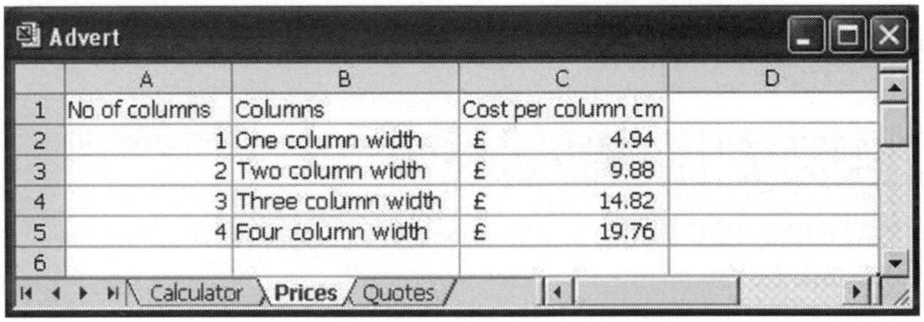

	A	B	C	D
1	No of columns	Columns	Cost per column cm	
2	1	One column width	£ 4.94	
3	2	Two column width	£ 9.88	
4	3	Three column width	£ 14.82	
5	4	Four column width	£ 19.76	
6				

Calculator \ **Prices** / Quotes /

Figure 10.11

3 Highlight cells A2 to C5 and name the area **Cost**.

4 Save the file as **Advert**.

5 Switch to the **Calculator** sheet.

6 Set up a combo box near cells B4 and C4, the Cell Link is **D4** and the Input Range is **Prices!B2:B5.**

7 Test that the combo box works as in Figure 10.12.

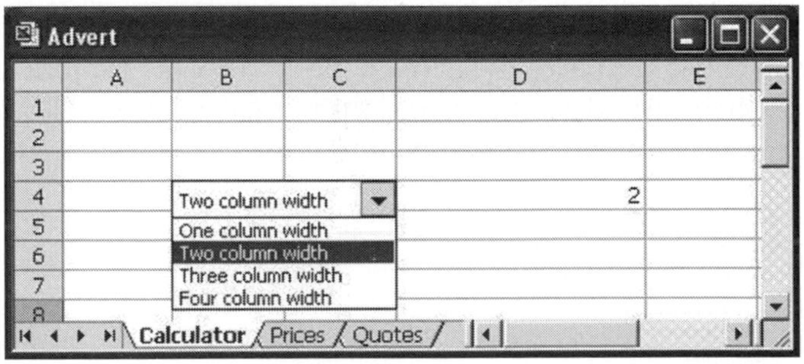

	A	B	C	D	E
1					
2					
3					
4		Two column width ▼		2	
5		One column width			
6		Two column width			
7		Three column width			
8		Four column width			

Calculator / Prices / Quotes /

Figure 10.12

8 In cell E4 use VLOOKUP to find the price per centimetre for that width. The formula is: **=VLOOKUP(D4,Cost,3).**

9   Format E4 to currency. Your spreadsheet should look like Figure 10.13.

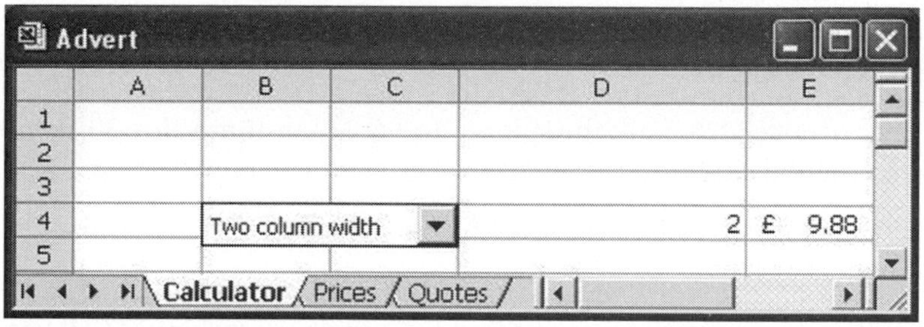

	A	B	C	D	E
1					
2					
3					
4		Two column width ▼		2	£ 9.88
5					

Calculator / Prices / Quotes

Figure 10.13

10 Add two option buttons near cells B8 and B10 as shown in Figure 10.14. Link the option buttons to D8.

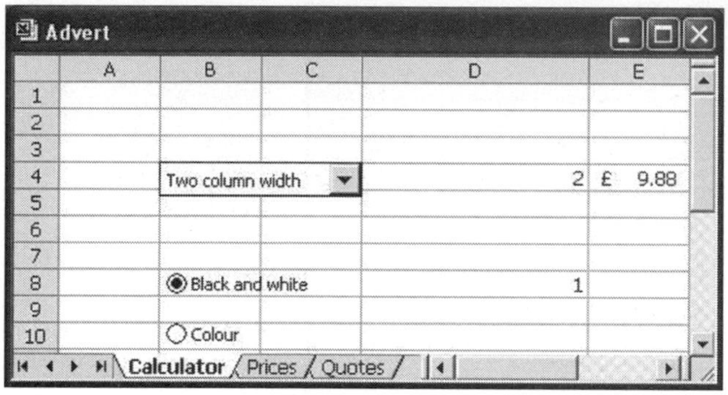

	A	B	C	D	E
1					
2					
3					
4		Two column width ▼		2	£ 9.88
5					
6					
7					
8		⦿ Black and white		1	
9					
10		○ Colour			

Calculator / Prices / Quotes

Figure 10.14

11 In E8 enter the formula **=IF(D8=1,1,1.5)**. The value of this cell will be 1 if Black and white is chosen or 1.5 if Colour is chosen. This is because colour advertisements are 1.5 times as expensive.

12 Add a check box near cell C12 as shown in Figure 10.15. Link the check box to cell D12.

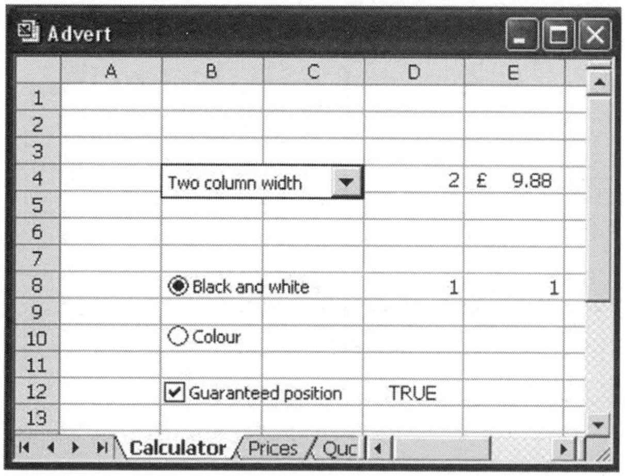

	A	B	C	D	E
1					
2					
3					
4		Two column width ▼		2	£ 9.88
5					
6					
7					
8		⦿ Black and white		1	1
9					
10		○ Colour			
11					
12		☑ Guaranteed position		TRUE	
13					

Calculator / Prices / Quc

Figure 10.15

13   In E12 enter the formula **=IF(D12=TRUE,5.1,0)**. Format the cell to currency.

14   In B6 enter **No of centimetres**. Merge together cells B6 and C6. (**Format, Cells, Alignment, Merge Cells.**)

15   Put a spinner over cell D6. Link the spinner to E6. Maximum value 30, minimum value 3, incremental change 1.

16   In E14 enter the formula **=E4*E6*E8+E12** to calculate the cost of the advertisement.

17   Use the test data in Figure 10.16 to test that the system is working. Then use some test data of your own.

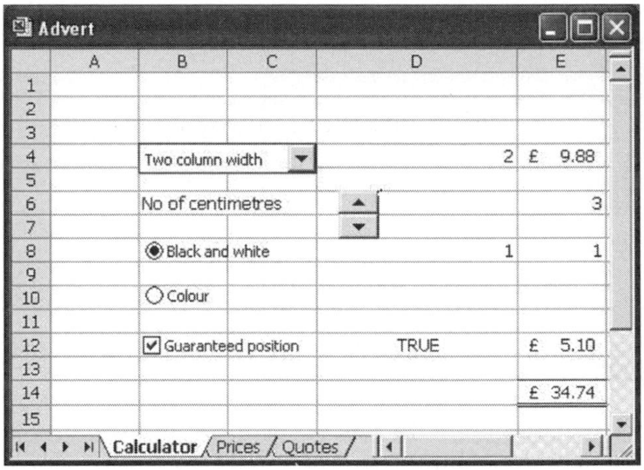

Figure 10.16

18   Format cells D4, E4, D8, E8, D12 and E12 to a white font to hide the contents of the cells. Add details of the newspaper at the top of the sheet as shown in Figure 10.17.

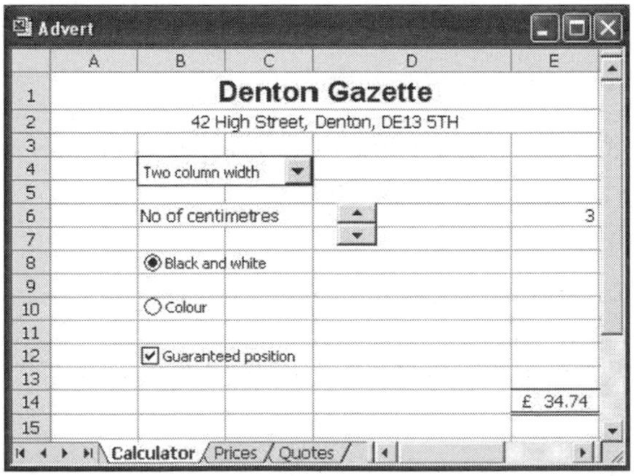

Figure 10.17

19   Save your file as **Advert**.

⊕ Unit 11 Macros

In this unit, you will learn how to speed up commonly used actions using:

○ macros;
○ macro buttons;
○ customized icons to run macros.

You will also learn how to create buttons and icons to run macros.

Introduction

A **macro** is a program that stores a series of Microsoft Excel commands so that they can be executed as a single command.

There are two ways to create a macro in Excel:

○ write the macro in Visual Basic or
○ record the macro.

Recording the macro is much easier than writing it in Visual Basic.

What macros are used for

Macros can be used in a variety of ways but common examples include:

○ formatting the screen (for example, by removing toolbars, scroll bars or the gridlines, setting print options or loading a front end);
○ navigating around a workbook (for example, moving to another sheet or selecting a cell);
○ manipulating data (for example, clearing a sheet ready for new data input, inserting new data into a file, automating data entry or sorting a table into order).

In this section you will record all three of these types of macro.

Worked example 1: Removing the gridlines from the screen

We often want to remove the gridlines from the screen so that it does not look like a spreadsheet.

Always work through the macro steps before recording them. In this example the steps are click on **Tools, Options** and click on the **View** tab. Uncheck the **Gridlines** box and click on **OK**.

We will use the workbook called **Invoice** that we used in Unit 9.

1   Load the file called **Invoice**.

2   Click on **Tools, Macro, Record New Macro**.

3   The record macro window opens as shown in Figure 11.1. Change the name of the macro to **GridOff**. (You cannot have spaces in a macro name.)

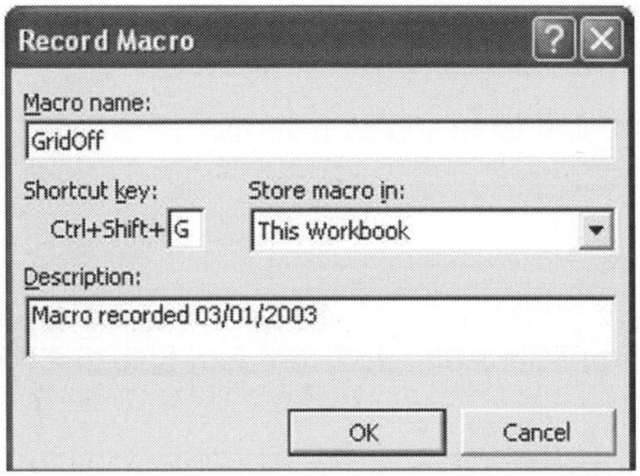

Record Macro

Macro name:
`GridOff`

Shortcut key: Store macro in:
Ctrl+Shift+ `G`   `This Workbook`

Description:
`Macro recorded 03/01/2003`

OK   Cancel

Figure 11.1

4   Press SHIFT + G to assign a **Shortcut key** to the macro and in the **Description** box give some brief details of your macro, by default it will display the date of recording.

Note

Excel uses many CTRL shortcut keys so always use CTRL and SHIFT to avoid replacing the defaults.

5   The default is to store the macro in **This Workbook** so click **OK**. The Stop Recording toolbar will appear as shown in Figure 11.2. You are now ready to record the steps in the macro.

Figure 11.2

6   Click on **Tools, Options** and click on the **View** tab. Uncheck the **Gridlines** box. Click on **OK**.

7   Click on the **Stop Recording** icon on the Stop Recording toolbar or click on **Tools, Macro, Stop Recording**.

8   Remember to save your file.

Exercise 1

(a) Record a macro called **GridOn** to put back the gridlines. This is similar to the previous macro except that the Gridlines box must be checked.

(b) Test that the macros work. Click on **Tools, Macro, Macros, GridOff, Run**. The gridlines should disappear.

(c) Run the **GridOn** macro in the same way.

Note

The shortcut ALT + F8 is useful for running macros.

Worked example 2: Switching to another worksheet

Still using the file **Invoice**, we will record a macro called **Data** to switch to Sheet2.

This may not seem very useful because you could just use the sheet tabs but eventually they will be removed. In this example there is only one step: to click on the **Sheet2** sheet tab.

1   Select **Sheet1** to start with.

2   Click on **Tools, Macro, Record New Macro** and call the new macro **Data**.

3   Click on the **Sheet2** sheet tab.

4   Click on **Stop Recording**.

5   Record another macro called **Invoice** to switch back to **Sheet1** of this workbook.

Viewing the macro coding

If you want to see what the Visual Basic coding of the recorded macro looks like, click on **Tools, Macro, Macros...** to display the macro window shown in Figure 11.3.

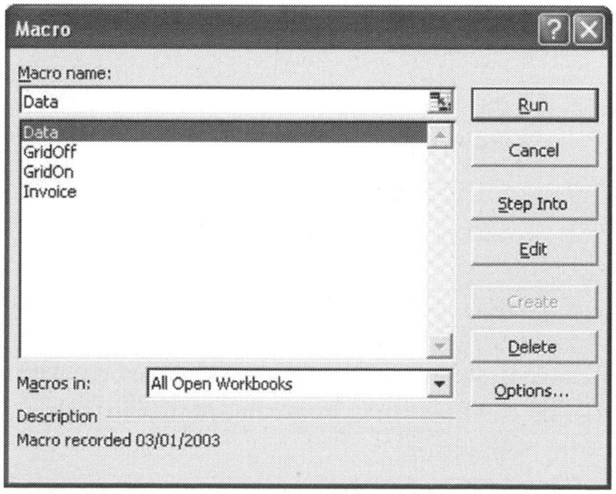

Figure 11.3

Click on the name **Data** and then **Edit**. The Visual Basic Editor will load as shown in Figure 11.4. We will look at the Visual Basic Editor in more detail later.

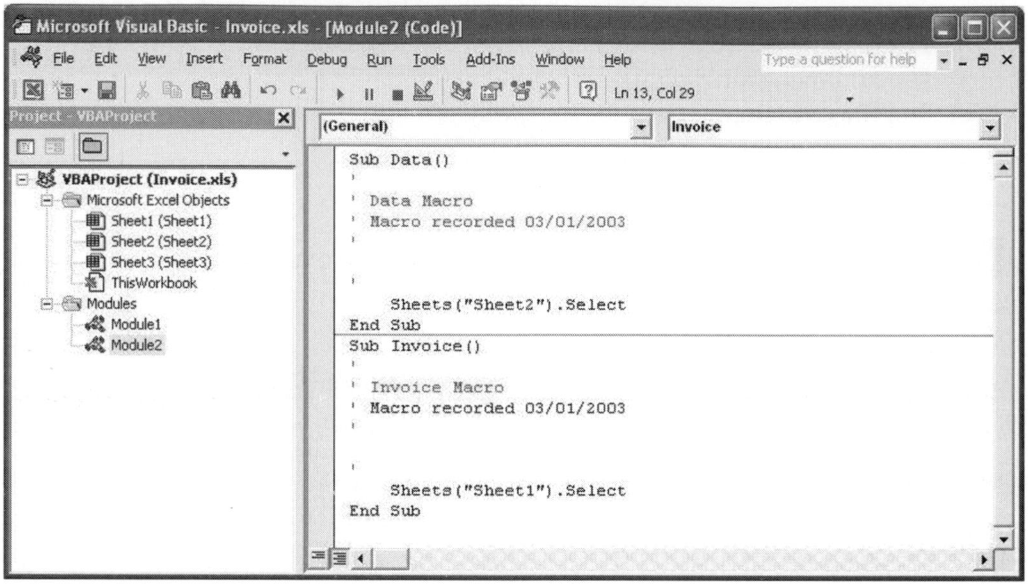

Figure 11.4

On the right of the screen is the main Visual Basic Editor window, where the macro coding will be displayed similar to this.

```
Sub Data()
'
' Data Macro
' Macro recorded 18/09/2002
'
'
Sheets("Sheet2").Select
End Sub
```

○ The first line is the name of the macro. All macros begin with **Sub**.
○ The next six lines in green are just information about the macro. They do not affect its behaviour.
○ The next line is the operation you have recorded, i.e. move to Sheet2.
○ The last line is the end of the macro. All macros end in **End Sub**.

Editing a macro

It is unlikely that you will want to edit this macro, but you can do so simply by editing the text. If you rename a worksheet, the macro coding does not automatically get updated. For example, if **Sheet2** was renamed **Prices**, you would need to change

```
Sheets ("Sheet2") .Select
```

into

```
Sheets ("Prices") .Select
```

To go back to Excel click on the **View Microsoft Excel** icon or click on **View, Microsoft Excel**.

Note   You can also use ALT + F11.

Worked example 3: Using a macro to clear data

A very important use of a macro is to clear data from a sheet ready for new data entry. For example, the invoice may need to be cleared ready for a new customer. The steps are to clear all the data in cells A14 to B17 and A19. See Figure 11.5.

1   Load the file **Invoice** if it is not already loaded.

	B	C	D	E
13	Catalogue No	Item	Unit Price	Price
14	1	Football shirts (Jarvis & Co)	£ 13.50	£ 175.50
15	12	Goalkeeper shirts (Skinner Bros)	£ 17.50	£ 17.50
16	21	Shorts (Jarvis & Co)	£ 8.99	£ 125.86
17	31	Pair socks (Jarvis & Co)	£ 6.99	£ 97.86
18		Striped shirts extra		£ -
19	◉ Plain		Sub Total	£ 416.72
20				
21	○ Stripes		VAT	£ 72.93
22				
23			Total	£ 489.65
24				

Sheet1 / Sheet2 / Sheet3 /

Figure 11.5

The data shown in Figure 11.5 will be cleared ready for another customer, as shown in Figure 11.6.

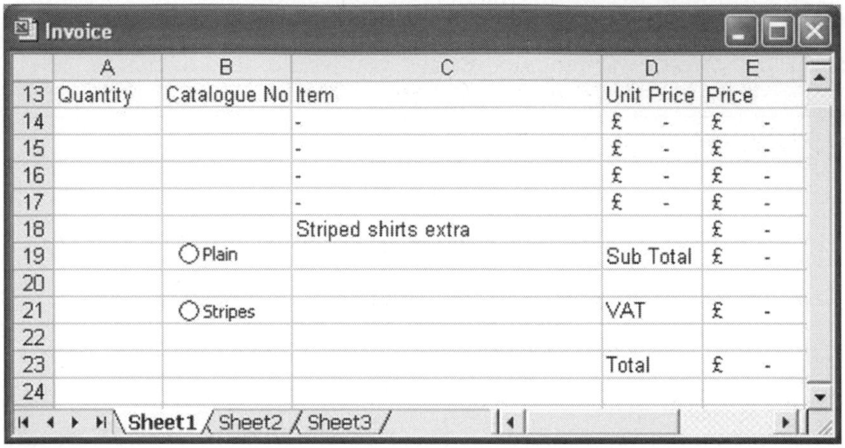

	A	B	C	D	E
13	Quantity	Catalogue No	Item	Unit Price	Price
14			-	£ -	£ -
15			-	£ -	£ -
16			-	£ -	£ -
17			-	£ -	£ -
18			Striped shirts extra		£ -
19		◯ Plain		Sub Total	£ -
20					
21		◯ Stripes		VAT	£ -
22					
23				Total	£ -
24					

Invoice — Sheet1 / Sheet2 / Sheet3

Figure 11.6

2   Start recording a new macro called **Clear**.

3   Highlight cells A14 to B17.

4   Select **Edit, Clear, All**.

5   Click on cell A19.

6   Select **Edit, Clear, All**.

7   Stop recording and test the macro.

Later you will use a macro to clear and store the data in an invoice.

Worked example 4: Using buttons to run macros

To run a macro, we must click on **Tools, Macro, Macros…** We then click on the name of the macro and then click on **Run**.

This is five mouse actions. By setting up a button we can cut this down to one action by simply clicking on a button.

1   Load the file **Invoice** if it is not already loaded. Select the **Sheet1** worksheet.

2   Turn on the Forms toolbar shown in Figure 11.7 by clicking on **View, Toolbars, Forms**.

Figure 11.7

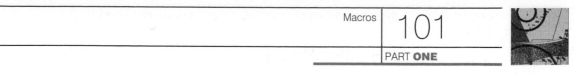

3   Click on the **Button** icon and drag out a button across columns F and G of the worksheet. (To align the button with the gridlines, hold the ALT key down as you drag.) You will see the Assign Macro window in Figure 11.8.

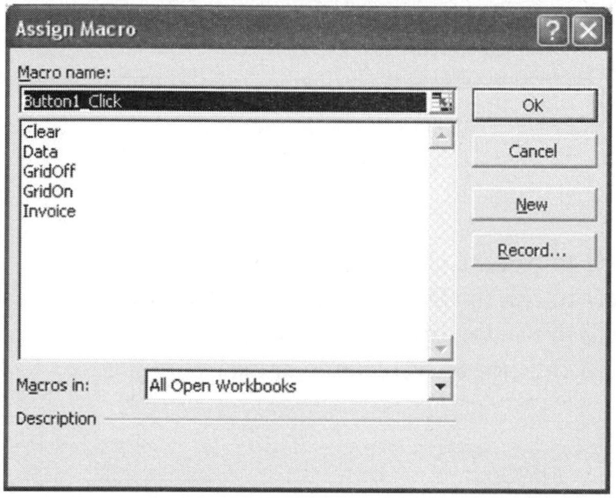

Figure 11.8

4   Click on the **GridOn** macro and click on **OK**.

5   Click on the button to rename the button text as shown in Figure 11.9.

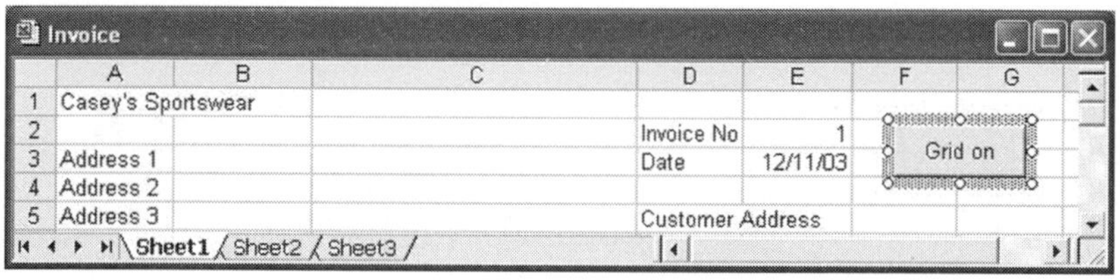

Figure 11.9

We have now combined several operations into one click of the mouse.

6   Add another button to run the **GridOff** macro as shown in Figure 11.10.

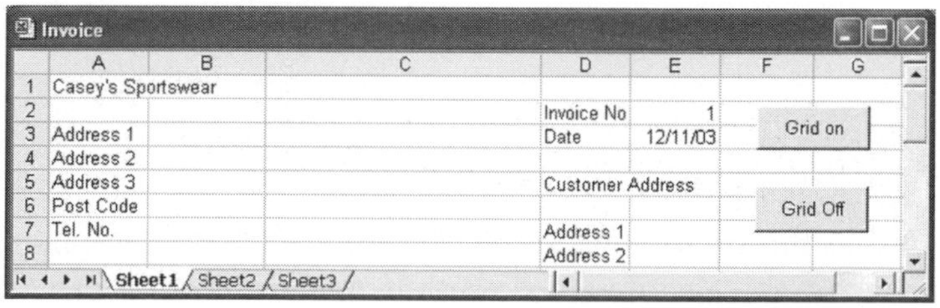

Figure 11.10

7   Test that both buttons work as expected.

Note

○ Right click on the button or use CTRL and click to select it so that you can move it, resize it, edit the text or assign a different macro.
○ Although a button appears on a worksheet and moves with the worksheet as you scroll up and down, it will not print.

Exercise 2

(a) Set up a button on Sheet1 to run the **Clear** macro. Label it **Clear data**.
(b) Set up a button on Sheet1 to run the **Data** macro. Label it **Edit data**.
(c) Set up a button on Sheet2 to run the **Invoice** macro.
(d) Test all your buttons. Your finished Sheet1 should appear as in Figure 11.11. Save your file.

	A	B	C	D	E	F	G
1	Casey's Sportswear						
2				Invoice No	1	Grid on	
3	Address1			Date	12/11/03		
4	Address2						
5	Address3			Customer Address		Grid off	
6	Postcode						
7	Tel. No.			Address1			
8				Address2			
9				Address3		Clear data	
10				Postcode			
11				Tel. No.			
12						Edit data	
13	Quantity	Catalogue No	Item	Unit Price	Price		
14			-	£ -	£ -		
15			-	£ -	£ -		
16			-	£ -	£ -		
17			-	£ -	£ -		
18			Striped shirts extra		£ -		
19		○ Plain		Sub Total	£ -		
20							
21		○ Striped		VAT	£ -		
22							
23	TRUE	☑ VAT		Total	£ -		

Sheet1 / Sheet2 / Sheet3

Figure 11.11

Designing your own buttons

You don't have to click on a button to run a macro. You could click on a graphic instead. It could be a graphic you have designed yourself, one from clip-art, an Excel **AutoShape** or even **WordArt**. See Figure 11.12.

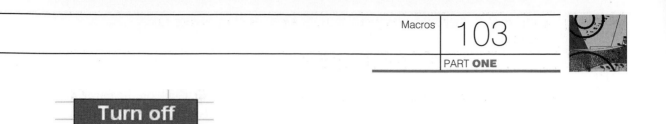

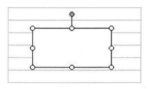

Figure 11.12

1 Turn on the Drawing toolbar with **View, Toolbars, Drawing**.

2 Click on **AutoShapes**. Click on **Basic Shapes** on the menu and choose a shape such as a **Rectangle**.

3 Drag out a rectangle on the screen as in Figure 11.13.

Figure 11.13

4 Right click on your shape. Click on **Format AutoShape** as in Figure 11.14 and choose a fill colour using the **Colors and Lines** tab.

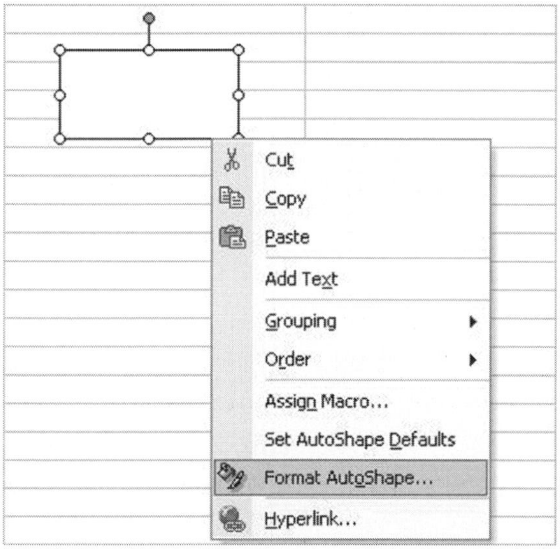

Figure 11.14

5 Right click on the shape again and click on **Add Text**. Type in the text and change colour, font and size in the normal way as in Figure 11.12.

6   Right click on the shape again and click on **Assign Macro**. Click on the name of the macro you want to run.

Setting up an icon on the toolbar to run a macro

Buttons are very useful for running macros, but they will not be on the screen if you scroll down or choose another worksheet. Another way of running a macro is to set up an icon on a toolbar.

Warning

Some networks restrict whether you can alter the settings. If you edit the toolbars to include new icons, these may not be there when you next log on.

It is a good idea to see if you can save your icons as you don't want to spend a lot of time setting up icons that won't save.

Suppose we want to add an icon to the Standard toolbar to run the macro called **GridOff**. We will use the **Invoice** file again.

1   Click on **Tools, Customize**. The Customize window appears as in Figure 11.15.

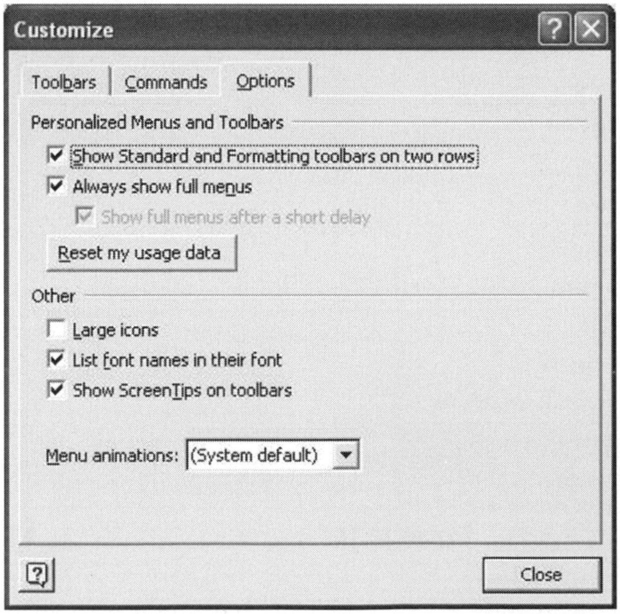

Figure 11.15

2   Click on the **Commands** tab as in Figure 11.16 and scroll down in the categories list until you see **Macros** and click on it. A 'smiley face' appears in the Commands box.

3   Drag the 'smiley face icon' on to the Standard toolbar and let go where you want the new icon to be placed as shown in Figure 11.16.

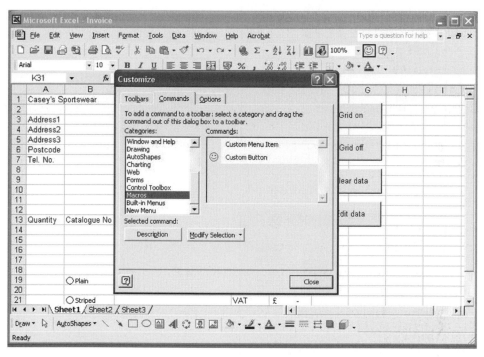

Figure 11.16

4   Right click on the 'smiley face icon'.

5   Click on **Change Button Image** to have a selection of possible icons as shown in Figure 11.17.

Figure 11.17

6   If you do not want one of the standard designs, you can customize them or create your own. Right click on the icon again and click on **Edit Button Image** to load a simple painting program to edit your icon as in Figure 11.18.

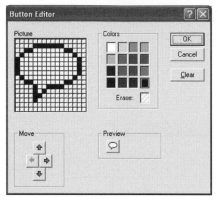

Figure 11.18

7   Edit your icon as you think suitable.

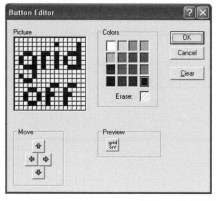

Figure 11.19

8   Right click on the icon again, click on **Assign Macro** and choose the **GridOff** macro.

9   Click on **Close** on the main dialogue box and test that the new icon works.

10 Set up an icon on the same toolbar to run the **GridOn** macro. Your toolbar will look like Figure 11.20.

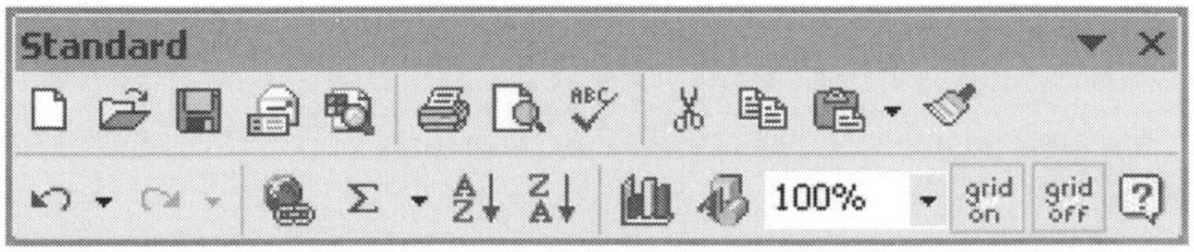

Figure 11.20

Note

You can also use this method to edit existing icons, for example to change the colour scheme on them.

○ You can add icons and text to the drop-down menus in exactly the same way.

○ To remove the icon. Right click on it, select **Customize** and drag the icon on to the **Customize window**.

Unit 12 Further macros

In this unit, you will learn how macros can be used to manipulate data and automate certain features in Excel.

Worked example 1: Setting up a macro to store data in another sheet

1   Load the file **Carpet** from Unit 10.

2   Enter the data in cells G1 and H1 as shown in Figure 12.1.

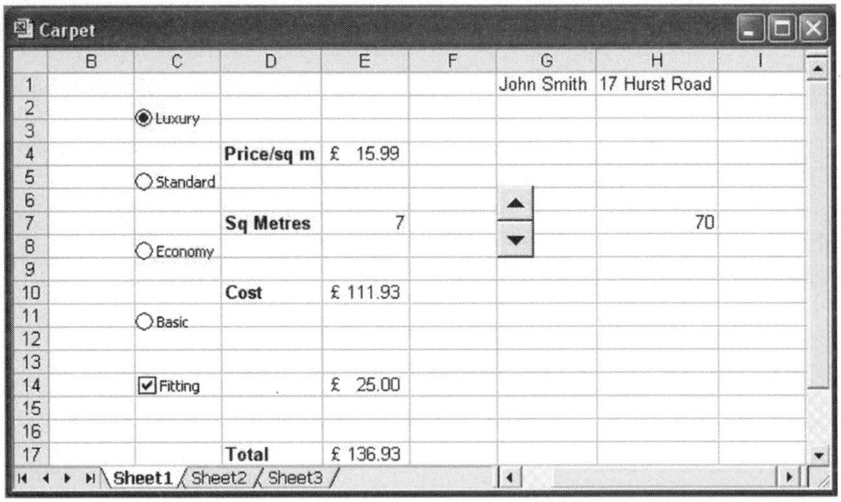

Carpet								
	B	C	D	E	F	G	H	I
1						John Smith	17 Hurst Road	
2		● Luxury						
3								
4			Price/sq m	£ 15.99				
5		○ Standard						
6						▲		
7			Sq Metres	7			70	
8		○ Economy				▼		
9								
10			Cost	£ 111.93				
11		○ Basic						
12								
13								
14		☑ Fitting		£ 25.00				
15								
16								
17			Total	£ 136.93				

Sheet1 / Sheet2 / Sheet3 /

Figure 12.1

This quote has been produced for John Smith of 17 Hurst Road. We need to move the name, address, the quote (£136.93) and store them in another sheet and get the screen ready for the next quote.

3   Switch to **Sheet3**, enter the column headings and widen the columns as shown in Figure 12.2.

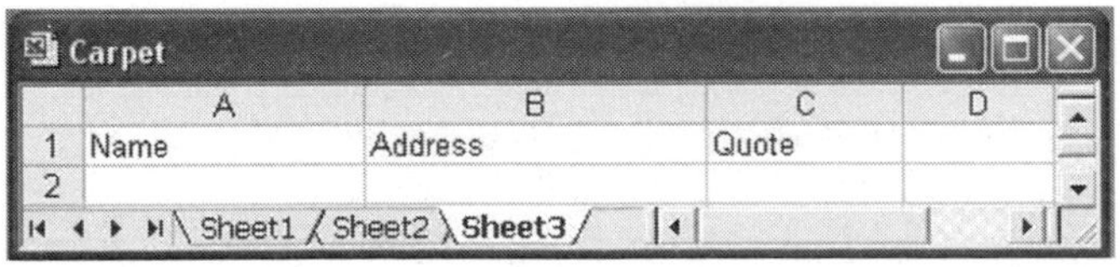

Carpet			
	A	B	C	D
1	Name	Address	Quote	
2				

 Sheet1 / Sheet2 \ Sheet3 /

Figure 12.2

4   Format column C to **Currency**.

5   Switch back to **Sheet1**. In cell I1 enter the formula **=E17**. This will pick up the value of the quote in E17 and display it in cell I1 as shown in Figure 12.3.

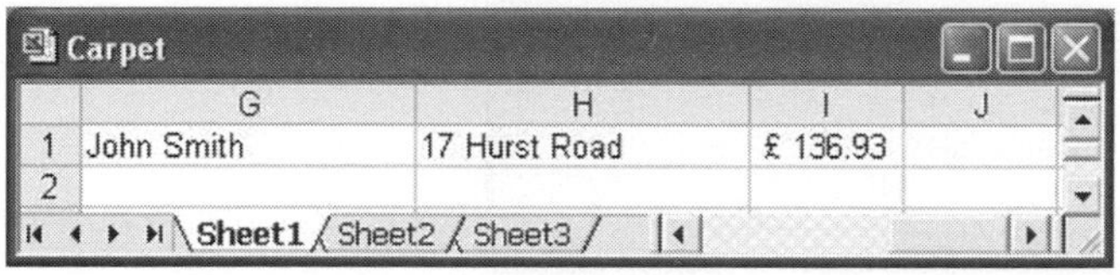

	G	H	I	J
1	John Smith	17 Hurst Road	£ 136.93	
2				

Sheet1 / Sheet2 / Sheet3 /

Figure 12.3

6   Start recording a macro by clicking **Tools, Macro, Record New Macro** and name it **Store.** (Choose a suitable shortcut key.)

7   Switch to **Sheet3**. Click on row heading 2 and click on **Insert, Rows**.

8   Switch back to **Sheet1**. Highlight cells G1, H1 and I1. Click on **Edit, Copy**.

9   Switch back to **Sheet3**. Click on cell A2 and click **Edit, Paste Special, Paste Values, OK**.

Note   If we just use **Edit**, **Paste** at this stage, the formulas and not the value of the quote will be pasted into Sheet3.

---

10   Switch back to **Sheet1**.

11   Press ESCAPE and return the cursor to cell G1.

12   Stop recording and add a button to run the macro.

13   Use the option buttons and the spinner to choose a different carpet. Enter a different name and address in G1 and H1. Save your file.

14   Run the macro again and test that it works as shown in Figure 12.4.

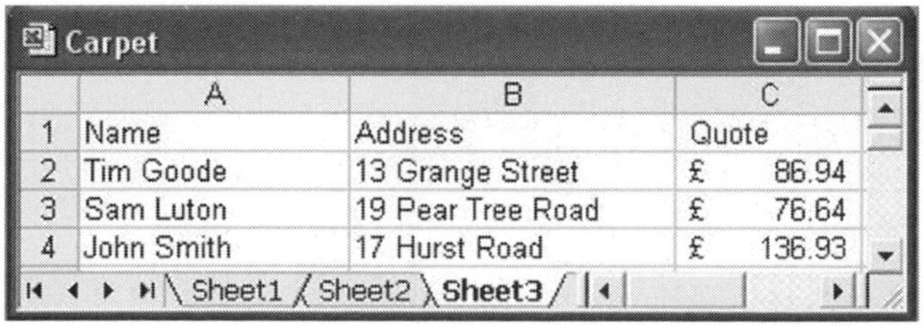

	A	B	C
1	Name	Address	Quote
2	Tim Goode	13 Grange Street	£ 86.94
3	Sam Luton	19 Pear Tree Road	£ 76.64
4	John Smith	17 Hurst Road	£ 136.93

Sheet1 / Sheet2 \ **Sheet3** /

Figure 12.4

Worked example 2: Updating sales figures

A shop stores details of the number of items in stock and the daily sales. These can be calculated using an Excel spreadsheet and automated using macros.

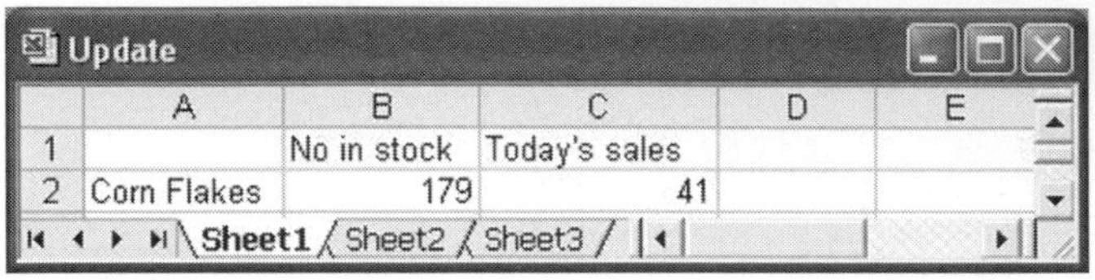

	A	B	C	D	E
1		No in stock	Today's sales		
2	Corn Flakes	179	41		

Sheet1 / Sheet2 / Sheet3

Figure 12.5

Every time the shop sells a packet of Corn Flakes, the number in C2 increases by one. We will set up a macro to automate this procedure.

The macro will add one to the number in C2 (41) and put the answer in D2. This will then be copied into C2 and D2 will be cleared.

1   Load Excel and set up the cells as shown.

2   Click on **Tools, Macro, Record New Macro**.

3   Call the macro **AddOne** and set up the shortcut key as CTRL + SHIFT +M.

4   Click on cell D2.

5   Enter the formula **=C2+1**.

6   Click on cell D2 again and select the **Copy** icon.

7   Click on cell C2 and click on **Edit, Paste Special, Values, OK**.

8   Click on cell D2 again and select **Edit, Clear, All**.

9   Stop recording.

10   Check that if you press CTRL + SHIFT +M, the number in C2 increases by 1.

11   Set up a button over cells D2 and E2 to run this macro as in Figure 12.6.

12   Save the file as **Update**.

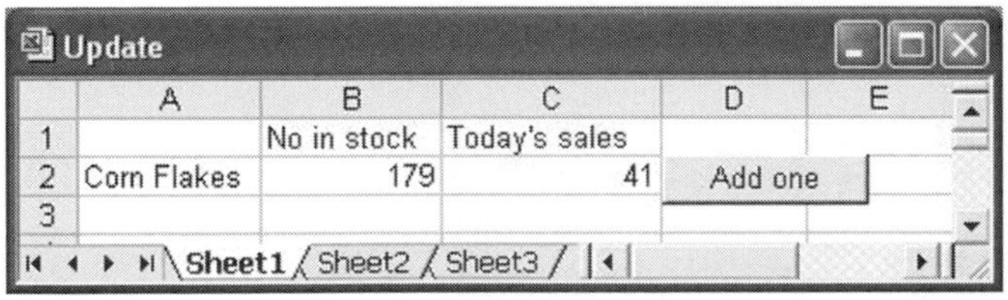

	A	B	C	D	E
1		No in stock	Today's sales		
2	Corn Flakes	179	41	Add one	
3					

Sheet1 / Sheet2 / Sheet3

Figure 12.6

Worked example 3: Updating stock levels

At the end of each day, the shopkeeper needs to update the stock levels and find out if new stock needs to be ordered.

The data is shown in Figure 12.6. The macro will take the number in C2 (41) away from the number in B2 (179). The answer (138) will be in a different cell, E2. This will then be copied into B2. C2 will then be reset to zero and E2 will be cleared. N.B. Do not worry if the button is over the cell E2.

We can record a macro to do the updating automatically as follows:

1 Click on **Tools, Macro, Record New Macro**. Change the name of the macro to **Update**.

2 Click on cell E2 and type in the formula **=B2 − C2**. Press ENTER. *(This works out the new number in stock.)*

3 Click on cell E2 again and click on **Edit, Copy**.

4 Click on cell B2 and click on **Edit, Paste Special, Values** and click on **OK**. *(The new number in stock is now in B2.)*

5 Click on cell C2 and type in **0**. Press ENTER.

6 Click on cell E2 and click on **Edit, Clear, All**.

7 Click on **Stop Recording**.

8 Set up a button over cells F2 and G2 to run the **Update** macro. Your spreadsheet should look like Figure 12.7.

	A	B	C	D	E	F	G
1		No in stock	Today's sales				
2	Corn Flakes	138	0	Add one		Update	
3							

Figure 12.7

9 Test the macro by entering a new figure for today's sales in C2.

10 Test that the number in stock has been updated correctly. Save the file.

Exercise

1   The school tuck shop stocks five chocolate bars listed in Figure 12.8.

	A	B	C	D
1		No in stock	Today's sales	
2	Boost	43	9	
3	Bounty	34	12	
4	Crunchie	19	19	
5	Mars	76	21	
6	Twix	39	6	
7				

Update

Sheet1 \ **Sheet2** / Sh

Figure 12.8

Record a macro called **Update2** to update all stock levels for all the products.

2   A developer wants to build a new shopping mall in town. A school geography class conduct a poll of shoppers about the new mall. The class want a simple click button system of voting as shown in Figure 12.9.

Survey

	A	B	C	D	E
1	In favour	Against	Don't know		
2	21	15	4	In favour	
3					
4					
5				Against	
6					
7					
8					
9				Don't know	
10					
11					

Sheet

Figure 12.9

The computer automatically counts the votes. Set up a system with three macros, so that each time you click on the button the appropriate number increases by one. Save the system as **Survey**.

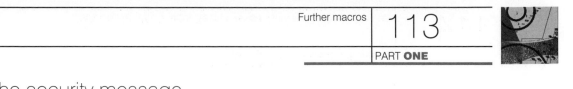

The security message

Figure 12.10

This message in Figure 12.10 appears when you open an Excel file with macros stored in it. It is a protection against viruses that may be stored in macros from an unreliable source.

Click on **Enable Macros** or the macros will not work.

You can disable this warning by clicking on **Tools, Macro, Security**.

Figure 12.11

The box in Figure 12.11 appears. Click on **Low** security. This may not be recommended but is all right if you have written the macros.

Controlling the start-up settings in Excel

The **Auto_open** macro is a macro that automatically runs when you load an Excel file.

You can use it to:

○ set the font;
○ set the font colour;
○ set the background colour;
○ turn on or off some of the toolbars;
○ remove the worksheet tabs;
○ remove the status bar at the bottom of the screen;
○ remove the formula bar;
○ remove the scroll bars;
○ remove the gridlines;
○ remove the row and column headings.

Note

○ There is another macro called the **auto_close** macro, which runs when you close an Excel file. You could use this to put back the controls when you exit from the file.
○ It is possible to disable the **auto_open** macro so that it does not run when the file has been loaded. Simply hold down the SHIFT key while the file is loading.

Setting up an Auto_open macro

We want our system to load without the appearance of a spreadsheet by removing the gridlines, sheet tabs, row and column headings etc.

The steps are:

1   Load the file **Invoice** and start recording a macro called **Auto_open**.

2   Click **Tools, Options**.

3   Uncheck the **Gridlines, Row and column headings, Sheet tabs, Scroll bars**.

4   Uncheck the **Formula bar** and **Status bar** and click on **OK**.

5   Stop recording.

6   Click **Tools, Macro, Visual Basic Editor** to view your macro code.

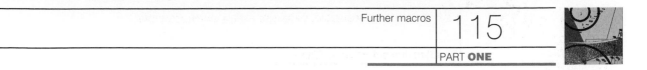

The coding of the **Auto_Open** macro will be as follows:

```
Sub auto_open()
    With ActiveWindow
        .DisplayGridlines = False
        .DisplayHeadings = False
        .DisplayHorizontalScrollBar = False
        .DisplayVerticalScrollBar = False
        .DisplayWorkbookTabs = False
    End With
    With Application
        .DisplayFormulaBar = False
        .DisplayStatusBar = False
    End With
End Sub
```

Record another macro called **Auto_close** to put them all back. Test the macros work when you open the file and close it.

The coding of the **Auto_close** macro will be as follows:

```
Sub auto_close()
    With ActiveWindow
        .DisplayGridlines = True
        .DisplayHeadings = True
        .DisplayHorizontalScrollBar = True
        .DisplayVerticalScrollBar = True
        .DisplayWorkbookTabs = True
    End With
    With Application
        .DisplayFormulaBar = True
        .DisplayStatusBar = True
    End With
End Sub
```

Developing systems

In Unit 10 we set up a file called **Advert** to calculate the prices of newspaper advertisements. We have now seen how to clear and move data using macros. The following example builds on the quote calculator and automatically stores details of quotes elsewhere in the system.

1   Load the file **Advert** from Unit 10 and increase the width of column D of the **Calculator** worksheet to 20. (**Format, Column, Width.**) See Figure 12.12.

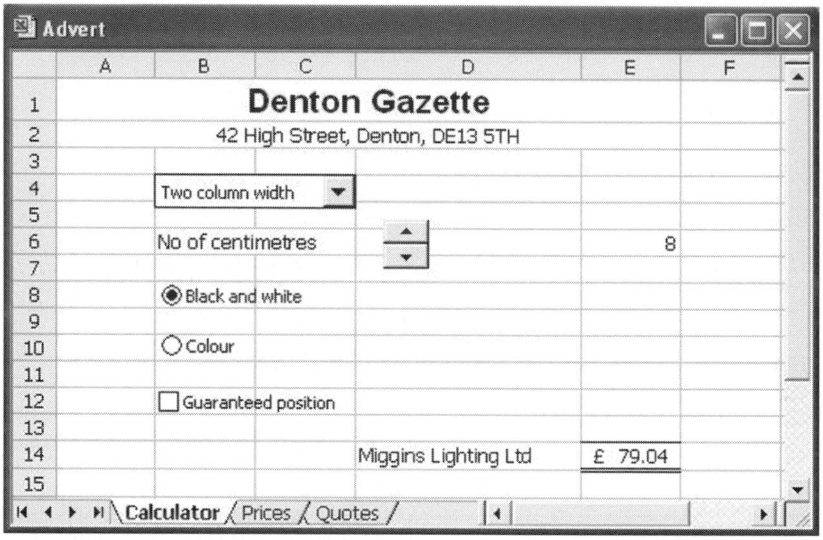

Figure 12.12

2   Enter the name of the customer (**Miggins Lighting Ltd**) in cell D14.

3   Switch to the **Quotes** sheet, increase the width of column A to 20 and enter the column headings as shown in Figure 12.13, format column B to currency.

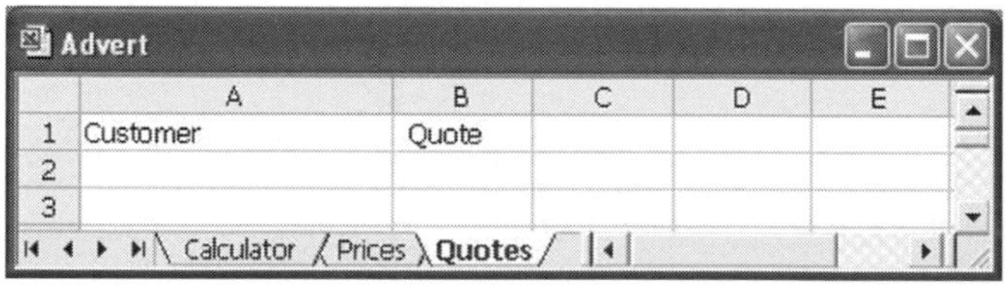

Figure 12.13

4   Go back to the **Calculator** sheet. Start recording a macro called **Filequote** with a shortcut key of CTRL and F. (**Tools, Macro, Record New Macro.**)

5   Switch to the **Quotes** sheet and highlight cells A2 to B2 and click on **Insert, Rows.**

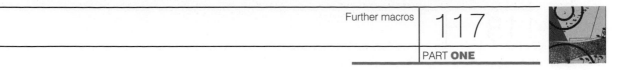
6   Go back to the **Calculator** sheet, highlight cells D14 to E14 and click on **Edit, Copy**.

7   Go back to the **Quotes** sheet and click on **Edit, Paste Special, Values, OK**.

8   Go back to the **Calculator** sheet and stop recording. As always when you have used **Copy**, press the ESC key to deselect.

9   Test the macro works for more customers as in Figure 12.14.

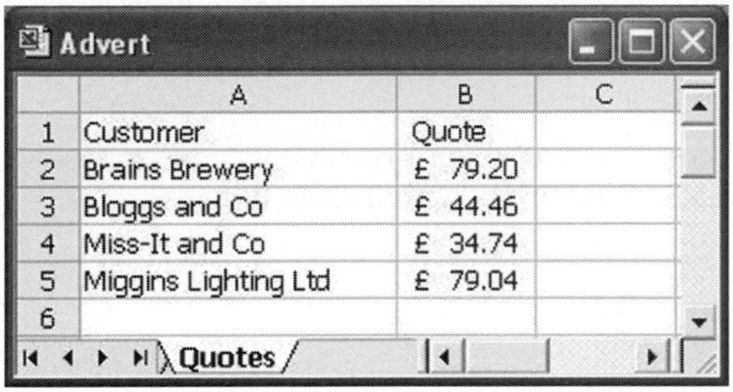

	A	B	C
1	Customer	Quote	
2	Brains Brewery	£ 79.20	
3	Bloggs and Co	£ 44.46	
4	Miss-It and Co	£ 34.74	
5	Miggins Lighting Ltd	£ 79.04	
6			

Figure 12.14

118

⊕ Unit 13 The Visual Basic Editor

In this unit you will learn how to use the Visual Basic Editor to customize certain features in Excel.

The Visual Basic Editor Window is used for entering commands in Excel's programming language Visual Basic, sometimes called VBA (Visual Basic for Applications).

Although you do not need to know anything about Visual Basic to record a macro, you need to know a little about Visual Basic if you want to do things such as:

○ edit macros recorded in Microsoft Excel;
○ set up message boxes and input boxes;
○ set up UserForms.

1 Load the file **Invoice** from Unit 11.

2 Click on **Tools, Macro, Visual Basic Editor** or press ALT + F11 to load the **Visual Basic Editor**.

There are three parts to the **Visual Basic Editor**, the **Project Explorer Window**, the **Properties Window** and the **Visual Basic Editor Window**.

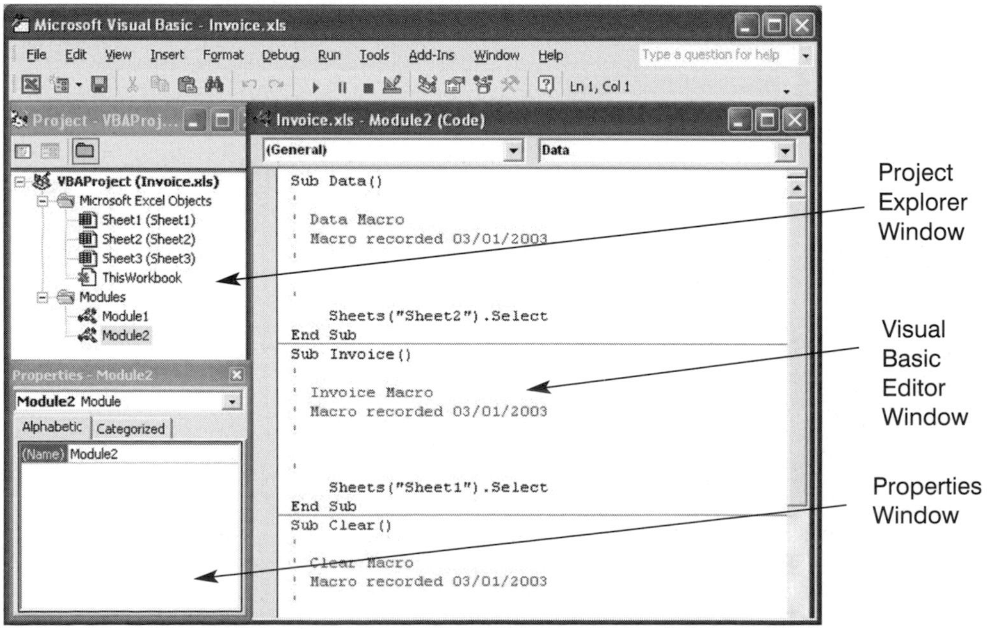

Figure 13.1

Make sure that the **Project Explorer** and the **Properties Window** are on the screen.

If they are turned off click on **View, Project Explorer** and **View, Properties Window**. Adjust the size of the windows and move them in the usual way so that they are in the positions shown in Figure 13.1.

○ **The Project Explorer Window** displays a list of the projects. Any open workbook is a project consisting of worksheets, modules (where macros and other Visual Basic code are stored) and UserForms.

If you double click on **Module1**, the coding for all the macros stored in Module 1 will appear in the Visual Basic Editor window.

Why is there sometimes a Module1 and a Module2?

If you record several macros in one session they will be stored in Module1. If later in another session, you record some more macros, they will be stored in Module 2 and so on. It will not affect the user if a macro is stored in Module1 or Module2.

○ The **Properties Window** displays the properties for the objects that make up the project, e.g. UserForms, Worksheets, Modules.

With just a little knowledge of Visual Basic it is possible to start customizing your systems. The next section uses a little Visual Basic and introduces Message Boxes and Input Boxes.

Message boxes

A message box is a small dialogue box that displays information and requests an action. An example appears in Figure 13.2, a helpline number is given and the user clicks OK.

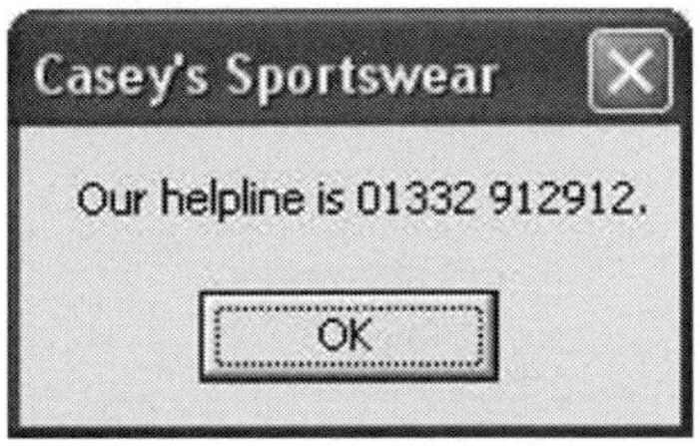

Casey's Sportswear

Our helpline is 01332 912912.

OK

Figure 13.2

Setting up a message box involves one command in Microsoft Visual Basic.

Worked example 1: Setting up a message box

1   Load the file **Invoice** (if it is not already loaded) and click on **Tools, Macro, Visual Basic Editor** to load the Visual Basic Editor.

2   Double click on Module1 in the Project Explorer window. Module1 should appear in the **Project Explorer** window. If it does not appear, click on **Insert, Module**.

3   Scroll down to the bottom of the macro coding in the main Visual Basic Editor window.

4   Enter the following text to set up a macro called Message1.

```
Sub Message1()
MsgBox "Our helpline is 01332 912912.", vbOKOnly, "Casey's Sportswear"
End Sub
```

Note

o The macro must begin with **Sub** and end with **End Sub**.
o You will not need to type in the **End Sub** part, when you enter a line beginning with Sub, the End Sub line is automatically inserted below.
o You can define the title (in this case Casey's Sportswear), the message (the helpline details) and the buttons as shown in Figure 13.2.
o vbOKOnly means you get just an OK button as shown in Figure 13.2.

5   Go back to Excel by clicking on the **View Microsoft Excel** icon.

6   Run the macro Message1 by clicking **Tools, Macro, Macros, Message1, Run** and you will see the message box shown in Figure 13.2.

Worked example 2: Displaying options on a message box

We might want the user to make a choice from a message box. The following example sets up a message box which has a **Yes** button and a **No** button. Clicking on **Yes** exits from Excel. Clicking on **No** does nothing.

1   Load the file **Invoice**.

2   Load the **Visual Basic Editor** and set up the following macro called **quit**.

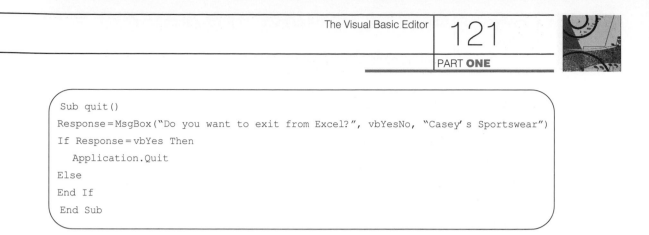

```
Sub quit()
Response=MsgBox("Do you want to exit from Excel?", vbYesNo, "Casey's Sportswear")
If Response=vbYes Then
   Application.Quit
Else
End If
End Sub
```

3 Run the macro and test the options **Yes** and **No**.

Figure 13.3

Exercise 1

1 Create a macro called *About* to set up a message box to say who created your system and give the date. Set up a button to run the macro.

Figure 13.4

2 In Unit 12 we looked at a system called **Survey** to computerize voting in a survey about a shopping centre. Suppose a pupil clicked the wrong button by mistake. By adding four lines at the start of each macro we can use a message box as a check on data entry.

```
Response=MsgBox("Do you want to vote in favour?", vbYesNo, "Check")
If Response=vbNo Then
End
End If
```

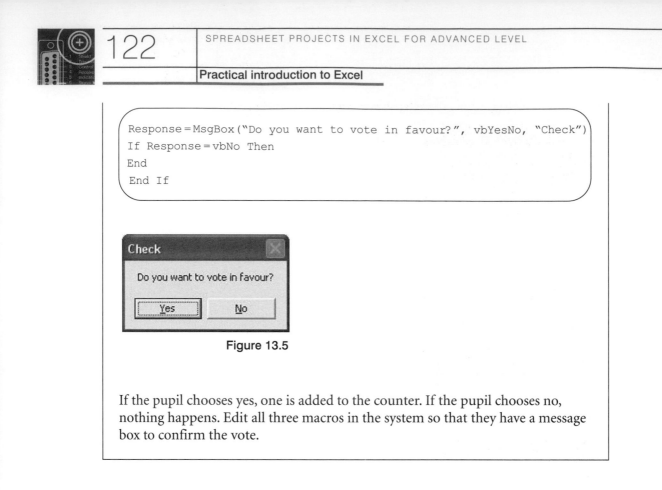

Figure 13.5

If the pupil chooses yes, one is added to the counter. If the pupil chooses no, nothing happens. Edit all three macros in the system so that they have a message box to confirm the vote.

Some useful message box settings

vbOKOnly	Displays the **OK** button only.
vbOKCancel	Displays the **OK** and **Cancel** buttons.
vbAbortRetryIgnore	Displays the **Abort**, **Retry**, and **Ignore** buttons.
vbYesNoCancel	Displays the **Yes**, **No**, and **Cancel** buttons.
vbYesNo	Displays the **Yes** and **No** buttons.

Message box icons

By adding an extra command, you can add one of four special icons to a message box. For example:

vbOKOnly + vbCritical displays the **OK** button and the **Critical Message** icon.

The command would look like this:

```
MsgBox "Created by C.A.Robins © 2003", vbOKOnly+vbCritical, "Information"
```

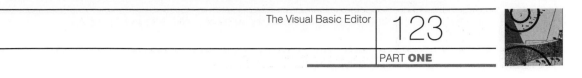

○ Use vbCritical for the **Critical Message** icon in Figure 13.6.

Figure 13.6

○ Use vbQuestion for the **Question Message** icon in Figure 13.7.

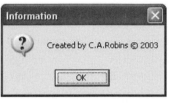

Figure 13.7

○ Use vbExclamation for the **Warning Message** icon in Figure 13.8.

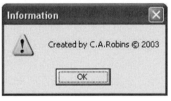

Figure 13.8

○ Use vbInformation for the **Information Message** icon in Figure 13.9.

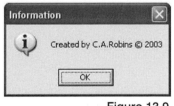

Figure 13.9

Exercise 2

1   Add the information message icon to the message box in exercise 1, question 1.

2   Add the warning query icon to the message boxes in exercise 1, question 2.

Worked example 3: Setting up an input box

An input box is another on-screen dialogue box. You can use it to enter data and paste the data into a cell.

1   Using the file **Invoice**, load the **Visual Basic Editor** by clicking on **Tools, Macro, Visual Basic Editor**.

2   Double click on **Module1** in the Project Explorer Window.

3   Scroll down to the bottom of the macro coding and type in this macro:

```
Sub ibox()
Dim value
Range("A14").Select
value = InputBox("How many football shirts?", "Casey's Sportswear")
ActiveCell.Value = value
End Sub
```

The macro does the following:

○ sets up a variable called value;
○ selects cell A14;
○ loads the input box in Figure 13.10.

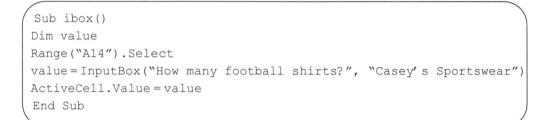

Figure 13.10

○ pastes the input data into cell A14.

Exercise 3

Load the file from Unit 12 called **Update**. Set up a macro to display an input box. The input box asks 'How many packets of Corn Flakes have been delivered today?' The answer is pasted into cell G2.

Extend the macro so that the number delivered today in G2 is added to the number in stock in cell B2.

Developing toggle button macros

Toggle buttons usually allow the user to switch between options at the click of a button.

In Unit 11, with the file **Invoice**, we set up a macro to turn the gridlines on and another to turn them off. It would be better to set up one macro to do both tasks, i.e. if the gridlines are visible, it will turn them off; if they are turned off, it will turn them on again. This is called a toggle macro.

We will set up a macro called GridToggle in Visual Basic to do this.

1   Click on **Tools, Macro, Macros, GridOff, Edit** and underneath the coding type this in:

```
Sub GridToggle()
    mygrid = ActiveWindow.DisplayGridlines
    ActiveWindow.DisplayGridlines = Not mygrid
End Sub
```

2   Set up a button to run this macro.
     The second line of the macro reads the old value asking 'Are the gridlines on or off?' The third line sets the new value to the opposite of the old value.

3   Set up a macro called **TabsToggle** to toggle the worksheet tabs on and off.

Developing systems

Summervale Auctions is a large auction house. They auction around 300 lots in one day. Bids go up £10 at a time. Summervale Auctions want a system that will:

(a) display the current lot number as shown in Figure 13.11;
(b) display the current bid;
(c) use a spinner to increase the bid by £10;
(d) use a macro automatically to add one to the lot number and reset the bid back to £10 after each sale has been recorded;
(e) keep a record of sales so far in Sheet2.

Figure 13.11 shows how the finished system might look.

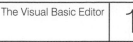

Figure 13.11

Getting started

1   Open a new Excel file and enter **Lot number** into cell A1, **1** into cell A2, enter **Bid** into cell B1 and enter **10** into cell B2. Format B2 to **Currency** and use the **Decrease Decimal** icon to format to no decimal places.

2   Format the widths of columns A and B as appropriate and add a spinner to increase the value of cell B2 by 10 (minimum value 10, incremental change 10, maximum value 3000).

Incrementing the lot number

We will not use a spinner for the lot number but set up a macro called **Add**.

1   Start recording a new macro called **Add**. (**Tools, Macro, Record New Macro.**)

2   Click on A3 and enter the formula **=A2+1**.

3   Click on A3 again and click on **Edit, Copy**. Click on A2 and click on **Edit, Paste Special, Values, OK**.

4   Click on A3 again and click on **Edit, Clear, All**. Click on **Stop Recording**. Test the macro adds one to the lot number.

Resetting the bid

We will now set up a macro to reset the bid to £10.

1   Switch to **Sheet2**.

2   Start recording a new macro called **SetBid**. (**Tools, Macro, Record New Macro.**)

3   Switch to Sheet1 and click on B2. Type **10** and press ENTER twice.

4   Click on **Stop Recording**.

Storing the bids

We will now set up a macro to store the successful bids in Sheet2.

1   Switch to **Sheet2** and put the headings **Lot number** and **Bid** in cells A1 and B1.

2   Format column B to currency, no decimal places. Select cell A2.

3   Switch to **Sheet1**. Start recording a new macro called **Store**. (**Tools, Macro, Record New Macro.**)

4   Highlight cells A2 and B2. Click on **Edit, Copy**.

5   Switch to **Sheet2**. (A2 should still be selected.)

6   Click on **Edit, Paste Special, Values, OK**.

7   Click on the **Relative Reference** icon (on the Stop Recording toolbar).

8   Use the arrow key to move down one cell to A3 and click on **Stop Recording**.

Combining the macros to automate the system

We can now edit the **Store** macro to store the data, add one to the lot number and reset the bid value to £10.

1 Click on **Tools, Macro, Macros**. Select the **Store** macro and choose **Edit**.

2 Click at the start of the last line (End Sub) and press ENTER twice.

3 On the first blank line type **SetBid** and on the second blank line type **Add**.

4 Save the macro. The coding will look like Figure 13.12. Switch back to Excel, go to **Sheet1** and add a button to run the **Store** macro.

```
auction.xls - Module1 (Code)

(General)                                              store

Sub store()
'
'  store Macro
'  Macro recorded 23/04/2003
'


'
     Range("A2:B2").Select
     Selection.Copy
     Sheets("Sheet2").Select
     Selection.PasteSpecial Paste:=xlPasteValues, Operation:=xlNone, SkipBlanks _
        :=False, Transpose:=False
     ActiveCell.Offset(1, 0).Range("A1").Select
SetBid
Add
End Sub
```

Figure 13.12

5 Test it all works as shown in Figure 13.13.

6 Fully customize your solution by adding **auto_open** and **auto_close** macros.

	A	B
	Lot number	Bid
1		
2	1	£60
3	2	£10
4	3	£70
5	4	£10
6	5	£100
7	6	£100
8	7	£20
9	8	£10

Auction — Sheet1 / Sheet2

Figure 13.13

⊕ Unit 14 UserForms

In this unit you will learn about UserForms and how they can be used as a user-friendly front end for an Excel workbook.

A UserForm is a way of providing a customized user-interface for your system. Sometimes it is called a dialogue box. A typical UserForm might look like the one in Figure 14.1 which we will set up in this unit.

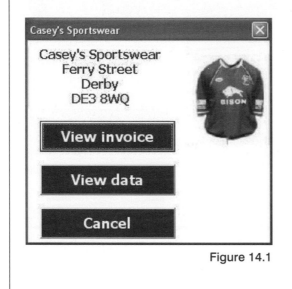

Figure 14.1

Worked example : Setting up a UserForm as a front end

1   Load the file **Invoice**.

This file contains macros called **Invoice** and **Data** to switch between the different worksheets.

2   Load the **Visual Basic Editor** by clicking on **Tools, Macro, Visual Basic Editor** or pressing ALT and F11.

3   Click on **Insert, UserForm** or click on the Insert UserForm icon. A blank UserForm will appear in the main Visual Basic Editor window as in Figure 14.2.

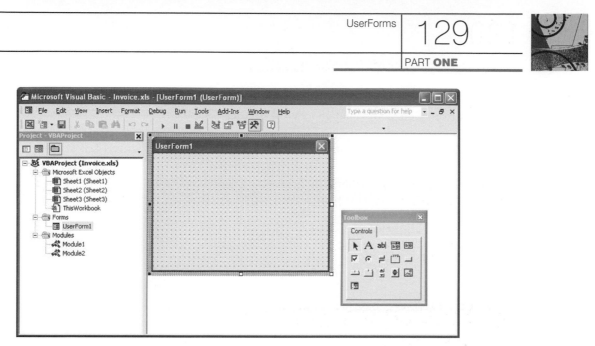

Figure 14.2

4   The Toolbox will also appear as shown in Figure 14.3. If it is not visible, click on the blank UserForm and click on **View, Toolbox**.

Figure 14.3

5   On the Toolbox, click on the **CommandButton** icon and drag out a rectangle on the UserForm near the middle, as shown in Figure 14.4.

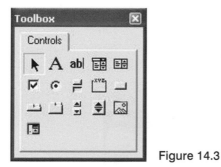

Figure 14.4

6   The text on the button will say **CommandButton1**. Edit this by clicking once on the button. Delete and change to **View invoice**.

7   Double click on the button. You will see the code shown in Figure 14.5.

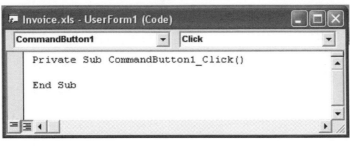

Figure 14.5

The cursor should be in the middle of these two lines. If not, click between the two lines.

8   Enter this text as shown in Figure 14.6.

```
Invoice
UserForm1.Hide
```

Figure 14.6

Invoice is the name of the macro that will run when you click on this button.

The command **UserForm1.Hide** removes the UserForm from the screen.

Note The spelling and the punctuation must be exactly as above or it won't work.

9　Click on **View, Object** or click on the **View Object** icon in the Project Explorer Window (top left of screen) shown in Figure 14.7 to go back to the plan of the UserForm.

Figure 14.7

10　In the same way add another button as shown in Figure 14.8 to run the other macro called **Data**.

11　Click on the **Label** icon in the Toolbox. Drag out a rectangle near the top of the UserForm and enter the name of the company. The UserForm will now look like Figure 14.8. Use the Format options to align and size the buttons.

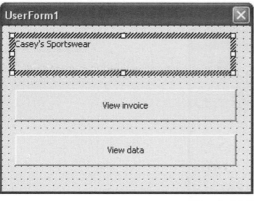

Figure 14.8

Using the Properties Window

The Properties Window at the bottom left-hand corner of the screen is used to set the properties of the UserForm. For example it is used to set the caption, the size, the colour, the font and any links to cells in the spreadsheet.

1   Select the label **Casey's Sportswear**. In the **Properties Window** (see Figure 14.9) scroll down to **Font**. Click on the three dots icon and set the size to **18**.

Properties - Label1

Label1 Label

Alphabetic	Categorized
(Name)	Label1
Accelerator	
AutoSize	False
BackColor	&H8000000F&
BackStyle	1 - fmBackStyleOpaque
BorderColor	&H80000006&
BorderStyle	0 - fmBorderStyleNone
Caption	Casey's Sportswear
ControlTipText	
Enabled	True
Font	Tahoma ...
ForeColor	&H80000012&
Height	24
HelpContextID	0

Figure 14.9

2   Scroll down to the **Text Align** property and select **2-fm TextAlignCenter** to centre the text.

3   Click off the label and on the UserForm. Select the **Caption** property to set the Caption to **Casey's Sportswear**. The UserForm will now look like Figure 14.10.

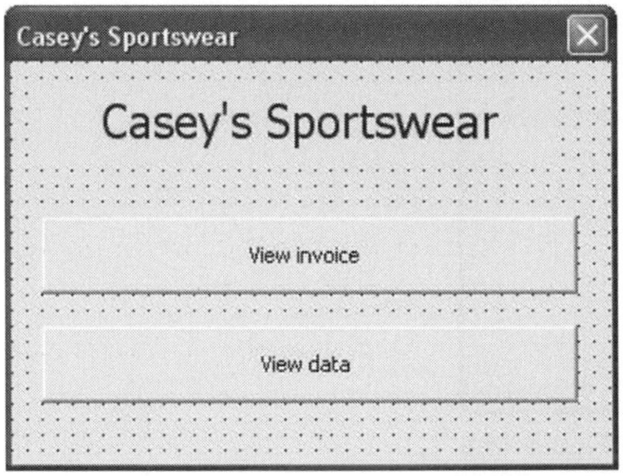

Casey's Sportswear

Casey's Sportswear

View invoice

View data

Figure 14.10

The UserForm is now set up.

4   Save your file by clicking on the Save icon. Test the UserForm by clicking on the **Run Sub/UserForm** icon or by pressing F5. The UserForm will load. Click on the Close icon (the X in the top right hand corner of the UserForm) to go back to the Visual Basic Editor.

> # Note
>
> If when you are in the Visual Basic Editor, you insert a second UserForm by mistake, you can delete it by clicking on File, Remove UserForm.

Setting up a macro to display your UserForm

Once you have designed a UserForm, you will need to set up a macro to display it. The macro will be set up in Visual Basic and once again, exact syntax is vital.

1   In Excel, click on **Tools, Macro, Visual Basic Editor**.

2   Double click on Module1 in the Project Explorer window, shown in Figure 14.11. If Module1 is not visible click on the + sign next to **Modules** in the Project Explorer window. Then double click on Module1.

Figure 14.11

3   You should see the coding for the macros you have already set up. Scroll down to the bottom and underneath the last macro text, type in the following:

```
Sub Box()
Load UserForm1
UserForm1.Show
End Sub
```

The two middle lines of code load the UserForm and display it on the screen. You will not need to type in the **End Sub** part as when you enter a line beginning with Sub, the End Sub line is automatically inserted below.

4   This sets up a macro called **Box**. Click on the **View Microsoft Excel** icon to go back to Excel.

5   Check the macro works using **Tools, Macro, Macros**. Click on **Box, Run**.

6   Test that the UserForm works for both buttons.

Set up an icon on the toolbars to run the **Box** macro. This will save time.

7   Go back to the Visual Basic Editor. Load the UserForm by double clicking on UserForm1 in the Project Explorer window.

8   In the Properties Window set the **Height** of the UserForm to 220 or extend the UserForm just by dragging downwards. Add an extra button as in Figure 14.12. Edit the text on the button to read **Cancel**. Double click on the new button and make the text read as follows:

```
Private Sub CommandButton3_Click()
End
End Sub
```

Figure 14.12

9   Save your file.

Each item on a UserForm such as a command button, a combo box or a text box is an object.

Each object has a unique name such as CommandButton1, TextBox6 or ComboBox4.

If you double click on the UserForm, you will see the code for each object. It will appear as follows:

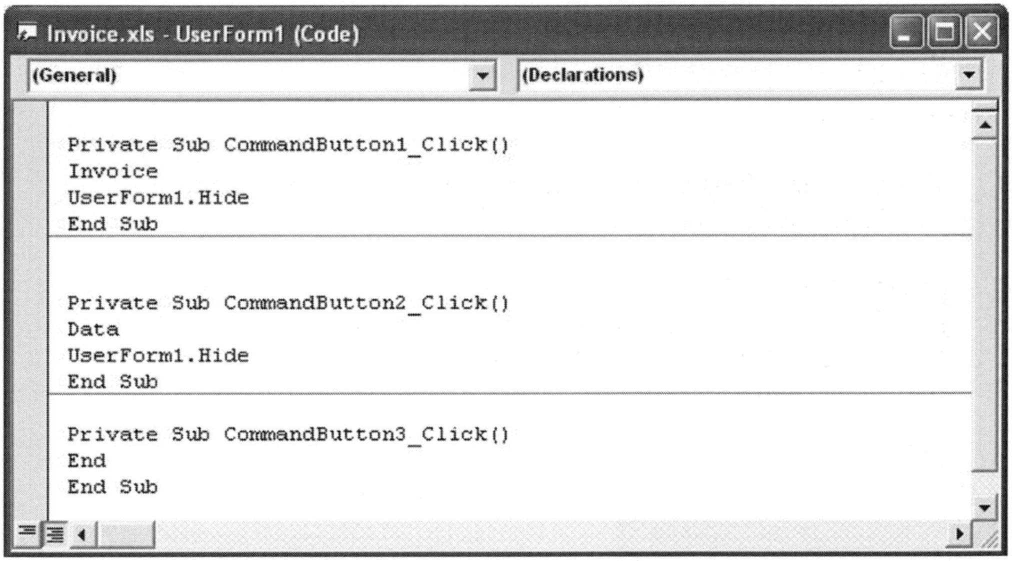

```
Invoice.xls - UserForm1 (Code)

(General)                    (Declarations)

    Private Sub CommandButton1_Click()
    Invoice
    UserForm1.Hide
    End Sub


    Private Sub CommandButton2_Click()
    Data
    UserForm1.Hide
    End Sub


    Private Sub CommandButton3_Click()
    End
    End Sub
```

Figure 14.13

Customizing your UserForm

You can develop your UserForm in a number of ways. For example by:

○ editing background colours;
○ changing the font;
○ adding an image;
○ resizing the UserForm.

The properties of each object are set up in the Properties Window.

1   Go back to the **Visual Basic Editor** and load the UserForm by double clicking on UserForm1 in the Project Explorer window as shown in Figure 14.14.

Figure 14.14

2   To edit the background colour, click on the UserForm. In the Properties Window, click on **BackColor**. Click on the drop-down arrow and choose **Palette** as in Figure 14.15. You have a variety of colours to choose from.

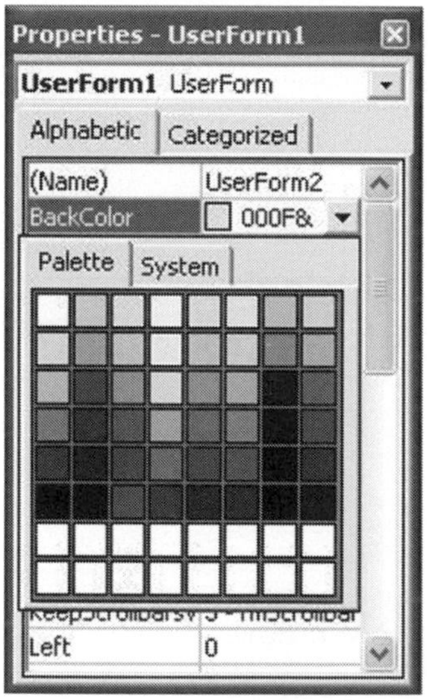

Figure 14.15

3   Click on one of the command buttons on the UserForm. Use the Properties Window to change the colour of the button, the colour of the text (**ForeColor**) and the font as required. Repeat this for the other buttons and the label.

4   To add a picture, click on the Image icon in the Toolbox and drag out a rectangle on the UserForm. Click on the row called **Picture** in the Properties Window. Double click on the icon with three dots to select a picture. Find the picture you require. Choose **PictureSizeMode 3** so that the picture resizes to fit.

5   Add a control tip text to your buttons using the Control Tip Text row of the Properties Window. Whatever you type in here appears on the screen as help text when you move the mouse over a control like a text box.

6   Resize the UserForm and the command buttons by dragging the controls in the normal way.

7   Save your file.

UserForms can be made to look eye-catching as shown in Figure 14.16.

Figure 14.16

⊕ Unit 15 Using UserForms to enter data

In this unit you will learn about how UserForms can be used to enter data into an Excel workbook.

Text boxes on a UserForm can be linked to cells in a spreadsheet and can be used for entering data. List boxes can be used to display data from the spreadsheet in the UserForm.

Obviously you can just type the data straight into the cells, but using a UserForm can make it easier for the user and gives greater control over data entry.

You can include other controls in a UserForm such as command buttons, combo boxes and option buttons as shown by the example in Figure 15.1 which we will set up in this unit.

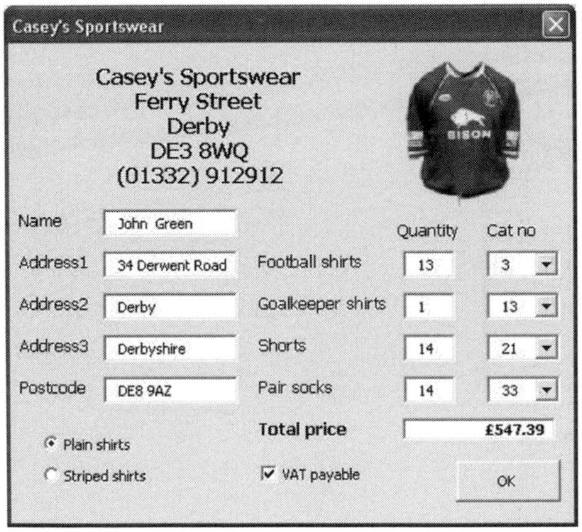

Casey's Sportswear

Casey's Sportswear
Ferry Street
Derby
DE3 8WQ
(01332) 912912

			Quantity	Cat no
Name	John Green			
Address1	34 Derwent Road	Football shirts	13	3
Address2	Derby	Goalkeeper shirts	1	13
Address3	Derbyshire	Shorts	14	21
Postcode	DE8 9AZ	Pair socks	14	33

○ Plain shirts
○ Striped shirts

Total price £547.39

☑ VAT payable   OK

Figure 15.1

Worked example: The football kit invoice

Setting up the UserForm

1   Load the file **Invoice** used in the previous unit.

We need to set up the UserForm to enter the customer's name and address and details of purchases, i.e. catalogue number, quantity, whether VAT is payable and whether the shirts are plain or striped. The total price will be displayed also.

2   Load the **Visual Basic Editor** by pressing ALT + F11. Insert a UserForm by clicking on **Insert, UserForm.** This will be called UserForm2.

3   Enlarge the UserForm so that it is 360 wide and 330 high. (These can be set using the **Width** and **Height** properties in the Properties Window.)

4   In the Properties Window, set the **Caption** to **Casey's Sportswear**. Add a label with the company address (use font size 12) and a suitable picture for a logo as shown in Figure 15.2.

Note   To go on to a new line in the label, press CTRL and ENTER.

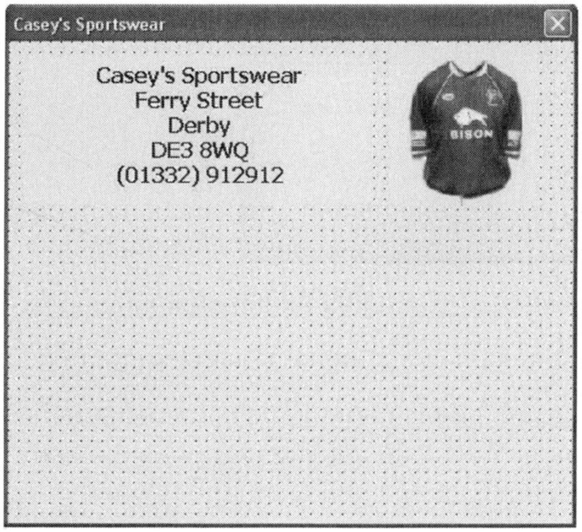

Casey's Sportswear
Ferry Street
Derby
DE3 8WQ
(01332) 912912

Figure 15.2

5   Add a Command Button at the bottom right on the UserForm as shown in Figure 15.3. Edit its text to **OK**.

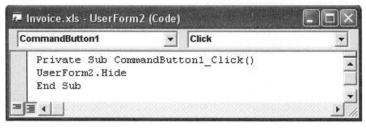

Figure 15.3

6   Double click on the button and add the text **UserForm2.Hide** as shown in Figure 15.4. This will close the User Form when OK is clicked.

Figure 15.4

7   Double click on Module1 in the Project Explorer Window. Scroll down to the bottom and add this macro:

```
Sub Details()
Load Userform2
Userform2.Show
End Sub
```

This sets up a macro called **Details** to load the UserForm.

8   Switch back to Excel to test that running the macro displays the UserForm.

Adding text boxes to enter details of purchase

1 Switch back to the Visual Basic Editor. Double click on UserForm2. Click on the **TextBox** icon in the Toolbox and drag out a box on the right-hand side of the UserForm as shown in Figure 15.5.

Figure 15.5

2 With the box selected, set the **Control Source** in the **Properties Window** to **A14** as shown in Figure 15.6.

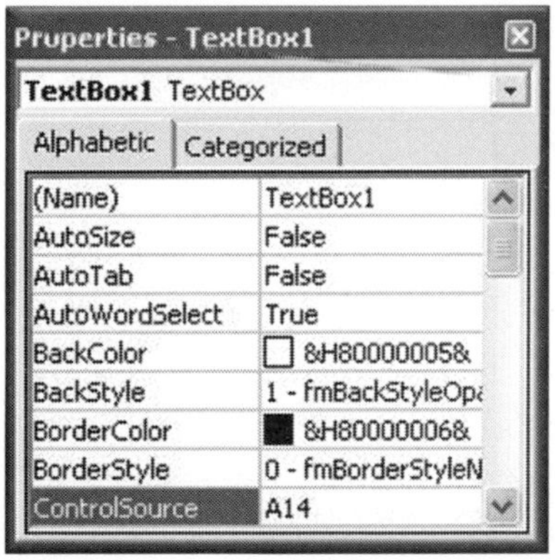

Figure 15.6

3   Click on the Label icon and drag out a box above the text box. Enter the text
Quantity into the Label as shown in Figure 15.7. Change the font and colour of
the text if required.

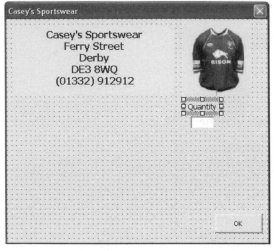

Figure 15.7

4   We now need to add extra text boxes and labels as shown in Figure 15.8.

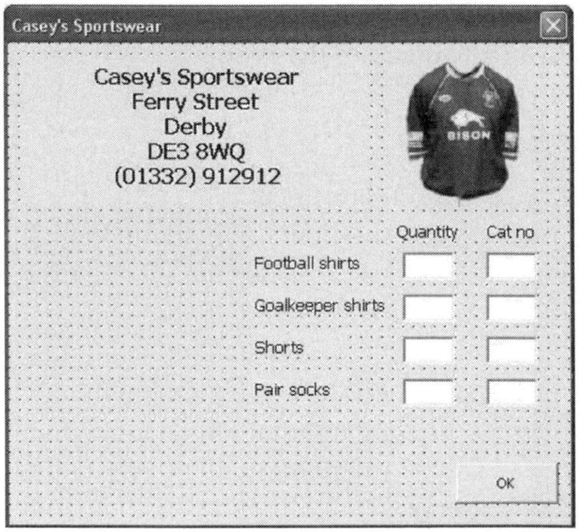

Figure 15.8

5   We need to set the **Control Source** for each text box as follows:
Football shirts catalogue number – **B14**
Goalkeeper shirts quantity – **A15**
Goalkeeper shirts catalogue number – **B15**
Shorts quantity – **A16**
Shorts catalogue number – **B16**
Pair of socks quantity – **A17**
Pair of socks catalogue number – **B17**

6   Switch back to Excel. Make sure that Sheet1 is showing and run the **Details**
macro. Test that as you enter data into the text boxes the data entered goes into
the correct cell as shown in Figure 15.9.

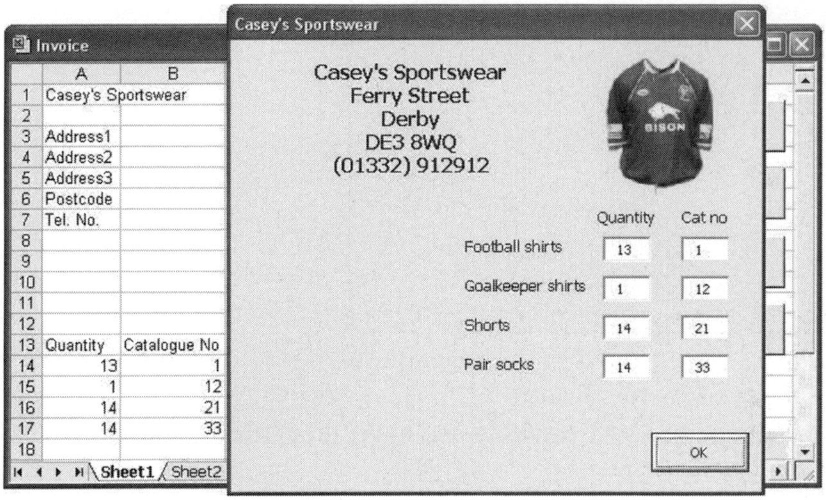

Figure 15.9

7   Save your file.

Adding a check box for VAT

We now want to add a check box to the UserForm to choose if VAT is payable.

1 Switch back to the Visual Basic Editor. Load UserForm2 by double clicking on UserForm2 in the Project Explorer Window.

2 Click on the **CheckBox** icon in the Toolbox and drag out a rectangle at the foot of the UserForm, as shown in Figure 15.10.

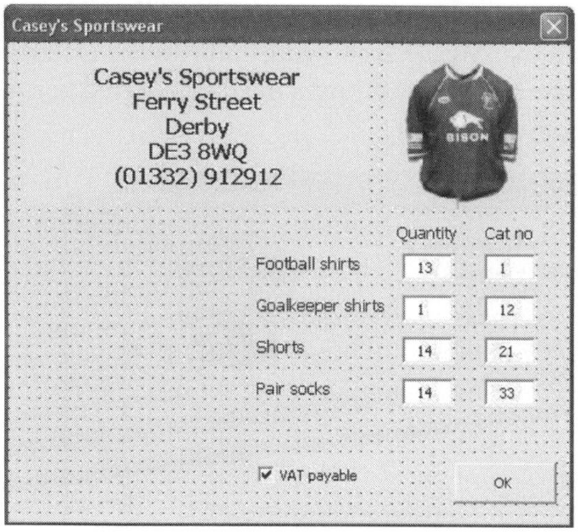

Figure 15.10

3 Edit the text to read **VAT payable** and in the Properties Window set the **Control Source** source to **A23**.

4 Switch to Excel and run the UserForm again. Test that the check box works.

Adding option buttons to select the type of shirt

We now want to add option buttons to the UserForm to choose striped or plain shirts.

1 In the Visual Basic Editor, use the **OptionButton** icon in the Toolbox to add two option buttons as shown in Figure 15.11. Set the **Control Source** for Plain shirts to **A18**.

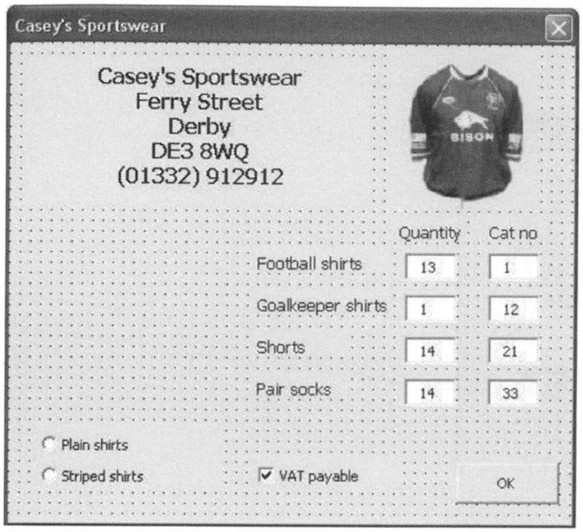

Figure 15.11

2   In Excel enter the formula **=IF(A18=TRUE,1,2)** into cell A19.

3   Run the details macro and test that the option buttons work.

Adding combo boxes to speed up data entry

As the catalogue number for football shirts can only be 1, 2 or 3, we can replace the top right text box on the UserForm with a combo box (drop-down box) giving a choice of 1, 2 or 3. This will speed up data entry and reduce the chance of mistakes. Set it up as follows:

1   In the Visual Basic Editor, load UserForm2 by double clicking on UserForm2 in the Project Explorer Window

2   Click on the top right text box. (It is in the football shirts row and the catalogue number column.) Press DELETE on the keyboard.

3   Click on the **ComboBox** icon in the Toolbox.

4   Drag out a box on the UserForm to replace the deleted text box as shown in Figure 15.12.

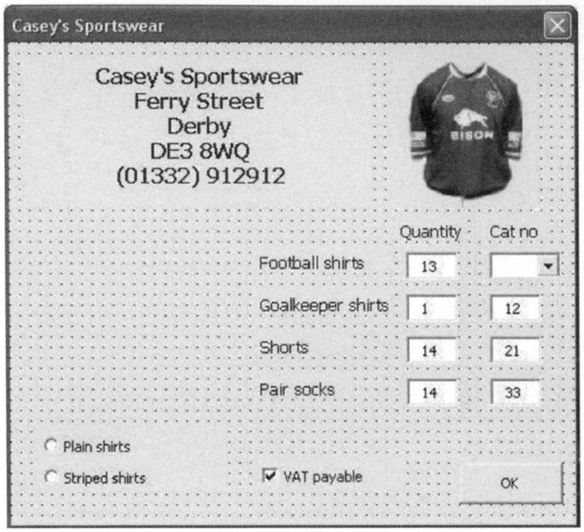

Figure 15.12

5   With the combo box still selected, set the **Control Source** in the properties window to cell **B14** and the Row Source to **Sheet2!A3:A5**.

6   Test the UserForm to ensure that it works and the items in the drop-down list are correct as shown in Figure 15.13.

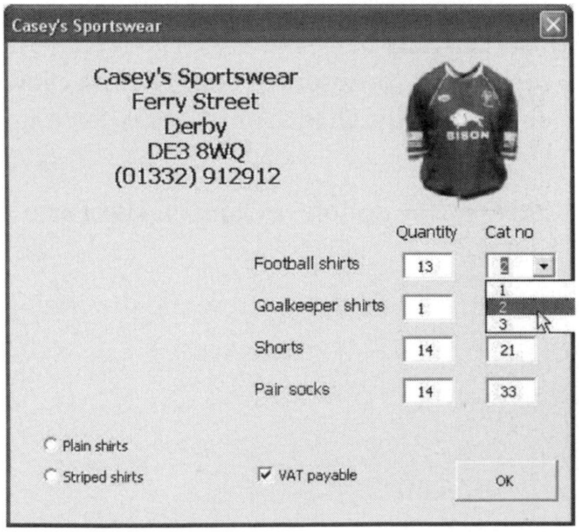

Figure 15.13

7   Develop the UserForm further by adding a combo box for the other three
    catalogue numbers as in Figure 15.14.

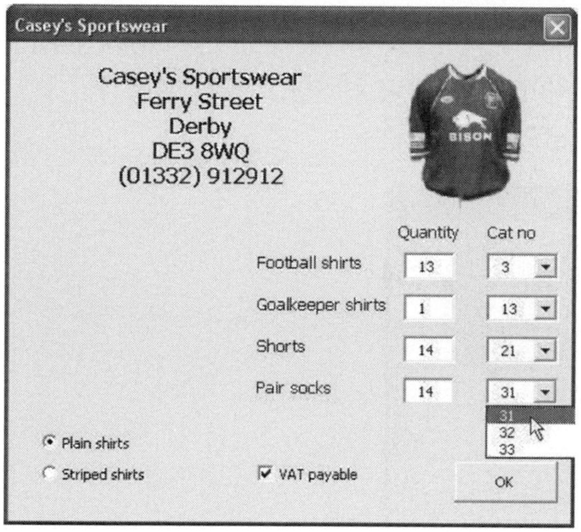

Figure 15.14

Adding text boxes for customer details

1   Add five text boxes on the left of the UserForm as shown in Figure 15.15.

2   Add the labels as shown.

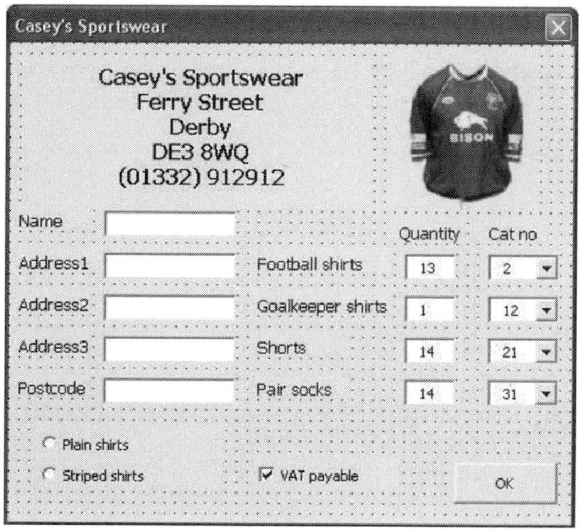

Figure 15.15

3   In the Properties Window set the **Control Source** for these text boxes to **E6** to **E10** respectively. This enables the name and address of the customer to appear on the UserForm.

4   Still in the Visual Basic Editor, click on the **ListBox** icon in the Toolbox. Drag out a box above the OK button, as shown in Figure 15.16.

5   Add a label **Total price** as shown.

Casey's Sportswear
Ferry Street
Derby
DE3 8WQ
(01332) 912912

	Quantity	Cat no
Football shirts	13	2
Goalkeeper shirts	1	12
Shorts	14	21
Pair socks	14	31

Name

Address1

Address2

Address3

Postcode

○ Plain shirts
○ Striped shirts

Total price
☑ VAT payable

OK

Figure 15.16

6   Select the list box. In the Properties Window, set the Row Source to **E23**, set the font to **bold** and align the text to the **right**.

7   Create a new macro called **Auto_open** as shown below so that UserForm2 is displayed when the file loads.

```
Sub Auto_open()
Load UserForm2
UserForm2.Show
End Sub
```

8   Save your file and test it thoroughly.

Unit 16 Running a system from a UserForm

In this unit you will learn how to develop and run a system from a UserForm.

Worked example: The ideal weight problem

Problem statement

Fitness, diet and healthy eating magazines often produce tables of ideal weights according to a person's sex and height as shown in Figure 16.1.

Weight						
	A	B	C	D	E	F
1		Men		Women		
2		Min	Max	Min	Max	
3	Height (cm)		Weight (kg)			
4	158	51	64	46	59	
5	160	52	65	48	61	
6	162	53	66	49	62	
7	164	54	67	50	64	
8	166	55	69	51	65	
9	168	56	71	52	66	
10	170	58	73	53	67	
11	172	59	74	55	69	
12	174	60	75	56	70	
13	176	62	77	58	72	
14	178	64	79	59	74	
15	180	65	80	60	76	
16	182	66	82	62	78	
17	184	67	84	63	80	
18						

Sheet1 / Sheet2 / Sheet3 /

Figure 16.1

- A system will be produced to allow a user to enter their sex and height.
- The system will calculate from tables the user's ideal maximum and minimum weight range.
- The output will be to screen with an option to print.

A brief design overview

A spinner will be used to enter a person's height in centimetres. It will be linked to cell J1.

Option buttons will be used to enter the user's sex. This will be linked to cell J2 which will store TRUE if male and FALSE if female.

J3 will be used to decide which columns to look up based on whether the user is male or female. The minimum weight for a man is in column 2. The minimum weight for a woman is in column 4. So if the user is a man, this cell will read 2. If the user is a woman, the cell will display 4.

Cell J4 will be used to look up the minimum value from either column 2 or column 4.

Cell J5 will be used to look up the maximum value from either column 3 or column 5.

Setting up the worksheet

1   Enter the details as shown in Figure 16.1 and save the file as **Weight**.

Note   You can download this file from **www.hodderictcoursework.co.uk**

2   Highlight the cells from A4 to E17 and give them the name **Table** using **Insert, Name, Define**.

3   Enter 170 into J1.
(This is the person's height.)

4   In J2 enter **TRUE**.
(TRUE represents Male, FALSE represents Female.)

5   In J3 enter **=IF(J2=TRUE,2,4)**.
(This shows which column to look in for the minimum weight. Column 2 for male, column 4 for female.)

6   In J4 enter **=VLOOKUP(J1,Table,J3)**.
(This looks up the minimum weight in either column 2 or column 4.)

7   In J5 enter **=VLOOKUP(J1,Table,J3+1)**.
(This looks up the maximum weight in either column 3 or column 5.)

The formulas are shown in Figure 16.2.

	J	K
1	170	
2	TRUE	
3	=IF(J2=TRUE,2,4)	
4	=VLOOKUP(J1,Table,J3)	
5	=VLOOKUP(J1,Table,J3+1)	
6		

Weight — Sheet1 / Sheet2 / Shee

Figure 16.2

The LOOKUP function in J4 and J5 looks up the minimum and maximum weights for the height in J1. For a male of height of 170, they should read 58 and 73.

Setting up the UserForm

1   Load the Visual Basic Editor Window by clicking on **Tools, Macro, Visual Basic Editor** or pressing ALT + F11.

2   Click on **Insert, UserForm** or click on the **Insert UserForm** icon.

3   In the Properties Window, set the Caption to **Your Ideal Weight**.

4   Also in the Properties Window, set the background colour to light grey as shown in Figure 16.3.

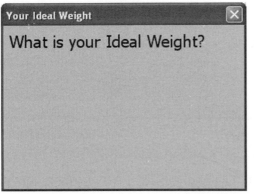

Figure 16.3

5   From the Toolbox use the Label tool to put the title **What is your Ideal Weight?** at the top of your UserForm.

6   Select the label and in the Properties Window, set the font size to 16. You may wish to set the background colour of the label too. The UserForm will look like Figure 16.4.

Figure 16.4

Setting up the spinner to adjust the height

1   Click on the Spin Button icon on the Toolbox and drag out a Spinner near the top of the UserForm. If the spinner is pointing horizontally, hold down the ALT key and resize the spinner so that it points vertically.

2   With the spinner still selected, set Max in the Properties window to **184**, Min to **158**, Small Change to **2** and then set the Control Source to **J1**.

3   Double click on the spinner and edit the text to read as follows:

```
Private Sub SpinButton1_Change()
Range("J1").Value = SpinButton1.Value
End Sub
```

This means that as you click the spinner, the value in cell J1 updates immediately.

4   Click on the **Close** icon to return to the UserForm.

5   Click on the **Run Sub/UserForm** icon to load the UserForm as shown in Figure 16.5 and test the spinner. It should alter the numbers in J1, J4 and J5.

	A	B	C	D	E	F	G	H	I	J
1		Men		Women						170
2		Min	Max	Min	Max					TRUE
3	Height (cm)		Weight (kg)							2
4	158	51	64	46	59					58
5	160	52	65	48	61					73
6	162	53	66	49	62					
7	164	54	67	50	64					
8	166	55	69	51	65					
9	168	56	71	52	66					
10	170	58	73	53	67					
11	172	59	74	55	69					
12	174	60	75	56	70					
13	176	62	77	58	72					
14	178	64	79	59	74					
15	180	65	80	60	76					
16	182	66	82	62	78					
17	184	67	84	63	80					
18										
19										

Your Ideal Weight

What is your Ideal Weight ?

Figure 16.5

6   Close the UserForm by clicking on the close icon. Return to the Visual Basic Editor and save your file.

7   In the Visual Basic Editor, click on the Text Box icon in the Toolbox and drag out a small text box underneath the spinner as shown in Figure 16.6 and set the Control Source in the Properties window to **J1**.

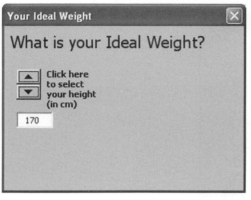

Figure 16.6

8   Add a label to your spinner as shown in Figure 16.6.

9   Click on the **Run Sub/UserForm** icon to test that the number in the text box goes up or down by 2 when the spinner is clicked. Save your file.

Adding option buttons to select Male or Female

1   Click on the Option Button icon in the Toolbox and add an option button to your UserForm. Edit the label to **Male** as in Figure 16.7 and set the Control Source to **J2**.

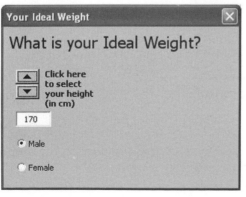

Figure 16.7

2   Add another option button labelled **Female**. You must not set the Control Source. Click on the **Run Sub/UserForm** icon to test that as you choose Female, the numbers change in J4 and J5. Save your file.

Adding list boxes to look up the weights

1   Click on the List Box icon in the Toolbox and add a list box to your UserForm as shown in Figure 16.8. Set the Row Source set to **J4**.

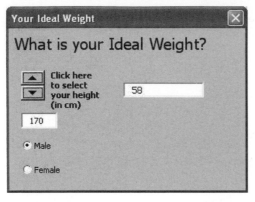

Figure 16.8

2   Add another list box with Row Source set to J5 and add labels as shown in Figure 16.9.

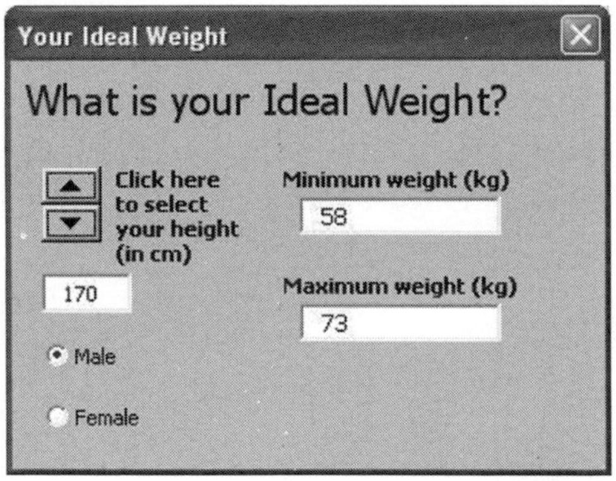

Figure 16.9

3   Click on the **Run Sub/UserForm** icon to test that as you click on the spinner, the maximum and minimum weights change. Save your file.

 Note   When linking a UserForm box to a cell with a formula or a lookup, use a **list box**.

Adding Print and Exit options using command buttons

1   Click on the Command Button icon in the Toolbox to add a command button as in Figure 16.10. Edit the text on the button to **Print**.

2   Double click on button. Edit the text so that it reads as follows:

```
Private Sub CommandButton1_Click()
UserForm1.PrintForm
End Sub
```

3   Add another command button. Edit the text on the button to **Exit**.

4   Double click on button. Edit the text so that it reads as follows:

```
Private Sub CommandButton2_Click()
Application.Quit
End Sub
```

Your Ideal Weight

What is your Ideal Weight?

Click here to select your height (in cm)

Minimum weight (kg)
58

170

Maximum weight (kg)
73

○ Male

○ Female   Print   Exit

Figure 16.10

5   Save your file. Click on the **Run Sub/UserForm** icon and test the buttons.

Finishing the system

1   Click on the Image icon in the Toolbox to add a suitable image to your UserForm as shown in Figure 16.11. Use the Picture property to select the image.

2 Enlarge the fonts of list boxes and centre the text as shown in Figure 16.11.

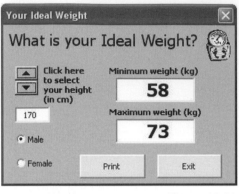

Figure 16.11

3 Click on **Insert, Module**. This opens a Visual Basic Editor window where macro coding is entered and stored.

4 Enter this macro in the Visual Basic Editor window:

```
Sub Auto_open()
Load UserForm1
UserForm1.Show
End Sub
```

This sets up an Auto_open macro to load the User Form when Excel loads.

5 Go back to Excel by clicking on the **View Microsoft Excel** icon.

6 Remove the gridlines by clicking on **Tools, Options** and unchecking **Gridlines**.

7 Highlight all the cells and hide the contents by setting the text colour to white.

8 Save your file.

9 Close the file. Reload the file and test that the system works.

Ideas for further development

You can develop the system further by:

○ removing row and column headings;
○ removing the toolbars;
○ removing the scroll bars;
○ removing the status bar, formula bar and tabs;
○ adding a second sheet storing the heights and weights in Imperial units;
○ setting up a UserForm for the user to select either Imperial or metric units.

Unit 17 Scenarios and pivot tables

Scenarios

> In this unit you will learn how to use scenarios to save different versions of the same worksheet.

Worked example

The Hotel Manhattan wants to plan their cash-flow. Their occupancy rates are around 70 to 80 per cent in summer and 50 to 60 per cent in winter. They can store various predictions for their income using **Scenarios**.

	A	B	C	D	E
1			Hotel Manhattan		
2	**Type of room**	**Price per night**	**No of rooms**	**Income if full**	
3	Single room	67	42	=B3*C3	
4	Double room	87	31	=B4*C4	
5	Suite	120	3	=B5*C5	
6	Penthouse	250	1	=B6*C6	
7				=SUM(D3:D6)	
8					
9	**Season**	**Month**	**No of days**	**Forecast occupancy**	**Revenue**
10	High season	May to September	153	1	=D10*C10*D7
11	Low season	October to April	212	1	=D11*C11*D7
12					=SUM(E10:E11)

Sheet1 / Sheet2 / Sheet3 /

Figure 17.1

1   Set up the spreadsheet as shown in Figure 17.1.

2   Format cells B3 to B6, D3 to D7 and E10 to E12 as currency.

3   Format cells D10 to D11 as percentages. (They will say 100%.)

The hotel has decided to investigate predictions based on:

○ 70 per cent occupancy all year round;

○ 60 per cent occupancy all year round;

○ 50 per cent occupancy all year round;

○ 70 per cent occupancy in high season and 50 per cent occupancy in low season.

We will set up four different **scenarios**. To set up scenarios:

4   Click on **Tools, Scenarios**. You will see the scenario manager shown in Figure 17.2.

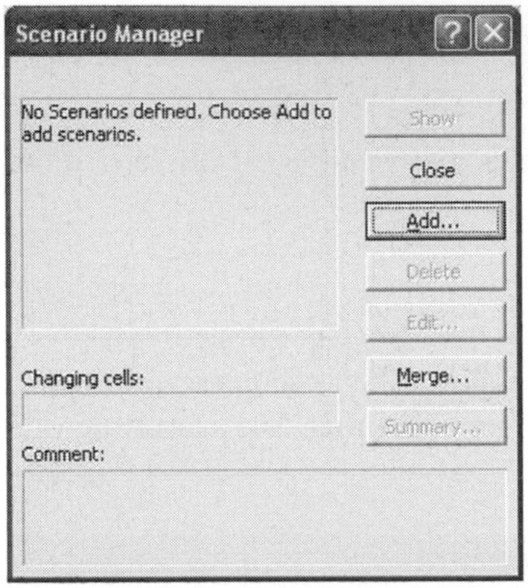

Figure 17.2

5   No scenarios exist at present so we need to add some. Click on **Add...**

6   Enter the name of the scenario – **70 per cent occupancy** – and the names of the two changing cells into the dialogue box as shown in Figure 17.3.

Figure 17.3

7   Click on **OK**.

8   Enter the value **70%** for each of the changing cells as shown in Figure 17.4 and click on **OK**.

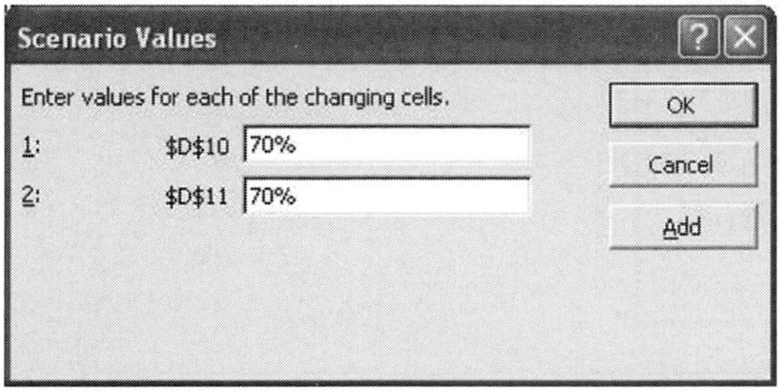

Scenario Values

Enter values for each of the changing cells.

1:        $D$10 70%

2:        $D$11 70%

OK

Cancel

Add

Figure 17.4

9   Add three more scenarios with the appropriate data.

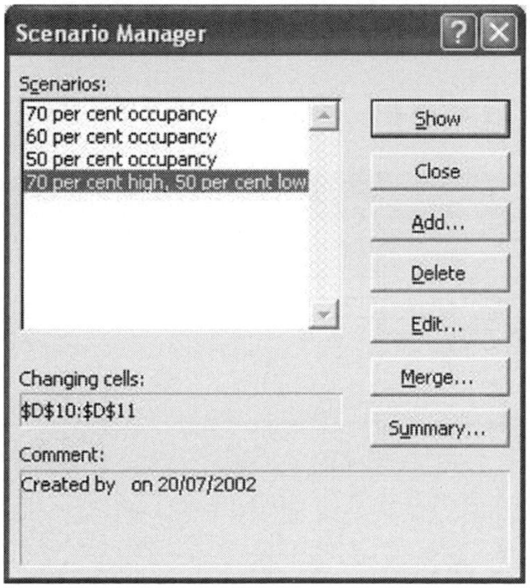

Scenario Manager

Scenarios:

70 per cent occupancy
60 per cent occupancy
50 per cent occupancy
70 per cent high, 50 per cent low

Show

Close

Add...

Delete

Edit...

Merge...

Summary...

Changing cells:

$D$10:$D$11

Comment:

Created by   on 20/07/2002

Figure 17.5

10 If you click on **Summary…** you will set up a new worksheet with a summary of all the scenarios. First the Scenario Summary box appears as shown in Figure 17.6.

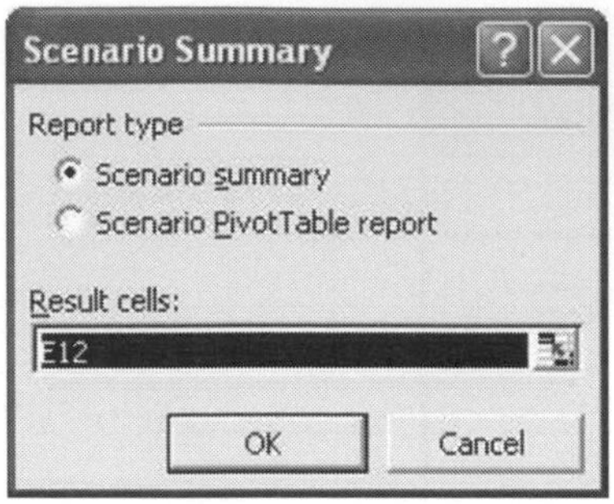

Figure 17.6

11 E12 is the cell with the total amount of the bill stored in it. This is the figure we want in our summary but we could click on any cell. Click on **OK**.

12 The summary looks like Figure 17.7.

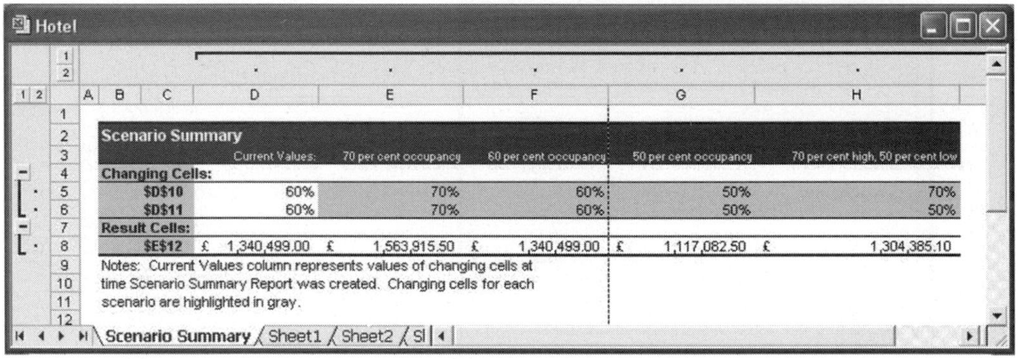

Figure 17.7

13 To load any of the scenarios:
   (a) Go back to Sheet1.
   (b) Click on **Tools, Scenarios**.
   (c) Click on the scenario required.
   (d) Click on **Show**.
   (e) Click on **Close**.

Note

The scenario summary does not update as you change figures in the spreadsheet. You will need to click on **Tools**, **Scenario** again and click on **Summary...** This will set up a new worksheet called Scenario Summary 2.

Pivot tables

In this section you will learn how to use pivot tables to group large amounts of data in an easy to read table.

Worked example

Hotel Manhattan has a file of its employees shown in Figure 17.8. A pivot table will allow us to group this information by department, by post and by sex to analyse exactly where the hotel pays wages.

	A	B	C	D	E	F	G	H
1	EMPL NO	SURNAME	FORENAME	DEPT	SALARY	DOB	POST	M/F
2	000262	Bird	Linda	Accommodation	£ 13,600	17/02/1976	Chef	F
3	000159	Caulder	Fraser	Restaurant	£ 14,200	05/06/1941	Chef	M
4	000267	Clark	Sarah	Reception	£ 11,090	31/10/1942	Receptionist	F
5	000297	Cook	Sally	Accommodation	£ 9,200	17/06/1953	Cleaner	F
6	000141	Dyson	Angela	Restaurant	£ 8,200	19/02/1958	Waitress	F
7	000011	Green	Julie	Accommodation	£ 9,200	20/06/1961	Cleaner	F
8	000185	Johnson	Rebecca	Restaurant	£ 7,900	22/12/1949	Waitress	F
9	000118	Jones	Robert	Restaurant	£ 7,400	17/08/1969	Waiter	M
10	000367	Khan	Wahir	Restaurant	£ 12,200	31/12/1958	Chef	M
11	000034	Noble	Marie	Restaurant	£ 8,150	14/06/1962	Waitress	F
12	000281	Patel	Niru	Restaurant	£ 7,600	01/05/1978	Waitress	F
13	000245	Powell	Sharon	Reception	£ 12,000	11/01/1966	Receptionist	F
14	000444	Robertson	Richard	Reception	£ 14,125	18/07/1960	Security Officer	M
15	000555	Robinson	Damion	Reception	£ 11,075	14/04/1978	Doorman	M
16	000190	Sands	Elizabeth	Accommodation	£ 8,500	04/04/1967	Cleaner	F
17	000247	Sands	Elaine	Accommodation	£ 9,600	18/12/1962	Cleaner	F

Figure 17.8

Note

1   Enter the data into a new worksheet and save it as **Workers**.

Notes

○ If you enter 000262, it will appears as 262 unless you type in an apostrophe first – '000262.

○ Note that in Excel XP, a small green triangle appears in the top left-hand corner of the cell. This is because it recognizes an error has occurred – a number is being stored as text. To remove the green triangle, highlight all the cells, click on the drop-down arrow and choose **Ignore Error** as shown in Figure 17.9.

	A	B	C	D	E	F	G	H
1	EMPL NO	SURNAME	FORENAME	DEPT	SALARY	DOB	POST	M/F
2	000262		Linda	Accommodation	£13,600	17/02/1976	Chef	F
3	000159			taurant	£14,200	05/06/1941	Chef	M
4	000267			eption	£11,090	31/10/1942	Receptionist	F
5	000297			ommodation	£ 9,200	17/06/1953	Cleaner	F
6	000141			taurant	£ 8,200	19/02/1958	Waitress	F
7	000011			ommodation	£ 9,200	20/06/1961	Cleaner	F
8	000185			taurant	£ 7,900	22/12/1949	Waitress	F
9	000118			taurant	£ 7,400	17/08/1969	Waiter	M
10	000367			taurant	£12,200	31/12/1958	Chef	M
11	000034			taurant	£ 8,150	14/06/1962	Waitress	F
12	000281			taurant	£ 7,600	01/05/1978	Waitress	F
13	000245	Powell	Sharon	Reception	£12,000	11/01/1966	Receptionist	F
14	000444	Robertson	Richard	Reception	£14,125	18/07/1960	Security Officer	M
15	000555	Robinson	Damion	Reception	£11,075	14/04/1978	Doorman	M
16	000190	Sands	Elizabeth	Accommodation	£ 8,500	04/04/1967	Cleaner	F
17	000247	Sands	Elaine	Accommodation	£ 9,600	18/12/1962	Cleaner	F

Context menu items shown in figure:
- Number Stored as Text
- Convert to Number
- Help on this error
- Ignore Error
- Edit in Formula Bar
- Error Checking Options…
- Show Formula Auditing Toolbar

Sheet1 / Sheet2 / Sheet3

Figure 17.9

○ If the date of birth appears as 17-Feb, highlight column F and click on **Format, Cells**, **Date** and choose the correct format.

2   Highlight the data and click on **Data, Pivot Table and Pivot Chart Report**. (**Data, Pivot Table Report** in Excel 97.)

3   It loads a wizard. Select **Microsoft Excel list or database** if not already selected and click on **Next**.

4   The next stage of the wizard asks where is the data that you want to use. Click on **Next**.

5   In Excel 97 the table shown in Figure 17.10 appears.

6   In Excel 2000 or Excel XP click on **New worksheet** and click on **Layout**. The table shown in Figure 17.10 appears.

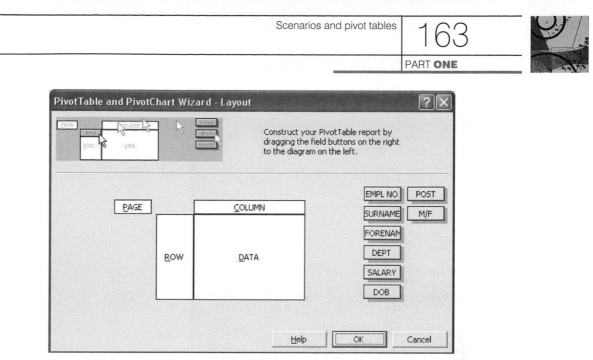

Figure 17.10

7   This is where you choose which data to group and display. Drag the fieldnames
    Dept and **Post** to where it says ROW. Drag **M/F** to where it says COLUMN and
    drag **Salary** to where it says DATA. When you drag **Salary** on to the middle of the
    page it becomes **Sum of SALARY**, as in Figure 17.11.

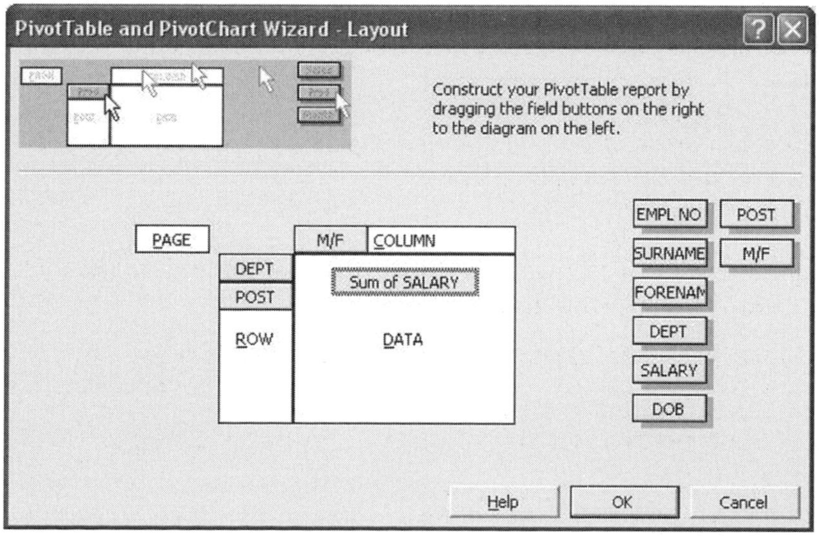

Figure 17.11

8   Click on **OK** and then click on **Finish**.

The pivot table will look like Figure 17.12.

	A	B	C	D	E
1					
2					
3	Sum of SALARY		M/F ▼		
4	DEPT ▼	POST ▼	F	M	Grand Total
5	Accommodation	Chef	13600		13600
6		Cleaner	36500		36500
7	Accommodation Total		50100		50100
8	Reception	Doorman		11075	11075
9		Receptionist	23090		23090
10		Security Officer		14125	14125
11	Reception Total		23090	25200	48290
12	Restaurant	Chef		26400	26400
13		Waiter		7400	7400
14		Waitress	31850		31850
15	Restaurant Total		31850	33800	65650
16	Grand Total		105040	59000	164040
17					

Sheet1 / Sheet2 / Sheet3

Figure 7.12

At a glance we can see total salaries paid, by department, by post and by sex.

Note If you alter the employees table, it does **not** alter the pivot table. To update the information you would need to create a new pivot table.

Exercise

The different departments of a company are charged on the basis of hours of internet use. The company has to distinguish between use for e-mail and use for the World Wide Web. Using the data in Figure 17.13, set up a pivot table to group the data, to show internet, intranet and total use for each department split into www and e-mail.

	A	B	C	D	E	F	G
	Forename	Surname	Section	Type	Internet use	Intranet use	Total
1							
2	Angela	Jones	Admin	email	4	6	10
3	Bertie	Galley	Finance	www	23	2	25
4	Heather	Jones	Security	email	2	7	9
5	Bill	Brown	Sales	email	3	3	6
6	Bill	Brown	Sales	email	16	4	20
7	Eileen	Sands	Finance	email	3	1	4
8	Elizabeth	Bird	Marketing	www	32	2	34
9	Charles	Bryant	Finance	email	21	9	30
10	Darren	Foreman	Finance	www	17	2	19
11	Olive	Hassent	Sales	email	8	0	8
12	Katie	Johnson	Marketing	email	10	3	13
13	Quinton	Harris	Sales	www	8	7	15
14							

Department — Sheet1 \ **Sheet2** / Sheet3 /

Figure 17.13

Note

You can download this file from **www.hodderictcoursework.co.uk**

⊕ Unit 18 Using Excel as a database

In this unit you will cover:
- ○ setting up, sorting and searching a database;
- ○ using Data Forms;
- ○ using AutoFilter;
- ○ using the Advanced Filter;
- ○ database functions.

A spreadsheet lends itself to storing and sorting lists of information, such as employees, customers, cars, students and so on.

More commonly files or lists such as this are called databases. Excel calls them **lists**.

Creating a data list

We are going to set up a simple **file** of properties for sale.

Each **record** in the file or row in the spreadsheet will hold details of the property.

The **fields** or columns in the spreadsheet will be Estate Agent, Area, Type, No of Bedrooms and Price as shown in Figure 18.1.

	Houses				
	A	B	C	D	E
1	**Agent**	**Area**	**Type**	**Bedrooms**	**Price**
2	Raybould & Sons	Hulland Ward	semi-detached	5	245000
3	Bagshaws	Etwall	detached	4	197500
4	Bagshaws	Etwall	detached	4	189950
5	Hall & Partners	Mickleover	detached	3	170000
6	Raybould & Sons	Littleover	bungalow	3	132000
7	Raybould & Sons	Etwall	detached	4	127000

Sheet1

Figure 18.1

Notes

- ○ When you enter the data you will notice that Excel stores previously entered data and carries out an AutoComplete for you. This saves you having to type in all the data. This can be turned off/on by choosing **Tools**, **Options**, clicking the **Edit** tab and checking the enable **AutoComplete**.
- ○ Calculated fields can be added by setting up the formulas in the appropriate column.

Sorting the file

Sorting can be done on the whole file or a named range of cells.

To produce a sorted list of houses by price:

1   Load the file **Houses**. Details of this file are found at the end of this unit.

Note   You can download this file from **www.hodderictcoursework.co.uk**

2   Click on any cell in the table such as A2 and click on **Data, Sort**. The Sort dialogue box in Figure 18.2 appears.

Figure 18.2

3   Click on the down arrow on the Sort by box, choose **Price** and click on **Descending**, click **OK**.

It is also possible to sort on more than one field, for example in agent order and then in price order.

1   Click on A2 or any cell in the table. From the menu choose **Data, Sort**.

2   Click on the down arrow on the Sort by box, choose **Agent** and click on **Ascending**.

3   Click on the down arrow on the first Then by box, choose **Price** and click on **Descending** and click **OK**.

This should produce a list sorted by Agent and then by Price.

Using a Data Form to search and edit a file

1 Load the file **Houses**.

2 Click on **Data, Form**.

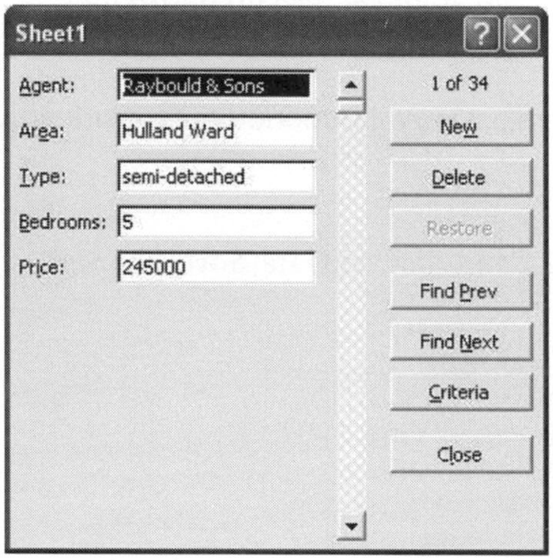

Figure 18.3

○ Click on **Find Next** to take you to details of the next house.

○ Click on **Find Prev** to take you to details of the previous house.

○ Click on **Delete** to enable you to remove a house from file.

○ Click on **New** to allow you to enter details of a new property (press TAB between entering fields).

You can use the Data Form to do simple searches

1 Click on **Criteria** and a blank form loads.

2 Enter **Etwall** in the field area and click on **Find Next** to scroll through the houses in Etwall.

You can narrow down the search:

1 Click on **Criteria** again and enter 3 in the **Bedrooms** field.

2 You can now scroll through the three-bedroomed houses in Etwall.

Exercise 1

Use the Data Form to answer the following questions:

1   Produce details of all houses for sale in Oakwood. How many are there?

2   A customer wants details of detached houses for sale in Mickleover. How many are there and what price are they?

3   A customer wants to purchase a house with three bedrooms in Littleover. Search for details. How many are there and what price are they?

Using AutoFilter to search the database

1   Load the file **Houses**.

2   Click on any cell in the data table, e.g. A2.

3   Click on **Data, Filter, AutoFilter**.

	A	B	C	D	E
1	Agent	Area	Type	Bedrooms	Price
2	Raybould & Sons	Hulland Ward	semi-detached	5	245000
3	Bagshaws	Etwall	detached	4	197500
4	Bagshaws	Etwall	detached	4	189950
5	Hall & Partners	Mickleover	detached	3	170000
6	Raybould & Sons	Littleover	bungalow	3	132000
7	Raybould & Sons	Etwall	detached	4	127000

Figure 18.4

Drop-down boxes appear by each field name as in Figure 18.4. If you click on the arrow it will give you a list of items in that field as in Figure 18.5.

	A	B	C	D	E
1	Agent	Area	Type	Bedrooms	Price
2	Raybould & Sons	Hulland Ward	(All)	5	245000
3	Bagshaws	Etwall	(Top 10...) (Custom...)	4	197500
4	Bagshaws	Etwall	bungalow	4	189950
5	Hall & Partners	Mickleover	detached	3	170000
6	Raybould & Sons	Littleover	semi-detached	3	132000
7	Raybould & Sons	Etwall	terraced detached	4	127000

Figure 18.5

It is easy to build up quick searches, e.g. bungalows in Mickleover.

1   Click on the Area field drop-down and choose **Mickleover**.

2   Then click on the Type field drop-down and choose **terraced**.

You should get the results in Figure 18.6.

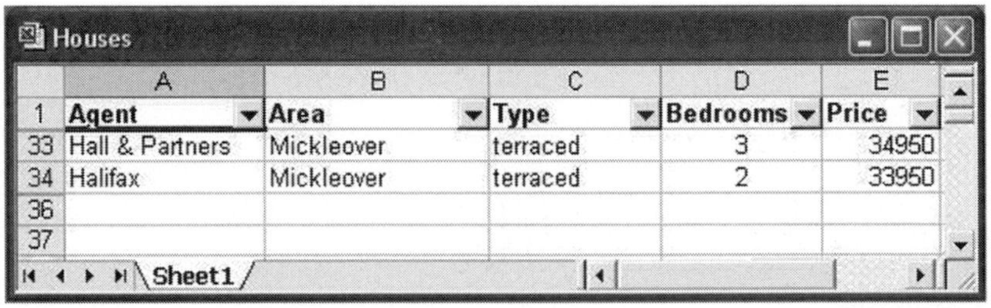

	A	B	C	D	E
1	Agent ▾	Area ▾	Type ▾	Bedrooms ▾	Price ▾
33	Hall & Partners	Mickleover	terraced	3	34950
34	Halifax	Mickleover	terraced	2	33950
36					
37					

Sheet1

Figure 18.6

Excel hides the rows that do not meet the criteria and displays the row numbers in blue.

To restore your data click on **Data, Filter, Show All**.

It is possible to do more advanced searching by choosing the custom option.

Filter 1

Suppose we wish to find properties in Mickleover or Littleover.

1   Choose the Area drop-down and click on **Custom**.

2   The dialogue box in Figure 18.7 appears. Fill it in as shown to output 18 houses.

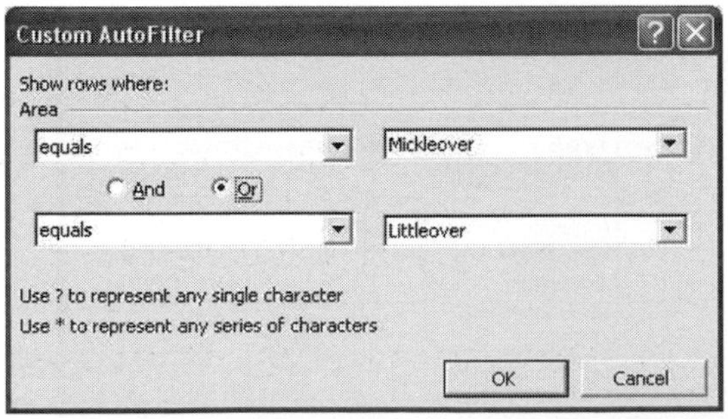

Figure 18.7

Filter 2

Suppose we wish to find properties with the price between £49,500 and £60,000.

1   Restore your data.

2   Click on the **Price** drop-down and click on **Custom**.

3   The dialogue box in Figure 18.8 appears. Fill it in as shown. Five houses should be output.

Custom AutoFilter

Show rows where:
Price

Is greater than	49500

● And   ○ Or

is less than	60000

Use ? to represent any single character
Use * to represent any series of characters

OK   Cancel

Figure 18.8

Some hints on using AutoFilter

To remove AutoFilter for a particular column, click on (**All**) from the drop-down list.

To remove all AutoFilters, click on **Data, Filter, Show All**.

You can use **AutoFilter** to find blank fields. If a column contains blanks you will see the entries (Blanks) and (NonBlanks) in the column's drop-down list.

If you wish to remove rows with blank entries then choose **NonBlanks**.

If you wish to find rows in which a column has no entry then choose **Blanks**.

Auto filtered data can be copied and pasted to other areas of the worksheet in the usual way; to automate this process you need to use the **Advanced Filter** option.

Exercise 2

Use **AutoFilter** and the file **Houses** to answer the following:

1   A customer wants details of houses for sale in Etwall. How many are there?

2   A customer wants to purchase a house with 4 bedrooms. Search for details. How many are there?

3   A customer requires details of detached houses in Mickleover. Search for details.

4   A customer requires a three-bedroomed house in Littleover. Search for details.

The Advanced Filter option

The Advanced Filter command allows you to search on more than two fields and offers increased options. The command can also be used to automate the moving of filtered data to another part of the worksheet.

Worked example 1

The first step is to define the cells that make up the database, this is called the **list range**.

1   Using the file **Houses** highlight the cells A1 to E35.

2   From the **Insert** menu choose **Name, Define** and call the range **Database** and click **OK**.

The next stage is to set up and define the **criteria range**. This is the range of cells which will store your search conditions.

3   Select the row headings in row 1 and copy and paste them to an area below your data list, we have chosen row 39.

4   In the rows below enter the search conditions as shown in Figure 18.9. We will produce a list of bungalows in Littleover.

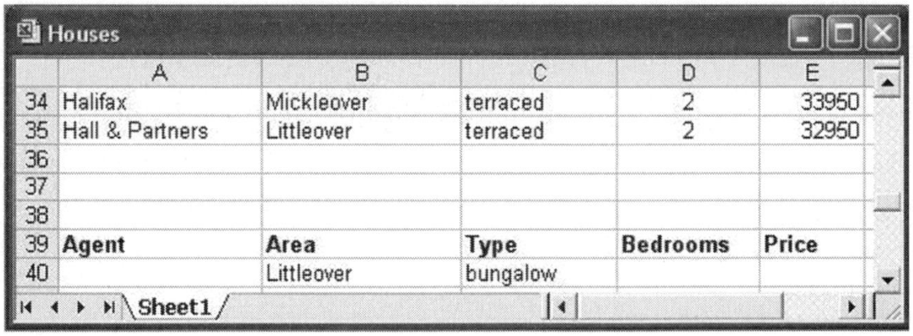

	A	B	C	D	E
34	Halifax	Mickleover	terraced	2	33950
35	Hall & Partners	Littleover	terraced	2	32950
36					
37					
38					
39	**Agent**	**Area**	**Type**	**Bedrooms**	**Price**
40		Littleover	bungalow		

Houses — Sheet1

Figure 18.9

5   Name the range A39 to E40 **criteria**.

6   Click on **Data, Filter, Advanced Filter**.

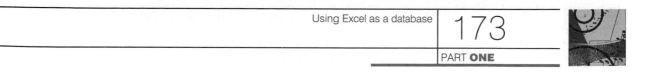

7   Enter the ranges shown in Figure 18.10.

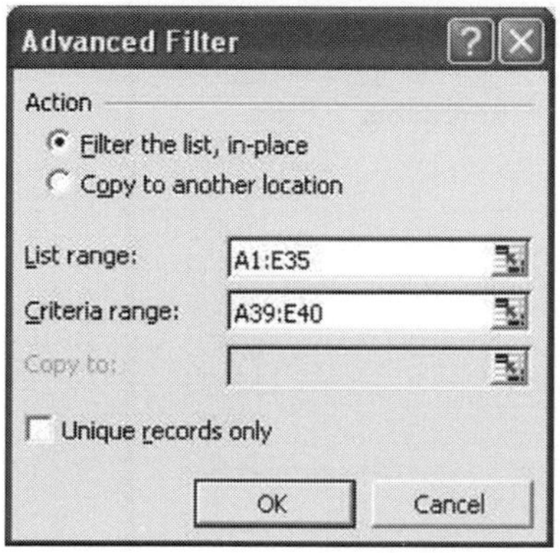

Figure 18.10

Clicking on **OK** should produce the filtered list in Figure 18.11 which displays one property. The selected row is highlighted in blue.

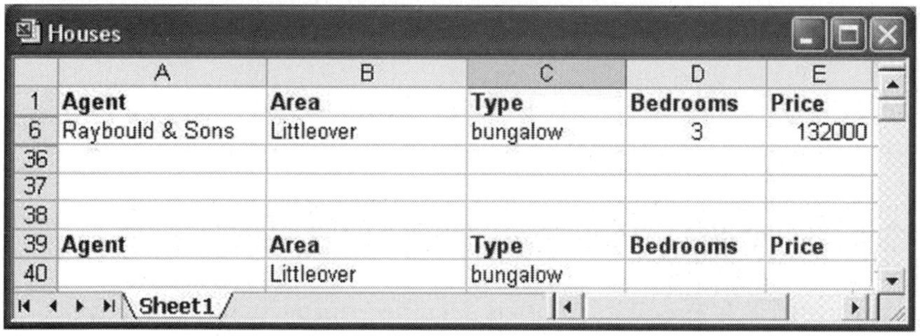

	A	B	C	D	E
1	Agent	Area	Type	Bedrooms	Price
6	Raybould & Sons	Littleover	bungalow	3	132000
36					
37					
38					
39	Agent	Area	Type	Bedrooms	Price
40		Littleover	bungalow		

Figure 18.11

Searches can be built up in the same way.

The search criteria in Figure 18.12 will list three-bedroomed properties in Mickleover or Etwall as shown in Figure 18.13.

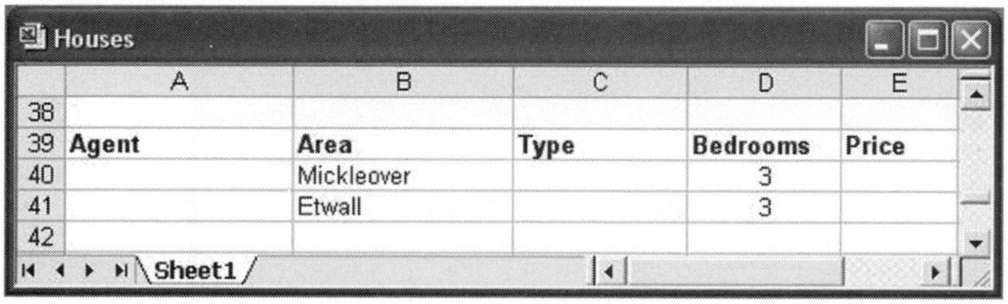

	A	B	C	D	E
38					
39	Agent	Area	Type	Bedrooms	Price
40		Mickleover		3	
41		Etwall		3	
42					

Figure 18.12

The criteria range is now A39:E41.

	A	B	C	D	E
1	**Agent**	**Area**	**Type**	**Bedrooms**	**Price**
5	Hall & Partners	Mickleover	detached	3	170000
12	Ashley Adams	Mickleover	bungalow	3	86950
13	Ashley Adams	Mickleover	bungalow	3	86950
18	Halifax	Etwall	semi-detached	3	65500
19	Ashley Adams	Etwall	semi-detached	3	65000
24	Ashley Adams	Mickleover	semi-detached	3	59950
26	Raybould & Sons	Mickleover	semi-detached	3	55000
28	Bagshaws	Etwall	terraced	3	49500
33	Hall & Partners	Mickleover	terraced	3	34950
36					
37					
38					
39	**Agent**	**Area**	**Type**	**Bedrooms**	**Price**
40		Mickleover		3	
41		Etwall		3	
42					

Figure 18.13

Exercise 3

Use the advanced filter option to answer the following questions.

1. A customer requires a three-bedroomed house in Littleover or Mickleover. Search for details.
2. A customer requires a property in the Allestree, Darley Abbey area. Search for details.
3. A customer requires a three-bedroomed detached property in Mickleover. Search for details.

Copying data to another location

1. Set up the search as shown in Figure 18.14 to find three-bedroomed properties in Etwall or Mickleover.

	A	B	C	D	E
38					
39	**Agent**	**Area**	**Type**	**Bedrooms**	**Price**
40		Mickleover		3	
41		Etwall		3	

Figure 18.14

2 Make sure your named criteria range is A39 to E41.

3 From the Data menu choose **Filter, Advanced Filter**.

4 In the dialogue box check **Copy to another location** and enter **A44** in the **Copy to** box as shown in Figure 18.15.

Advanced Filter

Action
- ○ Filter the list, in-place
- ● Copy to another location

List range: `$A$1:$E$35`

Criteria range: `$A$39:$E$41`

Copy to: `A44`

☐ Unique records only

[OK] [Cancel]

Figure 18.15

The search should produce the results in Figure 18.16.

	A	B	C	D	E
39	**Agent**	**Area**	**Type**	**Bedrooms**	**Price**
40		Mickleover		3	
41		Etwall		3	
42					
43					
44	**Agent**	**Area**	**Type**	**Bedrooms**	**Price**
45	Hall & Partners	Mickleover	detached	3	170000
46	Ashley Adams	Mickleover	bungalow	3	86950
47	Ashley Adams	Mickleover	bungalow	3	86950
48	Halifax	Etwall	semi-detached	3	65500
49	Ashley Adams	Etwall	semi-detached	3	65000
50	Ashley Adams	Mickleover	semi-detached	3	59950
51	Raybould & Sons	Mickleover	semi-detached	3	55000
52	Bagshaws	Etwall	terraced	3	49500
53	Hall & Partners	Mickleover	terraced	3	34950
54					

Houses — Sheet1

Figure 18.16

The output from the search is displayed in columns A to E in rows 44 to 53, which now become the named area **Extract**. Check by clicking the name box drop-down.

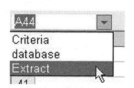

Figure 18.17

It is now possible to vary the criteria in the criteria range. Try changing the criteria to produce the output shown in Figure 18.18.

Houses

	A	B	C	D	E
39	Agent	Area	Type	Bedrooms	Price
40		Mickleover		2	
41		Etwall		2	
42					
43					
44	Agent	Area	Type	Bedrooms	Price
45	Halifax	Etwall	semi-detached	2	55500
46	Hall & Partners	Mickleover	semi-detached	2	52950
47	Bagshaws	Etwall	terraced	2	45000
48	Halifax	Mickleover	terraced	2	33950
49					

Sheet1

Figure 18.18

Using the database functions

Excel provides a number of **d** or **database** functions. Examples are **DCOUNT, DAVERAGE, DSUM, DMAX, DMIN.**

Database functions take the form **=Function(database,"field",criteria)** where:
- **Database** is the name of database range you have defined;
- **Field** is the column you wish to operate on;
- **Criteria** is the criteria range you have defined.

Worked example 2

We are going to use the database functions to analyse house prices in the Mickleover area.

1   Set up the criteria and headings as shown in Figure 18.19.

Houses

	A	B	C	D	E
39	Agent	Area	Type	Bedrooms	Price
40		Mickleover		2	
41					
42					
43	Number of houses				
44	Average price				
45	Maximum price				
46	Minimum price				
47	Total value				
48					

Sheet1

Figure 18.19

2   Make sure you have named the **database** and **criteria** ranges (A1:E35 and A39:E40).

3   Enter the formulas shown in Figure 18.20.

	A	B	C	D	E
	Houses				
	A	B	C	D	E
39	**Agent**	**Area**	**Type**	**Bedrooms**	**Price**
40		Mickleover		2	
41					
42					
43	**Number of houses**	=DCOUNT(Database,"price",Criteria)			
44	**Average price**	=DAVERAGE(Database,"price",Criteria)			
45	**Maximum price**	=DMAX(Database,"price",Criteria)			
46	**Minimum price**	=DMIN(Database,"price",Criteria)			
47	**Total value**	=DSUM(Database,"price",Criteria)			
48					

Figure 18.20

The results should be as in Figure 18.21.

	A	B	C	D	E	F	G
	Houses						
	A	B	C	D	E	F	G
39	**Agent**	**Area**	**Type**	**Bedrooms**	**Price**		
40		Mickleover		2			
41							
42							
43	**Number of houses**	2					
44	**Average price**	43450					
45	**Maximum price**	52950					
46	**Minimum price**	33950					
47	**Total value**	86900					
48							

Figure 18.21

When it works, try varying the search criteria, e.g. change the area to Littleover or the number of bedrooms to 3.

The houses file

Agent	Area	Type	Bedrooms	Price
Raybould & Sons	Hulland Ward	semi-detached	5	245000
Bagshaws	Etwall	detached	4	197500
Bagshaws	Etwall	detached	4	189950
Hall & Partners	Mickleover	detached	3	170000
Raybould & Sons	Littleover	bungalow	3	132000
Raybould & Sons	Etwall	detached	4	127000
Raybould & Sons	Willington	semi-detached	3	117500
Bradford & Bingley	Littleover	detached	5	99950
Bradford & Bingley	Oakwood	detached	4	92950
Bradford & Bingley	Oakwood	detached	4	92950
Ashley Adams	Mickleover	bungalow	3	86950
Ashley Adams	Mickleover	bungalow	3	86950
Bradford & Bingley	Borrowash	detached	3	85000
Ashley Adams	Allestree	semi-detached	3	82500
Bradford & Bingley	Mickleover	detached	5	79950
Bradford & Bingley	Littleover	detached	3	75950
Halifax	Etwall	semi-detached	3	65500
Ashley Adams	Etwall	semi-detached	3	65000
Halifax	Littleover	semi-detached	3	60000
Halifax	Littleover	semi-detached	3	60000
Halifax	Littleover	semi-detached	3	60000
Hall & Partners	Egginton	detached	3	59999
Ashley Adams	Mickleover	semi-detached	3	59950
Halifax	Etwall	semi-detached	2	55500
Raybould & Sons	Mickleover	semi-detached	3	55000
Hall & Partners	Mickleover	semi-detached	2	52950
Bagshaws	Etwall	terraced	3	49500
Hall & Partners	Littleover	terraced	2	48500
Halifax	Littleover	semi-detached	3	47500
Bagshaws	Darley Abbey	detached	4	46000
Bagshaws	Etwall	terraced	2	45000
Hall & Partners	Mickleover	terraced	3	34950
Halifax	Mickleover	terraced	2	33950
Hall & Partners	Littleover	terraced	2	32950

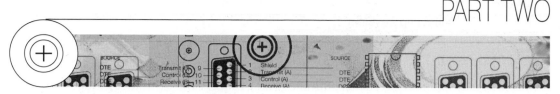

PART TWO

Setting up a system

⊕ Unit 19 Setting up the car insurance quotation system

The student should remember that the system demonstrated here is not being put forward for a particular grade at any level, it is fictitious and aims to show how the software features in Excel can be incorporated to produce a working system.

The system is made up of the following tasks:

1 setting up the Insurance Groups worksheet;
2 setting up the Multipliers worksheet;
3 setting up the Quotes worksheet;
4 preparing the quote – setting up the LOOKUP table;
5 preparing the quote – entering the multipliers;
6 calculating the total cost;
7 setting up the Customer's worksheet;
8 automating the filing of quotes;
9 clearing the current screen to enter a new quote;
10 designing the printed quote;
11 adding user options to the Quotes worksheet;
12 customizing the interface and some finishing touches;
13 adding the front end.

Note   Throughout the system development students are advised to keep a test log and record details of any tests carried out. Don't forget to save your work as you go along.

1 Setting up the Insurance Groups worksheets

(a) The user has provided data about the makes, models and insurance groups of cars. Enter the data into a worksheet as shown in Figure 19.1. Of course a real system would have far more cars.

	A	B	C	D	E
1	Number	Make	Model	IG	CarName
2	1	Peugeot	106	3	Peugeot 106
3	2	Peugeot	206	3	Peugeot 206
4	3	Peugeot	306	4	Peugeot 306
5	4	Peugeot	406	10	Peugeot 406
6	5	Peugeot	806	10	Peugeot 806
7	6	Ford	Ka	2	Ford Ka
8	7	Ford	Fiesta	4	Ford Fiesta
9	8	Ford	Escort	5	Ford Escort
10	9	Ford	Puma	9	Ford Puma
11	10	Ford	Focus	5	Ford Focus
12	11	Ford	Mondeo	8	Ford Mondeo
13	12	Ford	Galaxy	11	Ford Galaxy
14	13	Honda	Civic	9	Honda Civic
15	14	Honda	Prelude	14	Honda Prelude
16	15	Honda	Accord	8	Honda Accord
17	16	Reliant	Robin	6	Reliant Robin
18	17	Rover	100	3	Rover 100
19	18	Rover	200	6	Rover 200
20	19	Rover	400	8	Rover 400
21	20	Rover	800	12	Rover 800

Book1 — Groups

Figure 19.1

Note

You can download this file from **www.hodderictcoursework.co.uk**

(b) Rename the worksheet **Groups** by double clicking on the Sheet tab.

We are going to use a simplified format of the concatenate function to combine the Make and Model columns to give the full car name in column E.

(c) In cell E2 enter **=B2&" "&C2**. Make sure there is a space between the apostrophes.

(d) Copy the formula down the column by highlighting cells E2 to E21 and from the menu choosing **Edit, Fill, Down**.

(e) The column will need widening, click **Format, Column, AutoFit Selection** and enter the heading **CarName** in cell E1.

(f) Highlight the cells A1 to E21 and define them using the name **Groups** by clicking **Insert, Name, Define**.

We now need to add the insurance group costs.

(g) Enter the details as shown in Figure 19.2 in cells H1 to I21.

	A	B	C	D	E	F	G	H	I
1	**Number**	**Make**	**Model**	**IG**	**CarName**			**IG**	**Basic Cost**
2	1	Peugeot	106	3	Peugeot 106			1	£ 174.00
3	2	Peugeot	206	3	Peugeot 206			2	£ 180.00
4	3	Peugeot	306	4	Peugeot 306			3	£ 187.00
5	4	Peugeot	406	10	Peugeot 406			4	£ 194.00
6	5	Peugeot	806	10	Peugeot 806			5	£ 202.00
7	6	Ford	Ka	2	Ford Ka			6	£ 210.00
8	7	Ford	Fiesta	4	Ford Fiesta			7	£ 222.00
9	8	Ford	Escort	5	Ford Escort			8	£ 235.00
10	9	Ford	Puma	9	Ford Puma			9	£ 248.00
11	10	Ford	Focus	5	Ford Focus			10	£ 264.00
12	11	Ford	Mondeo	8	Ford Mondeo			11	£ 280.00
13	12	Ford	Galaxy	11	Ford Galaxy			12	£ 300.00
14	13	Honda	Civic	9	Honda Civic			13	£ 324.00
15	14	Honda	Prelude	14	Honda Prelude			14	£ 362.00
16	15	Honda	Accord	8	Honda Accord			15	£ 417.00
17	16	Reliant	Robin	6	Reliant Robin			16	£ 493.00
18	17	Rover	100	3	Rover 100			17	£ 600.00
19	18	Rover	200	6	Rover 200			18	£ 720.00
20	19	Rover	400	8	Rover 400			19	£ 838.00
21	20	Rover	800	12	Rover 800			20	£ 945.00

Figure 19.2

(h) Highlight the cells H1 to I21 and define them using the name **Costs** by
clicking **Insert, Name, Define**.

Your finished spreadsheet should appear as shown in Figure 19.2.

2 Setting up the Multipliers worksheet

(a) Click on the tab for Sheet2.

This sheet will store the multipliers used in calculating the insurance quote.

(b) Rename the worksheet **Multipliers** by double clicking on the Sheet tab.

(c) Enter the data into cells A1 to D34 as shown in Figure 19.3.

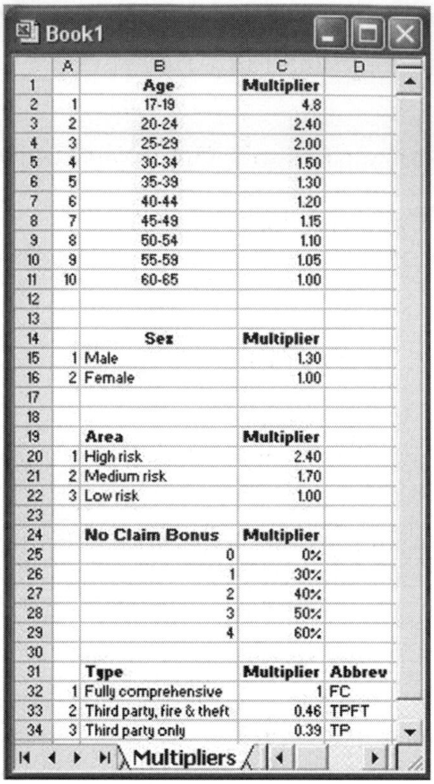

Book1

	A	B	C	D
1		**Age**	**Multiplier**	
2	1	17-19	4.8	
3	2	20-24	2.40	
4	3	25-29	2.00	
5	4	30-34	1.50	
6	5	35-39	1.30	
7	6	40-44	1.20	
8	7	45-49	1.15	
9	8	50-54	1.10	
10	9	55-59	1.05	
11	10	60-65	1.00	
12				
13				
14		**Sex**	**Multiplier**	
15	1	Male	1.30	
16	2	Female	1.00	
17				
18				
19		**Area**	**Multiplier**	
20	1	High risk	2.40	
21	2	Medium risk	1.70	
22	3	Low risk	1.00	
23				
24		**No Claim Bonus**	**Multiplier**	
25		0	0%	
26		1	30%	
27		2	40%	
28		3	50%	
29		4	60%	
30				
31		**Type**	**Multiplier**	**Abbrev**
32	1	Fully comprehensive	1	FC
33	2	Third party, fire & theft	0.46	TPFT
34	3	Third party only	0.39	TP

Multipliers

Figure 19.3

3 Setting up the Quotes worksheet

The next stage is to design the sheet which will display and calculate the quote.

(a) Double click on the tab for Sheet3 and rename the worksheet **Quotes**.

(b) Enter the data as shown in Figure 19.4 and set the width of column D to 20.

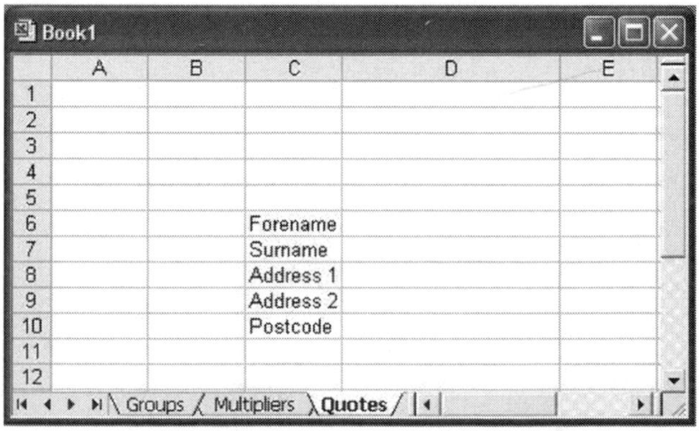

Book1

	A	B	C	D	E
1					
2					
3					
4					
5					
6			Forename		
7			Surname		
8			Address 1		
9			Address 2		
10			Postcode		
11					
12					

Groups / **Multipliers** \ **Quotes**

Figure 19.4

Adding the option buttons

Option boxes will be added to allow the user to select male or female.

(a) In cell C12 enter the label **Sex**.

(b) From the menu click **View, Toolbars, Forms** and select the **Option Button**.

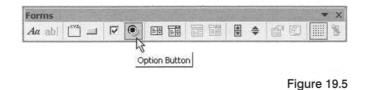

Figure 19.5

(c) Drag out two option buttons over cells D11 and D12, label one Male and the other Female.

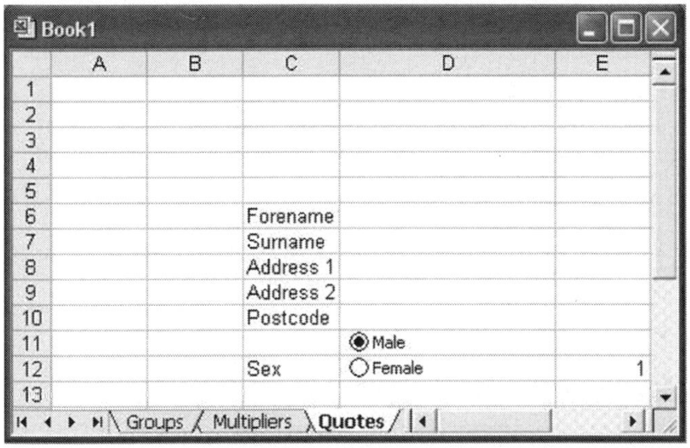

Figure 19.6

(d) Right click on one option button to call up the shortcut menu, click on **Format Control** and set the cell link to E12 as shown in Figure 19.8.

Figure 19.7

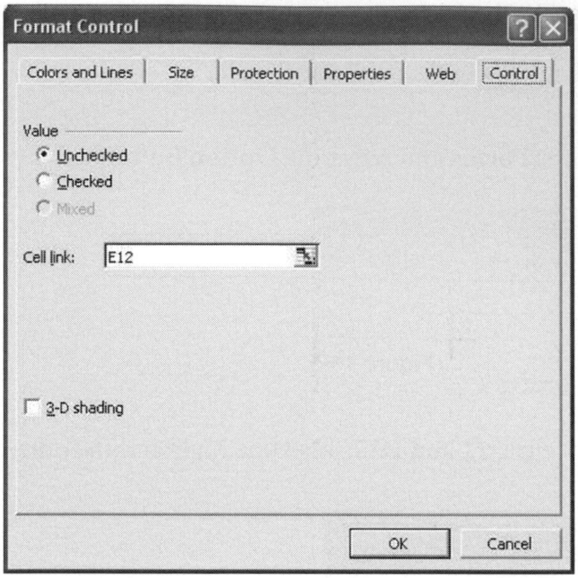

Format Control ? X

| Colors and Lines | Size | Protection | Properties | Web | Control |

Value
- ⦿ Underchecked
- ○ Checked
- ○ Mixed

Cell link: E12

☐ 3-D shading

OK   Cancel

Figure 19.8

Adding combo boxes

Combo boxes are now added to allow the user to select the type of car and age group of the driver.

(a) In cell C14 enter the label **Car**.

(b) From the menu click on **View, Toolbars, Forms** and select **Combo Box**.

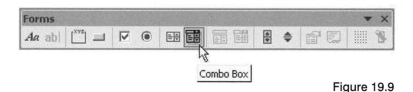

Combo Box

Figure 19.9

(c) Drag out a combo box over cell D14.

(d) Right click on the combo box to call up the shortcut menu, click on **Format Control** and set the cell link to E14 and set the input range to **Groups!E2:E21**.

(e) Test that your combo box lists the names of the available cars as in Figure 19.10.

(f) In cell C16 enter the label **Age**.

(g) Drag out another combo box over cell D16 and link the control to E16.

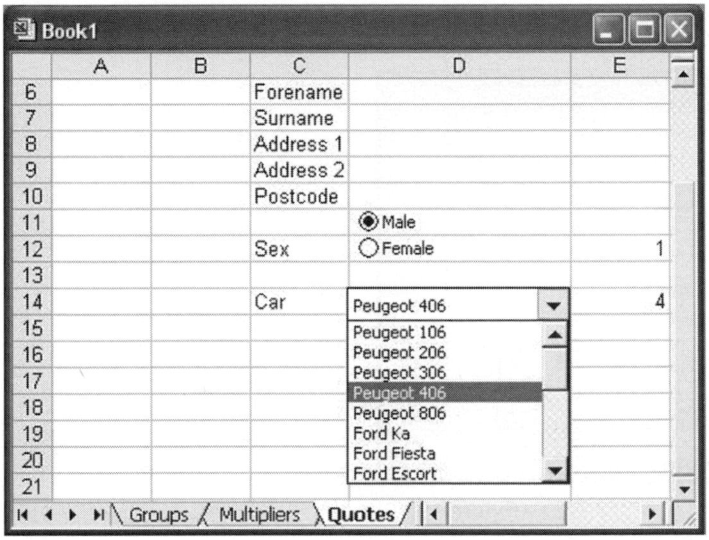

Figure 19.10

(h) Enter the input range as **Multipliers!B2:B11**. This can be done by switching to the sheet Multipliers and dragging across the cell range B2 to B11.

(i) Test that your combo box appears as shown in Figure 19.11.

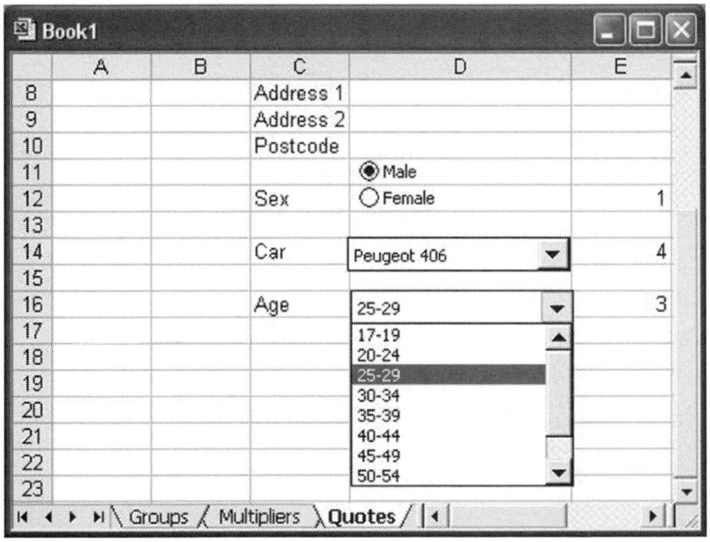

Figure 19.11

Your sheet should appear as shown in Figure 19.12.

	A	B	C	D	E
5					
6			Forename		
7			Surname		
8			Address 1		
9			Address 2		
10			Postcode		
11				⦿ Male	
12			Sex	○ Female	1
13					
14			Car	Peugeot 406 ▼	4
15					
16			Age	25-29 ▼	3
17					

Groups / Multipliers / **Quotes** /

Figure 19.12

Adding list boxes

List boxes are now added to allow the user to select the area of risk and insurance types.

(a) In cell C18 enter **Area** and in cell C20 enter **Type**.

(b) From the menu choose **View, Toolbars, Forms** and select **List Box**.

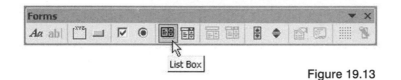

Figure 19.13

(c) Drag out a list box over cell D18. Link the control to cell E18. Enter the input range as **Multipliers!B20:B22**.

(d) Drag out another list box over cells D20. Link the control to cell E20. Enter the input range as **Multipliers!B32:B34**.

(e) Use the handles on the controls to position and resize as necessary.

Adding a check box

A check box will be used to declare an extra driver.

(a) In cell C22 enter the label **Driver**.

(b) From the menu click **View, Toolbars, Forms** and select **Check Box**.

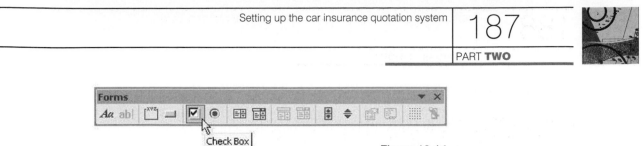

Figure 19.14

(c) Drag out a check box over cell D22 and link the control to E22. Change the label to **Extra Driver**.

At this stage your spreadsheet should appear as in Figure 19.15.

	A	B	C	D	E	F
5						
6			Forename			
7			Surname			
8			Address 1			
9			Address 2			
10			Postcode			
11				◉ Male		
12			Sex	○ Female	1	
13						
14			Car	Ford Fiesta ▼	7	
15						
16			Age	60-65 ▼	10	
17						
18			Area	Medium risk ▲	3	
19				Low risk ▼		
20			Type	Third party, fire & theft ▲	3	
21				Third party only ▼		
22			Driver	☑ Extra driver	TRUE	
23						

◄ ► ►► \ Groups / Multipliers \ **Quotes** /

Figure 19.15

Adding a spinner

A spinner will be used to set the number of years' no claims bonus where appropriate. A **LOOKUP** function will find the percentage discount allowed depending on the years' no claims bonus.

(a) In cell C24 enter the heading **No claims**. In D23 and E23 enter the headings **Years** and **Per cent**. Right align *Years* and centre *Per cent*.

(b) From the menu click **View, Toolbars, Forms** and select **Spinner**.

Figure 19.16

(c) Drag out a spinner control over the left side of cells D24 and D25.

(d) Link the spinner to cell D24. Set the maximum value to 4, minimum value to 0 and increment 1 as in Figure 19.17. This implies that a driver can have up to 4 years' no claims bonus.

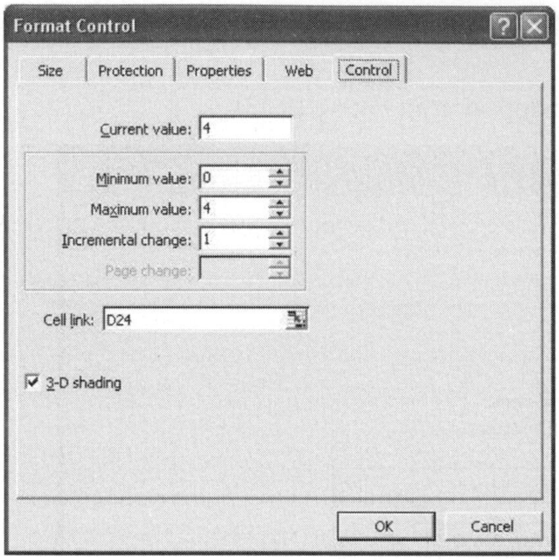

Figure 19.17

(e) In cell E24 enter the formula **=VLOOKUP(D24,Multipliers!B25:C29,2)** and format the cell to percentage.

This function will look in the Multipliers sheet for the percentage discount available.

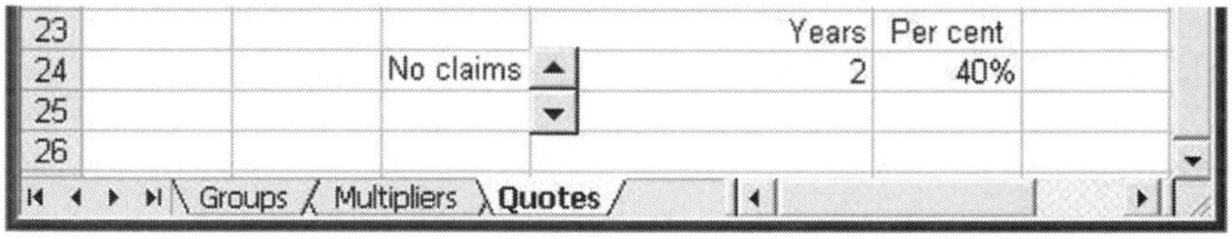

Figure 19.18

Note

The sheet at present may look a little untidy and cramped, we will deal with the layout later.

4 Preparing the quote – setting up the LOOKUP table

(a) In cells F6 to F14 enter the factors needed to calculate the insurance quotes as shown in Figure 19.19. You will need to change the width of column F to 11.

	A	B	C	D	E	F	G
5							
6			Forename			Make	
7			Surname			Model	
8			Address 1			IG	
9			Address 2			Sex	
10			Postcode			Age	
11				◉ Male		Risk	
12			Sex	○ Female	1	Extra Driver	
13						No claims	
14			Car	Peugeot 406 ▼	4	Type	

Groups / Multipliers \ **Quotes** /

Figure 19.19

(b) In G6 enter the formula: **=VLOOKUP(E14,Groups,2)**.

This will pick up the numeric value of the car chosen which is stored in E14, find it in the named area Groups and return the make from the second column.

(c) In G7 enter the formula: **=VLOOKUP(E14,Groups,3)**.

This will pick up the numeric value of the car chosen which is stored in E14, find it in the named area Groups and return the model from the third column.

(d) In G8 enter the formula: **=VLOOKUP(E14,Groups,4)**.

This will pick up the numeric value of the car chosen which is stored in E14, find it in the named area Groups and return the insurance group from the fourth column.

These cells should now display the make, model and insurance group of the car chosen in the combo box, e.g. a Peugeot 406 is Group 10.

(e) In cell G9 enter the formula: **=VLOOKUP(E12,Multipliers!A15:C16,2)**.

When the option box is clicked male returns the value 1 in E12 and female returns the value 2. The **LOOKUP** function looks across to the Multipliers sheet and returns Male or Female.

(f) In G10 enter the formula **=VLOOKUP(E16,Multipliers!A2:C11,2)**.

The combo box which stores the age returns a value in E16. The LOOKUP function finds this value in the Multipliers sheet and returns the actual age e.g. a 1 returns 17-19.

(g) In G11 enter the formula **=VLOOKUP(E18,Multipliers!A20:B22,2)**.

The list box which stores the risk returns a value in E18. The LOOKUP function finds this value in the Multipliers sheet and returns the actual risk, e.g. a 1 returns High risk.

(h) In G12 enter the formula: **=IF(E22=TRUE,"Yes","No")**.

If the check box for the extra driver is checked E22 takes the value TRUE, if unchecked E22 takes the value FALSE. The function returns Yes or No in G12.

(i) In G13 enter the formula **=D24**.

This looks up and returns the number of years' no claims discount.

(j) In G14 type in the formula: **=VLOOKUP(E20,Multipliers!A32:D34,4)**.

This displays the abbreviation for the insurance type in cell G14.

Your spreadsheet should appear as shown in Figure 19.20.

	A	B	C	D	E	F	G	H
5								
6			Forename			Make	Peugeot	
7			Surname			Model	406	
8			Address 1			IG	10	
9			Address 2			Sex	Male	
10			Postcode			Age	25-29	
11				⦿ Male		Risk	Medium risk	
12			Sex	○ Female	1	Extra Driver	No	
13						No claims	2	
14			Car	Peugeot 406 ▼	4	Type	FC	
15								
16			Age	25-29 ▼	3			
17								
18			Area	High risk ▲	2			
19				Medium risk ▼				
20			Type	Fully comprehensive ▲	1			
21				Third party, fire & theft ▼				
22			Driver	☐ Extra driver	FALSE			
23					Years Per cent			
24			No claims ▲		2	40%		
25			▼					

◄ ► ►│ \ Groups / Multipliers \ **Quotes** /

Figure 19.20

(k) Test your spreadsheet by changing the details in the combo boxes etc. and making sure that the correct changes take place in column G.

5 Preparing the quote – entering the multipliers

The next stage is to look up and store the multiplier associated with each factor.

(a) In cell H8 enter the formula: **=VLOOKUP(G8,Costs,2)**.

This formula looks up the basic insurance cost for a car in that group, e.g. a Peugeot 406 is Group 10 and should display 264.

(b) In cell H9 enter the formula: **=VLOOKUP(E12,Multipliers!A15:C16,3)**.

If Male is selected this cell should display 1.3. If Female is selected it displays 1. (This is because males are considered 1.3 times more likely to be in an accident than females.)

(c) In cell H10 enter the formula: **=VLOOKUP(E16,Multipliers!A2:C11,3)**.

This displays the multiplier for that age grouping, e.g. for someone aged 25–29 it should display 2.

(d) In cell H11 enter the formula: **=VLOOKUP(E18,Multipliers!A20:C22,3)**.

This displays the multiplier for the chosen risk, e.g. for a medium risk area it should display 1.7.

(e) In cell H12 enter the formula: **=IF(E22=TRUE,1.3,1)**.

This displays the multiplier for extra drivers, e.g. if the box is checked it should display 1.3. Otherwise it will display 1.

(f) In cell H14 enter the formula: **=VLOOKUP(E20,Multipliers!A32:C34,3)**.

This displays the multiplier for the type of insurance, e.g. for fully comprehensive it should display 1.

Your spreadsheet should appear as shown in Figure 19.21.

	A	B	C	D	E	F	G	H
5								
6			Forename			Make	Peugeot	
7			Surname			Model	406	
8			Address 1			IG	10	264
9			Address 2			Sex	Male	1.3
10			Postcode			Age	25-29	2
11				⦿ Male		Risk	Medium risk	1.7
12			Sex	○ Female	1	Extra Driver	No	1
13						No claims	2	
14			Car	Peugeot 406 ▾	4	Type	FC	1
15								
16			Age	25-29 ▾	3			
17								
18			Area	High risk ▲	2			
19				Medium risk ▾				
20			Type	Fully comprehensive ▲	1			
21				Third party, fire & theft ▾				
22			Driver	☐ Extra driver	FALSE			
23					Years	Per cent		
24			No claims ▲		2	40%		
25			▾					

Groups / Multipliers \ **Quotes** /

Figure 19.21

6 Calculating the total cost

We now will use the basic cost and the multipliers to work out the real cost of the insurance.

(a) Enter the headings **Total without discount**, **No claims discount** and **Total cost** in cells F16, F18 and F20.

(b) Use **Format, Column, Width** to set the width of column F to 20.

(c) In H16 enter **=H8*H9*H10*H11*H12*H14**.

(d) In H18 enter **=H16*E24**.

(e) In H20 enter **=H16-H18**.

(f) Format the totals in H16 to H20 to currency.

Your spreadsheet should appear like the one shown in Figure 19.22.

	A	B	C	D	E	F	G	H
5								
6			Forename			Make	Peugeot	
7			Surname			Model		406
8			Address 1			IG		10	264
9			Address 2			Sex	Male	1.3
10			Postcode			Age	25-29	2
11				⦿ Male		Risk	Medium risk	1.7
12			Sex	○ Female	1	Extra Driver	No	1
13						No claims		2
14			Car	Peugeot 406 ▼	4	Type	FC	1
15								
16			Age	25-29 ▼	3	Total without discount		£1,166.88
17								
18			Area	High risk ▲ Medium risk ▼	2	No claims discount		£466.75
19								
20			Type	Fully comprehensive ▲ Third party, fire & theft ▼	1	Total cost		£700.13
21								
22			Driver	☐ Extra driver	FALSE			
23					Years Per cent			
24			No claims ▲		2 40%			
25			▼					

H ◀ ▶ H \ Groups / Multipliers \ **Quotes** /

Figure 19.22

7 Setting up the Customers worksheet

We need to set up a worksheet area to file away quotes.

(a) Insert a new worksheet and name it **Customers**.

(b) Set the font size for the whole sheet to 8 point.

(c) Set up the header row as shown in Figure 19.23.

(d) Format column O to currency.

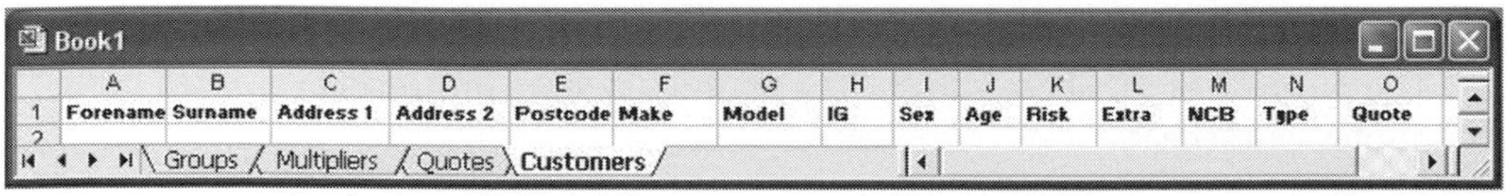

Figure 19.23

8 Automating the filing of quotes

We will set up a macro called **Filequote** to file quotes in the new **Customers** worksheet. We need to start by creating room on screen for the control buttons that will take the user around the system.

(a) Reduce the width of columns A and B on the Quotes worksheet to 2.00.

This creates room to the right of the screen and starts to give the user interface a balance.

When a quote is given we will need to file it away.

This can be a very long task and needs to be done very carefully and as always should be planned and practised before recording takes place.

(b) Enter some sample customer quote details including name and address.

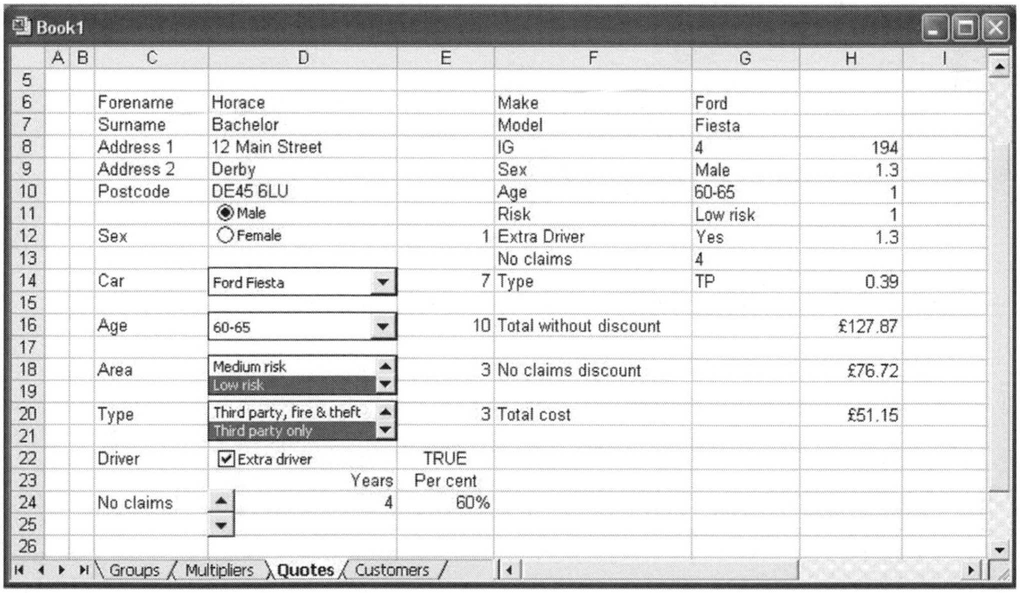

Figure 19.24

(c) Insert another new worksheet and name it **Data**.

The purpose of the sheet is to act as a temporary store for the data entered in the quotes worksheet.

(d) Set up the **Data** worksheet with the same column headings as the **Customers** worksheet. Use copy and paste to help you.

(e) Enter the formulas as shown in Figure 19.25. Format column O to currency. Set the font size to 8 point.

	A	B	C	D	E	F	G	H	I	J	K	L	M	N	O
1	Forename	Surname	Address 1	Address 2	Postcode	Make	Model	IG	Sex	Age	Risk	Extra	NCB	Type	Quote
2	=Quotes!D6	=Quotes!D7	=Quotes!D8	=Quotes!D9	=Quotes!D10	=Quotes!G6	=Quotes!G7	=Quotes!G8	=Quotes!G9	=Quotes!G10	=Quotes!G11	=Quotes!G12	=Quotes!G13	=Quotes!G14	=Quotes!H20
3															

Groups / Quotes / Multipliers / Customers \ Data /

Figure 19.25

The data will appear as in Figure 19.26.

	A	B	C	D	E	F	G	H	I	J	K	L	M	N	O
1	Forename	Surname	Address 1	Address 2	Postcode	Make	Model	IG	Sex	Age	Risk	Extra	NCB	Type	Quote
2	Horace	Bachelor	12 Main Street	Derby	DE45 6LU	Ford	Fiesta	4	Male	60-65	Low risk	Yes	4	TP	£51.15
3															

Groups / Quotes / Multipliers / Customers \ Data /

Figure 19.26

When a new quote is made the data is automatically picked up on this worksheet. This row of data then needs copying and pasting to the **Customers** worksheet.

The steps in the macro are:

(f) Make sure you have the correct data on the **Quotes** worksheet.

(g) Start recording a new macro called **Filequote**.

(h) Switch to the **Customers** worksheet.

(i) Select row 2 (by clicking on the row number 2) and insert a row.

(j) Switch to the **Data** worksheet.

(k) Select row 2 and click on **Edit, Copy**.

(l) Switch to the **Customers** sheet.

(m) Select cell A2 and click **Edit**, **Paste Special**, **Values** and click **OK**.

(n) Click on the bold icon to turn off the bold text.

(o) Click on a free space in the spreadsheet area.

(p) Stop recording.

(q) Add a button on the right-hand side of the **Quotes** worksheet near cells I14 to J15 to run the **Filequote** macro. Label the button **File Quote**.

Enter some different sample data into the **Quotes** worksheet and test that the **Filequote** macro works as expected. The oldest quotes will be at the bottom as in Figure 19.27.

	A	B	C	D	E	F	G	H	I	J	K	L	M	N	O
1	Forename	Surname	Address 1	Address 2	Postcode	Make	Model	IG	Sex	Age	Risk	Extra	NCB	Type	Quote
2	Alanna	Crowe	12 Fortescue Ro	Derby	DE5 9PK	Ford	Ka		2	Female	30-34	High risk	No	1	FC	£ 453.60
3	Charles	George	63 Arthur Street	Derby	DE16 6TY	Honda	Civic		9	Male	45-49	Low risk	Yes	3	TPFT	£ 110.86
4	Horace	Bachelor	12 Main Street	Derby	DE45 6LU	Ford	Fiesta		4	Male	60-65	Low risk	Yes	4	TP	£ 51.15
5															

Groups / Quotes / Multipliers \ **Customers** / Data /

Figure 19.27

9 Clearing the current screen to enter a new quote

When the quote has been filed away we clearly need to clear the screen ready for a new quote.

We will record a macro called **Clearscreen** to carry out the process. As always, plan and practise the macro before recording.

There is a difficulty with this process. It is not just a case of selecting cells and clicking **Edit, Clear, All**.

A number of the cells contain complex formulas and we do not wish to clear them from the spreadsheet.

When recording the macro we need to clear the name and address in cells D6 to D10 and simply delete the numbers returned by the various controls in column E.

The steps are:

(a) Switch to the **Quotes** worksheet.

(b) Start recording a new macro called **Clearscreen**.

(c) Highlight cells D6 to D10.

(d) From the menu click on **Edit, Clear, All**.

(e) Highlight cells E12 to E22 and click on **Edit, Clear, Contents**.

(f) Highlight cell D24 and click on **Edit, Clear, Contents**.

(g) Return the cursor to cell D6.

(h) Stop recording.

(i) Add a button at the bottom right-hand side of the **Quotes** worksheet near cells G24 to H24 to run the **Clearscreen** macro. Label the button **Clear Screen**.

(j) Enter some more data and test the macro.

The macro should clear the data and place the cursor in position for the next quote.

Improving the screen layout (optional)

There are many small things we can do to the Quotes worksheet to improve its layout and make it more user-friendly as shown in Figure 19.28.

(a) Format the text in columns C and F to bold. You will need to increase the width of column C to around 10.

(b) The data in cells E12 to E22 and cells H8 to H14 does not need to be seen. The simplest way to hide this data is to format the colour of the text to white.

(c) Align the data in cells G6 to G14 to the left of the cell.

	A	B	C	D	E	F	G	H	I	J
5										
6			**Forename**	Roy		**Make**	Peugeot			
7			**Surname**	Marshall		**Model**	806			
8			**Address 1**	2 Hall Road		**IG**	10			
9			**Address 2**	Derby		**Sex**	Male			
10			**Postcode**	DE34 8PL		**Age**	30-34			
11				⦿ Male		**Risk**	Medium risk			
12			**Sex**	○ Female		**Extra Driver**	Yes			
13						**No claims**	2			File Quote
14			**Car**	Peugeot 806 ▼		**Type**	FC			
15										
16			**Age**	30-34 ▼		**Total without discount**		£1,137.71		
17										
18			**Area**	High risk ▲		**No claims discount**		£455.08		
19				Medium risk ▼						
20			**Type**	Fully comprehensive ▲		**Total cost**		£682.62		
21				Third party, fire & theft ▼						
22			**Driver**	☑ Extra driver						
23				Years	Per cent				Clear Screen	
24			**No claims**	▲ 2	40%					
25				▼						

Figure 19.28

You may see the #N/A error message. This occurs when an item such as the age or type of car has not been selected. It is possible to use an IF statement to detect blank cells in the data entry area and replace the errors generated with a blank. If cells in the data entry area do not contain a blank then the functions in column G will operate as normal.

(d) Edit the formulas to appear as shown in Figure 19.29. Use of copy and paste may help.

	G	H
6	=IF(E14="","",VLOOKUP(E14,Groups,2))	
7	=IF(E14="","",VLOOKUP(E14,Groups,3))	
8	=IF(E14="","",VLOOKUP(E14,Groups,4))	=IF(G8="","",VLOOKUP(G8,Costs,2))
9	=IF(E12="","",VLOOKUP(E12,Multipliers!A15:C16,2))	=IF(E12="","",VLOOKUP(E12,Multipliers!A15:C16,3))
10	=IF(E16="","",VLOOKUP(E16,Multipliers!A2:C11,2))	=IF(E16="","",VLOOKUP(E16,Multipliers!A2:C11,3))
11	=IF(E18="","",VLOOKUP(E18,Multipliers!A20:B22,2))	=IF(E18="","",VLOOKUP(E18,Multipliers!A20:C22,3))
12	=IF(E22="","",IF(E22=TRUE,"Yes","No"))	=IF(E22=TRUE,1.3,1)
13	=IF(D24="","",D24)	
14	=IF(E20="","",VLOOKUP(E20,Multipliers!A32:D34,4))	=IF(E20="","",VLOOKUP(E20,Multipliers!A32:C34,3))
15		
16		=IF(D6="","",H8*H9*H10*H11*H12*H14)
17		
18		=IF(D6="","",H16*E24)
19		
20		=IF(D6="","",H16-H18)

H ◀ ▶ H \ Groups \ **Quotes** / Multipliers / Customers / Data /

Figure 19.29

(e) The formula in E24 also needs changing to
=IF(D24="","",VLOOKUP(D24,Multipliers!B25:C29,2)).

10 Designing the printed quote

The next stage is to design the layout of the printed quote and set it up to take the data from the **Quotes** worksheet.

(a) Insert a new sheet and rename it **Printed Quote**.

(b) Set up rows 1 to 8 to display the letterhead as shown in Figure 19.30 using the **Drawing** toolbar in Excel.

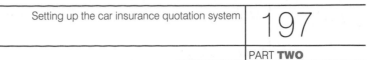

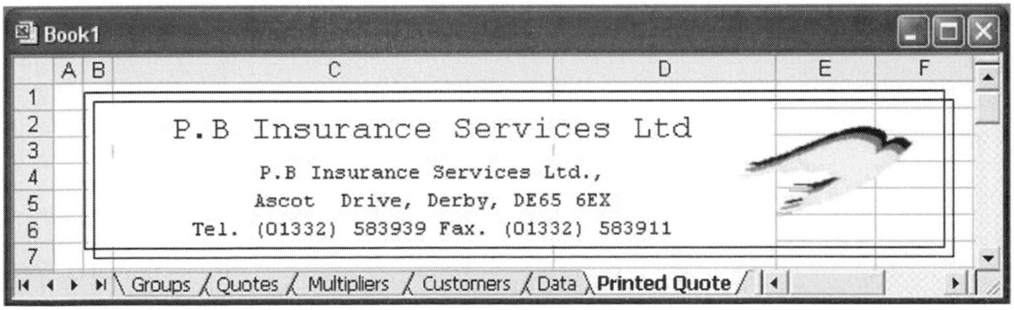

Figure 19.30

The letterhead is made up of the following:

○ Column A and B are formatted to width 2.
○ Column C is width 40 and column D is width 20.
○ A text box containing PB Insurance Services Ltd, Courier New font size 16 point.
○ A text box containing the address in Courier New font size 10 point.
○ Format both text boxes to have no border.
○ Insert a suitable logo.
○ Insert two rectangles the same size (use copy and paste) around the letterhead.
○ Do not go to the right of column F.
○ Make sure the rectangles are formatted to **No Fill**.

Hints

(c) Set up rows 8 to 32 to display the headings and formulas as shown in Figure 19.31.

	C	D
8	Date	=TODAY()
9		
10	Insurance quotation for:	
11	=Quotes!D6&" "&Quotes!D7	
12	=Quotes!D8	
13	=Quotes!D9	
14	=Quotes!D10	
15		
16	Make	=Quotes!G6
17	Model	=Quotes!G7
18	Age	=Quotes!G10
19	Sex	=Quotes!G9
20	Extra driver	=Quotes!G12
21	Insurance type	=VLOOKUP(Quotes!E20,Multipliers!A32:B34,2)
22	Years no claims bonus	=Quotes!D24
23		
24	Quotation	=Quotes!H20
25		
26	Quotation valid until	=TODAY()+14
27		
28	Signed on behalf of PB Insurance Services Ltd	
29		
30		
31		
32	Paul Bryant, Managing Director	

Book1

\ Groups / Quotes / Multipliers / Customers / Data \ Printed (

Figure 19.31

The formulas link to the **Quotes** worksheet and display the quote data.

(d) Remove the gridlines and align column D to the left.

(e) Format D24 to **Currency**.

(f) To print accurately you may need to adjust your print margins.

The final quote will look like Figure 19.32.

P.B Insurance Services Ltd

P.B Insurance Services Ltd.,
Ascot Drive, Derby, DE65 6EX
Tel. (01332) 583939 Fax. (01332) 583911

Date   29/12/2002

Insurance quotation for:
Roy Marshall
2 Hall Road
Derby
DE34 8PL

Make   Peugeot
Model   806
Age   30-34
Sex   Male
Extra driver   Yes
Insurance type   Fully comprehensive
Years no claims bonus   2

Quotation   £682.62

Quotation valid until   12/01/2003

Signed on behalf of PB Insurance Services Ltd

Figure 19.32

11 Adding user options to the quotes worksheet

On the quotes worksheet we already have buttons to file a quote and to clear a quote from the screen. We need to offer the following additional options:

○ Print a quote
○ View all quotes
○ Edit groups
○ Edit multipliers
○ Exit

Macros need to be set up to automate each option and a button added for each macro. Remember to practise and plan the steps before recording each macro.

Print a quote

We need to record a macro to print a quote. Call the macro **Printquote**.
The steps are:

(a) Start recording.

(b) Switch to the **Printed Quote** sheet by clicking its tab.

(c) From the menu choose **File, Print** and click **OK**.

(d) Click on the **Quotes** tab to return to the **Quotes** sheet.

(e) Stop recording.

(f) Add a button to the Quotes sheet by dragging a button across cells I17 and J18, name it **Print Quote**.

View all quotes

This is a simple macro called **Viewquotes** which will switch from the **Quotes** sheet to the **Customers** sheet.

The steps are:

(a) Start recording.

(b) Click on the **Customers** worksheet

(c) Stop recording.

(d) Add a button to cells I20 to J21 of the **Quotes** worksheet and call it **View Quotes**.

Edit groups

In exactly the same way as above, record a macro to move to the **Groups** worksheet and position the button across cells I7 and J8 of the **Quotes** worksheet. Label the button **Edit Groups** and call the macro **Editgroups**.

Edit multipliers

In exactly the same way, record a macro to move to the **Multipliers** worksheet and position the button across cells I10 and J11 of the **Quotes** worksheet. Label the button **Edit Multipliers** and call the macro **Editmultipliers**.

Exit

Position the button across cells I23 and J24. We will set up the macro later.

Don't forget that you can get the spacing between macro buttons even by selecting them all and clicking on **Draw, Align or Distribute, Distribute Vertically** (on the Drawing toolbar).

To link the system together macros need to be recorded to return the user from each of the **Groups**, the **Multipliers** and the **Customers** worksheets. Name the macro **Quotes** and attach a button to it labelled **Return to Quote** in an appropriate place on each worksheet.

12 Customizing the interface and some finishing touches

Your system should now be working and appear as shown in Figure 19.33.

	C	D	E	F	G	H	I	J
1								
2								
3								
4								
5								
6	**Forename**	Roy		**Make**	Peugeot			
7	**Surname**	Marshall		**Model**	806		Edit Groups	
8	**Address 1**	2 Hall Road		**IG**	10			
9	**Address 2**	Derby		**Sex**	Male			
10	**Postcode**	DE34 8PL		**Age**	30-34		Edit Multipliers	
11		◉ Male		**Risk**	Medium risk			
12	**Sex**	○ Female		**Extra Driver**	Yes			
13				**No claims**	2		File Quote	
14	**Car**	Peugeot 806 ▼		**Type**	FC			
15								
16	**Age**	30-34 ▼		**Total without discount**		£1,137.71		
17							Print Quote	
18	**Area**	High risk ▲		**No claims discount**		£455.08		
19		Medium risk ▼						
20	**Type**	Fully comprehensive ▲		**Total cost**		£682.62	View Quotes	
21		Third party, fire & theft ▼						
22	**Driver**	✔ Extra driver						
23		Years	Per cent		Clear Screen		Exit	
24	**No claims** ▲	2	40%					
25		▼						

Groups \ **Quotes** / Multipliers / Customers / Data / Printed Quote /

Figure 19.33

It is not essential but with a little use of lines, boxes, colour fills and a logo, it is possible to transform the look and feel of your system interface to the one in Figure 19.34.

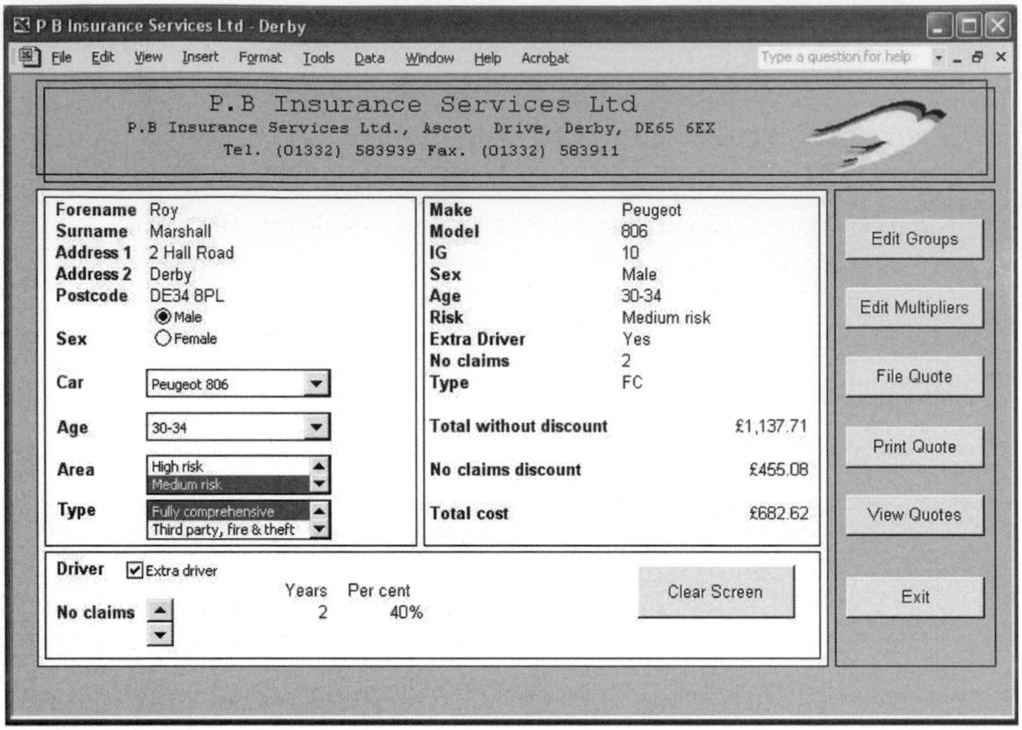

Figure 19.34

Adding the auto_open macro

In Excel the **auto_open** macro runs when the file is opened.

We want our system to load without the appearance of a spreadsheet by removing the gridlines, sheet tabs, row and column headings etc.

We will record a macro called **auto_open**.

The steps are:

(a) Start recording.

(b) Click **Tools, Options**.

(c) Uncheck the **Gridlines**, **Row and column headings**, **Sheet tabs**, **Scroll bars**.

(d) Uncheck the **Formula bar** and **Status bar** and click on **OK**.

(e) Click **View, Toolbars** and remove the **Standard** and **Formatting toolbars** (if present).

(f) Stop recording.

Click **Tools, Macro, Visual Basic Editor** to view your macro code.

```
Sub auto_open()
'
'  auto_open Macro
'  Macro recorded 13/01/2003
'
'
    With ActiveWindow
Application.Caption = "PB Insurance Services Ltd"
        .DisplayGridlines = False
        .DisplayHeadings = False
        .DisplayHorizontalScrollBar = False
        .DisplayVerticalScrollBar = False
        .DisplayWorkbookTabs = False
    End With
    With Application
        .DisplayFormulaBar = False
        .DisplayStatusBar = False
    End With
    Application.CommandBars("Standard").Visible = False
    Application.CommandBars("Formatting").Visible = False
End Sub
```

(g) Insert the line *Application.Caption = "PB Insurance Services Ltd"* and change your filename to Derby; this code replaces the Microsoft Excel header as shown in Figure 19.35.

P B Insurance Services Ltd - Derby

File   Edit   View   Insert   Format   Tools   Data   Window   Help   Acrobat   Type a question for help

Figure 19.35

Adding the auto_close macro

When we close our system down, Excel looks to run an **auto_close** macro if present.

On leaving the system we want to restore Excel's original settings.

We will record a macro called **auto_close**.

The steps are:

(a) Start recording.

(b) Click on **Tools, Options**.

(c) Check the **Gridlines**, **Row and column headings**, **Sheet tabs**, **Scroll bars**.

(a) Check the **Formula bar** and **Status bar** and click on **OK**.

(e) Click **View, Toolbars** and restore the **Standard** and **Formatting toolbars**.

(f) Stop recording.

Click **Tools, Macro, Visual Basic Editor** to view your macro code.

```
Sub auto_close()
'
' auto_close Macro
' Macro recorded 13/01/2003
'
'

  With ActiveWindow
    .DisplayGridlines = True
    .DisplayHeadings = True
    .DisplayHorizontalScrollBar = True
    .DisplayVerticalScrollBar = True
    .DisplayWorkbookTabs = True
  End With
  With Application
    .DisplayFormulaBar = True
    .DisplayStatusBar = True
  End With
    Application.CommandBars("Standard").Visible = True
    Application.CommandBars("Formatting").Visible = True
End Sub
```

The macro as it stands merely restores the Excel settings, we want to save and close our application down. If you have added an application caption we also need to remove that.

Add the following lines before the End Sub;

```
    Application.Caption = Empty
    ActiveWorkbook.Save
    Application.Quit
```

These lines of code clear the caption, save the current workbook and close down Excel.

Assign this macro to the button on the Quotes worksheet labelled Exit.

13 Adding the front end

The last stage is to add the front end shown in Figure 19.36 to the system.

```
PB Insurance Services Ltd                                    [X]

          P.B Insurance Services Ltd

            P.B Insurance Services Ltd
                   Ascot Drive
                      Derby
                    DE65 6EX
              Tel. (01332) 583939
              Fax. (01332) 583911




   ┌─────────┐   ┌─────────────┐   ┌─────────┐
   │  Exit   │   │    Enter    │   │  About  │
   └─────────┘   └─────────────┘   └─────────┘
```

Figure 19.36

The **Exit** button will close down the system, **Enter** will move to the **Quotes** interface and the **About** button will give system details.

(a) Load the Visual Basic Editor by clicking on **Tools, Macro, Visual Basic Editor**.

(b) Click on **Insert, UserForm**.

(c) In the **Properties Window** for the **User Form** (at the bottom left of the screen) set the **Caption** to PB Insurance Services Ltd, the **Height** to 320 and **Width** to 400.

(d) Using the **Text Box** and **Image** tools add the company details and logo as shown in Figure 19.36.

(e) Add three **Command Buttons**; by default they are called CommandButton1, 2 and 3. Edit the button labels to **Exit**, **Enter** and **About**.

(f) Double click on each of the buttons in turn. The window in Figure 19.37 will appear. It is now just a case of tinkering with the code.

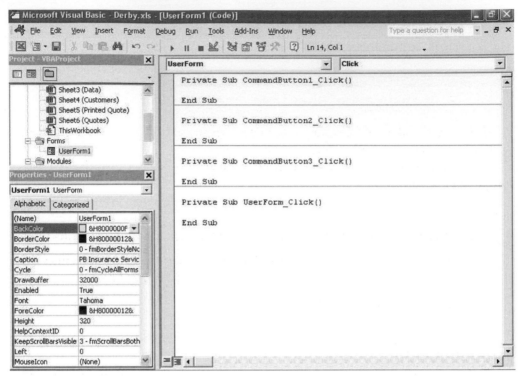

Figure 19.37

The code should be as follows:

The **Exit** button (closes the system down)

```
Private Sub CommandButton1_Click()
Application.Quit
End Sub
```

The **Enter** button (hides the User Form and runs a macro called Start)

```
Private Sub CommandButton2_Click()
UserForm1.Hide
Start
End Sub
```

The **About** button (runs a Message box)

```
Private Sub CommandButton3_Click()
MsgBox "Spreadsheet Projects in Excel for Advanced Level by Mott and Rendell", vbOKOnly, "PB Insurance Services"
End Sub
```

We also need to make a few changes to our **auto_open** macro. We now want it to load the UserForm. When we select enter on the User Form we want to remove the UserForm and then run a macro called Start which effectively runs the original auto_open macro.

Edit the macro as follows:

(a) In Excel click on **Tools, Macro, Macros**. Select **auto_open** and choose **Edit**.

(b) Delete the name **auto_open** in the first line and replace it with **start** like this:

```
Sub start()
'
' auto_open Macro
```

(c) At the end of this macro, type in the following new macro:

```
Sub auto_open()
Load UserForm1
UserForm1.Show
End Sub
```

Note
You can add the line **ScreenUpdating = False** to this macro to reduce the screen flicker.

(d) Finally, test the system thoroughly. When you are satisfied that it is fully working, add cell protection where appropriate.

PART THREE

Documenting a system

⊕ Unit 20 Documenting the car insurance quotation system

An ICT project is much more than just setting up the solution using Microsoft Excel. You must also include documentation covering the analysis of the system, its design, its implementation, testing, a user guide and evaluation.

The documentation provided here follows closely the **AQA AS level ICT** specification. You will find other courses require a similar approach but always refer to the specification guidelines.

Examples of courses are:

○ the coursework components for students studying **A/S** and **A levels** in **ICT**;
○ the mandatory unit in Spreadsheet Design for students studying the **Advanced Subsidiary** and **Advanced VCE** in **ICT**;
○ the Computing project component for students studying **A/S** and **A levels** in **Computing**.

Advanced Subsidiary courses in ICT tend to focus on encouraging students to specify and design a solution to a task set externally or chosen by the student themselves. The student is expected to implement, test and fully document their solution. A process of ongoing recording and development is often encouraged.

The following pages show you how to document your solution by looking at some of the documentation provided with the PB Insurance Services Ltd system.

Remember

The documentation here is not supposed to be complete but each section offers examples, pointers and hints to what is considered good practice.

Advanced courses in ICT encourage the student to analyse and design a solution to a real problem for a real user. The problem tends to be more complex and leads to the implementation of a system by the student.

Julian Mott and Ian Rendell have written another coursework book: **Database Projects in Access for Advanced Level**. This provides further exemplar materials which may be of use to both students and teachers.

PB Insurance Services Ltd Car Insurance Quotes

Contents

1 Specification
   (a) Problem statement
   (b) Resources available
   (c) End-user requirements
   (d) Input, output and processing requirements
   (e) Design
   (f) Sub-tasks to the solution
   (g) Test strategy
   (h) Test plan

2 Implementation

3 User testing
   (a) Test results
   (b) User testing

4 User guide

5 Evaluation

1 Specification

In this section you need to give a clear description of your identified problem and establish clearly the requirements. You will need also to state the inputs, processes and outputs needed. Clear design plans along with strategies and plans for testing should be presented.

(a) Problem statement

This should be a description of the problem to be solved. It might briefly include: details of the user or business, its purpose, the information processing involved, some of the problems it has and some detail as to what you are going to try and solve.

PB Insurance Ltd

Paul Bryant runs a small car insurance brokers.

He works full-time from his Derby office. He has a part-time assistant who tends to work evenings and weekends.

He has developed a loyal customer base who regularly ring the office when car insurance renewal is due. To maintain customer relations and develop his business by attracting new clients, he often conducts business at the home of his customers.

To calculate the insurance quote Paul uses his calculator and a table of insurance ratings.

All cars are allocated to an insurance group (IG) number. The more expensive and powerful the car, the higher the rating, e.g. a Ford Puma is IG 9.

Insurance group costs

IG	BASIC COST
1	£ 174.00
2	£ 180.00
3	£ 187.00
4	£ 194.00
5	£ 202.00
6	£ 210.00
7	£ 222.00
8	£ 235.00
9	£ 248.00
10	£ 264.00
11	£ 280.00
12	£ 300.00
...	...

The insurance group basic price is then adjusted according to a range of criteria.

The younger you are the more you are considered a risk and hence the more you pay. For example, a person aged 20–24 has a factor of 2.4.

So a 21-year old driving a Ford Puma would pay **£248 × 2.4 = £595.20**.

Age factors

AGE	MULTIPLIER
17–19	4.80
20–24	2.40
25–29	2.00
30–34	1.50
35–39	1.30
40–44	1.20
45–49	1.15
50–54	1.10
55–59	1.05
60–65	1.00

Age is not the only factor that comes into play.

If you are male you are considered a higher risk than if you are female by a factor of 1.3.

Hence if the 21-year-old driver of the Ford Puma was male he would pay
£248 × 2.4 × 1.3 = £773.36.

Sex factors

SEX	MULTIPLIER
Male	1.30
Female	1.00

Other factors that are taken into account are the type of area you live in which is classified as high, medium or low risk.

Area factors

AREA	MULTIPLIER
High risk	2.40
Medium risk	1.70
Low risk	1.00

Insurance types available are third party, third party fire and theft, and fully comprehensive.

Insurance type factors

TYPE	MULTIPLIER	ABBREVIATION
Fully comprehensive	1	FC
Third party, fire & theft	0.46	TPFT
Third party only	0.39	TP

An extra driver can be added to the policy by adding a factor of 1.3. No claims discount is available as the table below shows:

No claims discounts

NO CLAIM BONUS	MULTIPLIER
0	0%
1	30%
2	40%
3	50%
4	60%

Paul more often than not is issuing his quotes over the phone. It is quite a lengthy process using his calculator and reference tables and quotes are handwritten or word-processed which in turn is lengthy. He would like to automate the system and make better use of his PC. When he makes customer visits, he would like to be able to take a laptop-computer for the purpose of issuing quotes.

(b) Resources available

The purpose of this section is to look at the hardware and software resources available to the user and make appropriate comment or recommendations. Try and look at this in relation to the problem you are trying to solve. It is not a case of just listing a typical PC specification. You might also consider printer options and the backup facilities needed.

Resources available

In the office Paul has a Pentium 4 with 128Mb of memory. The operating system is Windows XP and the Office XP suite is installed including Excel XP. He has a powerful Epson Laser printer for the high quality printing he will need.

He also has available an older laptop, Pentium 400 with 64 Mb of memory, with Windows 98 and Office 97 installed. He will have to install the Office XP suite and consider upgrading his laptop to 128Mb. It is neither advisable nor practical to move the laser printer around so out of office work can only be done on screen.

Working between the two machines will require careful attention to transferring and backing up files between the machines.

Paul and his assistant are reasonably competent with the day-to-day use of a PC and will only need simple instructions to get started.

(c) *End-user requirements*

1 A solution is required to be able to give a quick quote accurately and efficiently.
2 The solution must produce multiple copies of the quote.
3 The solution should enable phone enquiries to be dealt with far more quickly than at present.
4 Issued quotes need to be stored with the facility to view at a later date.
5 Quotes should be issued with a professional look on letter-headed paper.
6 The solution must be user friendly, yet have a professional look and feel.
7 The solution should be easy to transfer easily between the laptop and office-based PC.

Clearly establishing the requirements is the key to your solution. If you are clear what you are setting out to achieve many parts of the documentation will fall into place easily, particularly the testing and evaluation. When you consider the above requirements you might ask yourself:

○ How many multiple copies?
○ How quick and how accurate does the quote have to be?
○ What makes a solution user friendly?
○ How quickly does a phone enquiry have to be dealt with to be an improvement on the present situation?
○ How will you ensure the solution is transferable?

(d) Input, output and processing requirements

Establish exactly what your solution must do (**the processes**), the data that is needed to do it (**input**) and what it is supposed to do (**output**). These need to be clearly stated. You cannot design a solution without this detail!

Much of the detail required here for our example has been stated earlier in this unit where the process of calculating the quote was explained.

Input requirements

Customer details to include:
- Forename
- Surname
- Address
- Sex
- Make and model of car
- Age of driver in grouped format, e.g. 40–45
- Type of insurance, fully comprehensive, third party fire and theft or third party
- Area risk assessment given as high, medium or low
- Extra driver to be declared or not
- No claims discount up to a maximum of 60% for 4 years no claims

Insurance details to include:
- Insurance group ratings for makes of cars
- Multiplying factors to be allocated to sex, age of driver, area risk and insurance type

Processing requirements

- Details of insurance group will be looked up from a table
- Details of multiplying factors to be used will be looked up from a table
- Data will be transferred from the client details area on screen to the customers area
- The cost of the quote will be calculated with and without no claims discount
- Quote details will be stored for future reference

Output requirements

- Full quote details on screen to include customer name, address, car details, the cost of insurance with and without VAT including detail of the no claims discount available.
- Fully customized and professionally printed output with company logo and header containing company address and phone/fax numbers, issue date, full quote details with the quote expiry date clearly shown.

(e) Design

The project should be broken down into clear sub-tasks or modules, which should relate to the users' requirements. Produce design plans for each sub-task.

Your design plans should be done away from the computer.

Design plans are probably best done by hand. You could use A3 paper and/or use a blank grid from an Excel spreadsheet.

Good spreadsheet designs will include details of:

- sheet naming, named cells and cell ranges;
- validation and cell protection;
- cell formatting;
- fonts and graphics;
- labels and formulas used;
- links between sheets;
- general sheet layouts;
- interfaces and screen designs;
- macros and macro buttons;
- any customized outputs to include details of page layout.

(f) Sub-tasks to the solution

I will break the car insurance problem down into the following sub-tasks:

1 **The Insurance Groups worksheet**

2 The Multipliers worksheet

3 **The Quotes worksheet**
   (a) **customer details section**
   (b) **quote details section**
   (c) **the calculation**

4 The Customers worksheet

5 Macros are needed to:
   (a) file the quotes
   (b) **clear the screen**

6 The printed quote worksheet

7 **The Start-up screen and options**

The designs for the sub-tasks highlighted in bold are shown in the following diagrams.

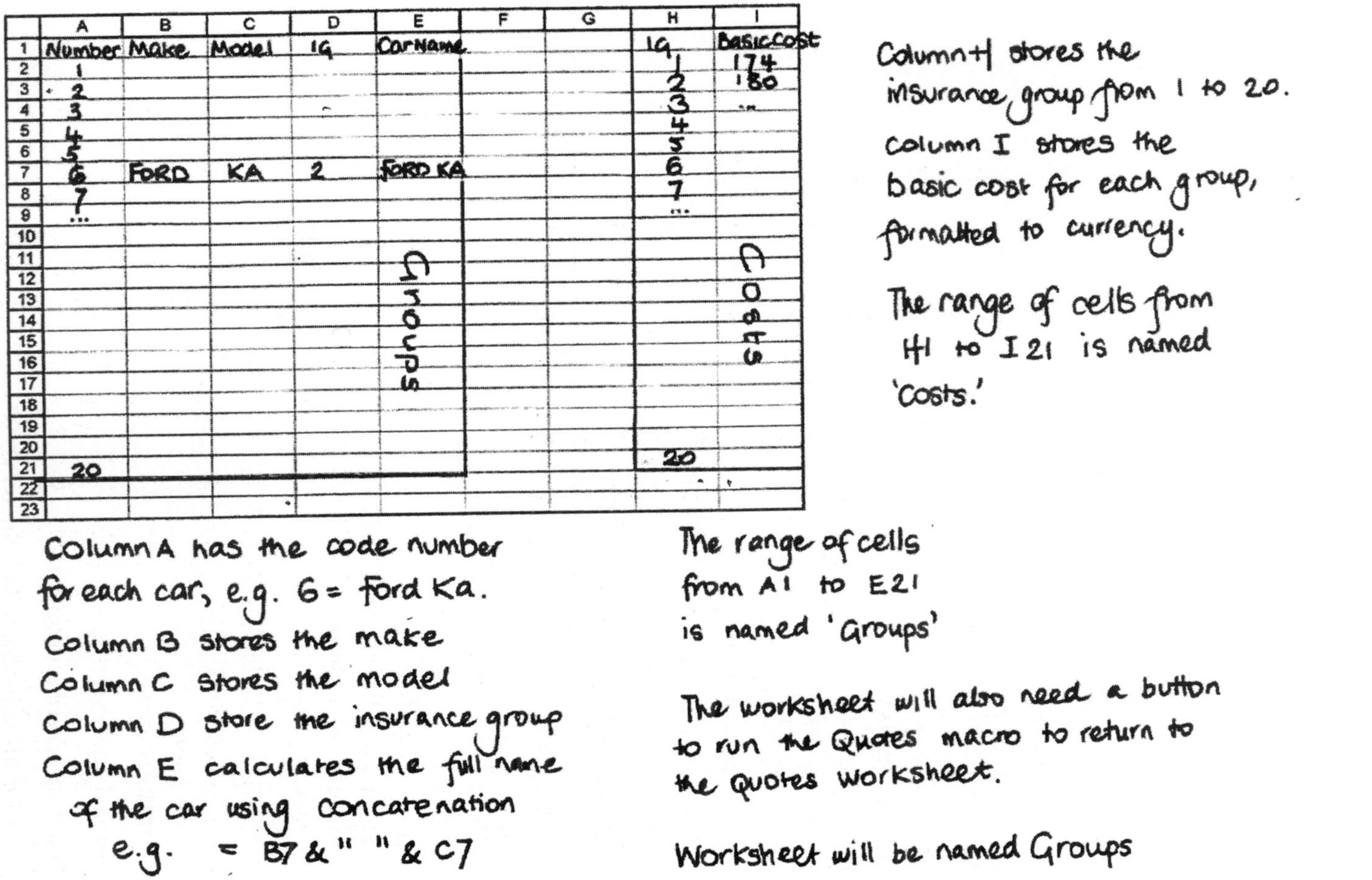

Column H stores the insurance group from 1 to 20.

Column I stores the basic cost for each group, formatted to currency.

The range of cells from H1 to I21 is named 'Costs.'

The range of cells from A1 to E21 is named 'Groups'

The worksheet will also need a button to run the Quotes macro to return to the Quotes worksheet.

Worksheet will be named Groups

	A	B	C	D	E	F	G	H	I
1	Number	Make	Model	IG	CorName			IG	BasicCost
2	1							1	174
3	2							2	180
4	3							3	
5	4							4	
6	5	FORD	KA	2	FORD KA			5	
7	6							6	
8	7							7	
9	...							...	
10									
11									
12									
13									
14									
15									
16									
17									
18									
19									
20									
21	20							20	
22									
23									

Groups

Costs

Column A has the code number for each car, e.g. 6 = Ford Ka.

Column B stores the make

Column C stores the model

Column D store the insurance group

Column E calculates the full name of the car using concatenation

e.g. = B7 & " " & C7

Figure 20.1

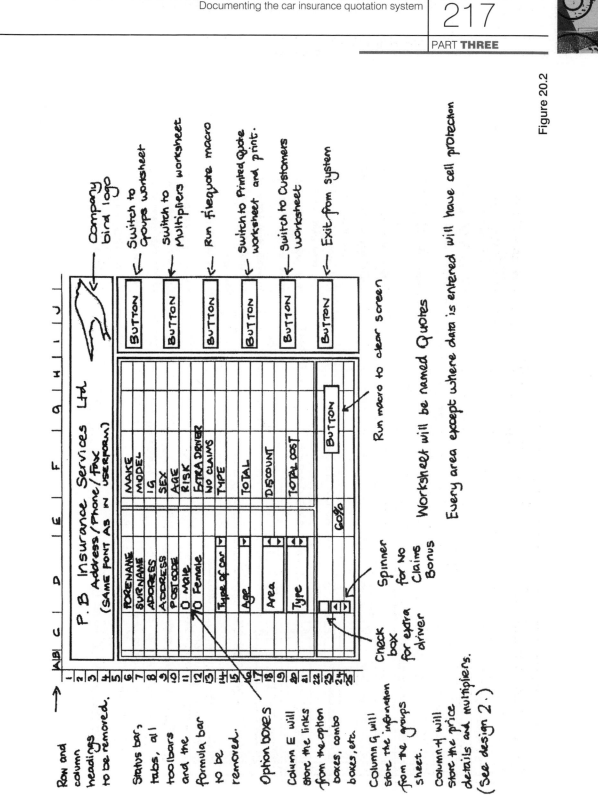

Figure 20.2

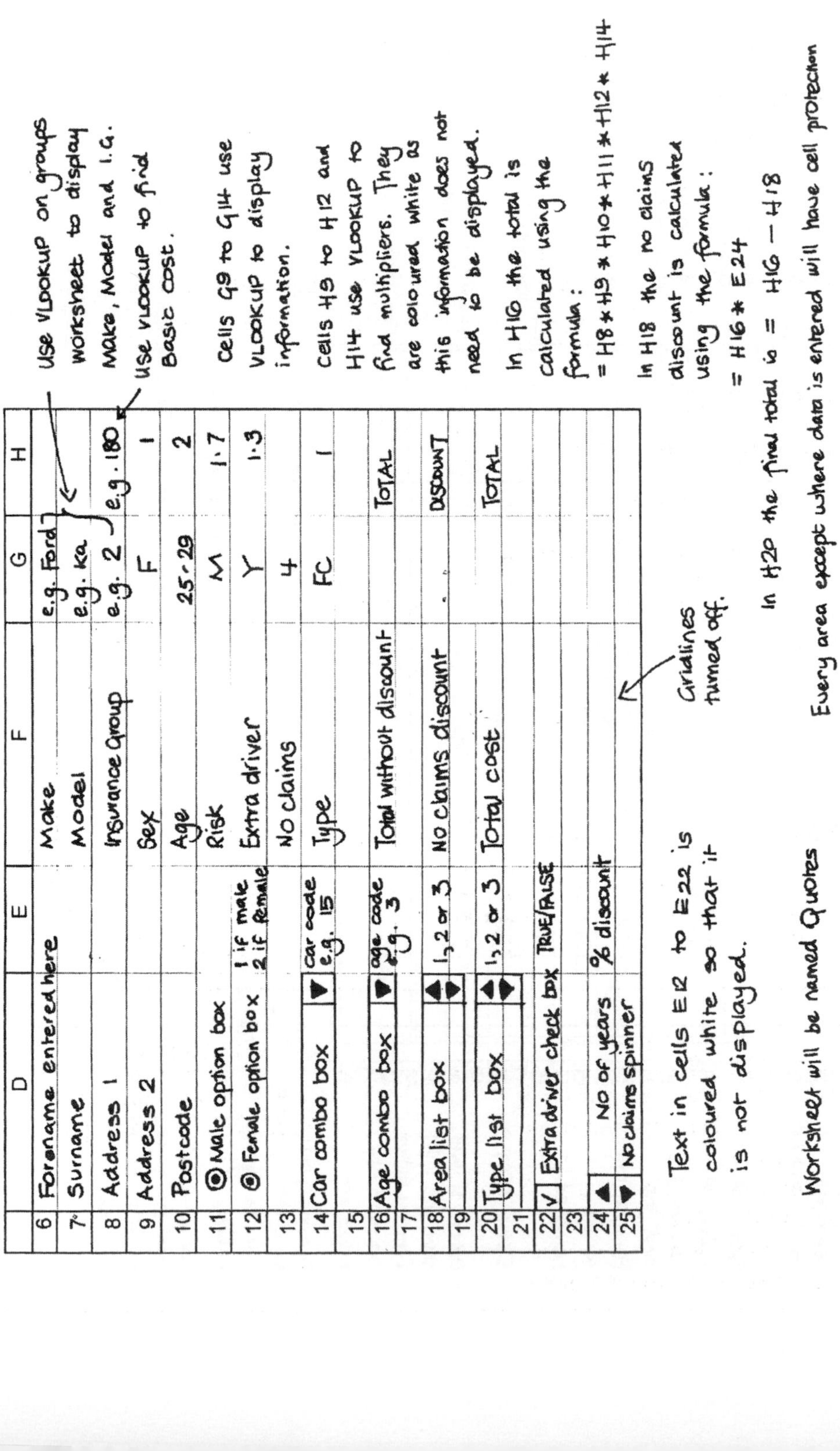

	D	E	F	G	H
6	Forename entered here		Make	e.g. Ford	
7	Surname		Model	e.g. ka	
8	Address 1		Insurance group	e.g. 2	e.g. 180
9	Address 2		Sex	F	1
10	Postcode		Age	25-29	2
11	◉ Male option box		Risk	M	1.7
12	◉ Female option box	1 if male 2 if female	Extra driver	Y	1.3
13			No claims	4	
14	Car combo box	car code e.g. 15	Type	FC	1
15					
16	Age combo box	age code e.g. 3	Total without discount		TOTAL
17					
18	Area list box	1,2 or 3	No claims discount		DISCOUNT
19					
20	Type list box	1,2 or 3	Total cost		TOTAL
21					
22	Extra driver check box	TRUE/FALSE			
23					
24	No of years	% discount			
25	No claims spinner				

Use VLOOKUP on groups worksheet to display Make, Model and I.G.

Use VLOOKUP to find basic cost.

Cells G9 to G14 use VLOOKUP to display information.

Cells H9 to H12 and H14 use VLOOKUP to find multipliers. They are coloured white as this information does not need to be displayed.

In H16 the total is calculated using the formula:
$$= H8 * H9 * H10 * H11 * H12 * H14$$

In H18 the no claims discount is calculated using the formula:
$$= H16 * E24$$

In H20 the final total is = H16 − H18

Gridlines turned off.

Text in cells E12 to E22 is coloured white so that it is not displayed.

Worksheet will be named Quotes

Every area except where data is entered will have cell protection.

Figure 20.3

Sub-Task 5b Design

Macro to clear the screen (after quote has been filed)

The macro must:

1 select the Quotes worksheet;

2 select cells D6 to D10;

3 clear these cells;

4 select cells E12, E14, E16, E18, E20, E22 and D24 (using CTRL and click);

5 clear the contents.

Sub-Task 7 Design

The Start-up screen and options

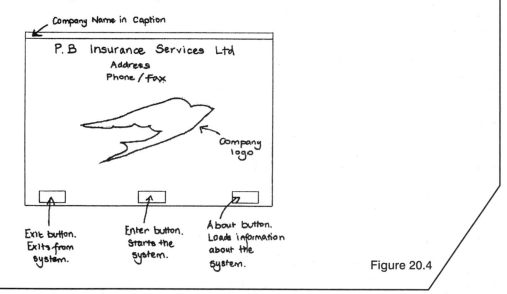

Figure 20.4

Design dos	Design don'ts
• Present your plans in a format such that a reasonably competent person could take them and make a start on setting up your solution. You could get another student to try them out. • Make them legible and neat. This person must be able to read them.	• Don't use screen dumps from the actual solution as part of your design plans.

Note If your solution has many similar features, e.g. interfaces or outputs, you could just design one of them in detail showing all the common features. The others could then be listed with details of the features that are different perhaps shown in a tabular format.

(g) Test strategy

Testing is an integral part of developing an IT solution. Your design should include a test strategy and a test plan.

The test strategy describes the different types of testing or approaches that will take place. It is a general overview of the way in which you will test your solution.

Most solutions are made up of different parts: the individual calculations on worksheets and the links and processes between sheets. There will be different routes through the solution and, importantly, different outputs. One or more users may also be involved.

The test strategy will outline the order of testing, the types of testing, the approaches (in this case we might choose different customers) and involve the end-user who will test the solution on both his systems.

The test plan says exactly what you will test, what the test (input) data will be and what the expected output data should be. Particular attention should be given to check that the output from the solution (in this case the insurance quotation) is correct and the full requirements are met.

Tests in the test plan should:

○ be numbered;
○ state the purpose of the test;
○ specify the test data to be used, if any;
○ outline the expected result;
○ cross-reference to clear hard copy usually in the form of a screen dump;
○ provide evidence of the actual results plus any comments;
○ outline any corrective action needed or taken.

Where appropriate test data should include typical data and, if possible, extreme, invalid or awkward data. This does not mean every single cell or operation, you need to be able to focus on key features where you suspect there could be problems.

You might be encouraged to adopt a test as you develop the solution approach. Students invariably do this without documenting the work they have done. Details of corrective action need to be recorded. Rarely do solutions work first time and you should not be afraid to report on problems.

It is not necessary to perform dozens of similar tests. For example, if data validation has been applied to many cells, it is not necessary to repeat the same test on each cell. Just clearly document one and reference the others.

(h) Test plan

The Insurance Groups worksheet

TEST NUMBER	PURPOSE OF TEST	TEST DATA USED	EXPECTED OUTCOME	ACTUAL OUTCOME AND COMMENTS
1	Test the CONC function in column E combines contents of columns B and C	All makes and models in named range Groups	Make and Model combined with space in between	

Setting up the Quotes worksheet – testing the input controls for entering the driver details

TEST NUMBER	PURPOSE OF TEST	TEST DATA USED	EXPECTED OUTCOME	ACTUAL OUTCOME AND COMMENTS
2	Test Option buttons (Sex)	Click on male/female	Returns 1 or 2 in E12	
3	Test Combo box (Car) returns correct values	Ford Ka	Returns 6 in E14	
4	Test Combo box (Age) returns correct values	60-65	Returns 10 in E16	
5	Test Area List box returns correct values	Low risk	Returns 3 in E18	
6	Test Type List box returns correct values	Fully comprehensive	Returns 1 in E20	
7	Test Check box returns TRUE/FALSE	Check the check box and uncheck it	Returns TRUE/FALSE in E22	
8	Test the Spinner control and LOOKUP return correct discount	Increment spinner to 2 years	40% should be looked up and returned in E24	

Preparing the quotes – testing the VLOOKUP and other functions

TEST NUMBER	PURPOSE OF TEST	TEST DATA USED	EXPECTED OUTCOME	ACTUAL OUTCOME AND COMMENTS
9	Test VLOOKUP in G6, G7, G8 returns correct values from the named range Groups	Peugeot 406 is chosen from D14 returning 4 in E14	Car details and IG returned in G6, G7, G8 – Peugeot 406 IG 10	
10	Test VLOOKUP in G10 and G14 returns correct values from the named worksheet Multipliers	Age 40-44 Type Fully comprehensive	40-44 and FC returned in G10 and G14	
11	Test VLOOKUP functions in G9 and G11 return correct values from the worksheet Multipliers	Choose Male and High Risk	Male and High Risk returned in G9 and G11	
12	Test IF function in G12 returns correct value	Check Extra driver in E22	Yes is returned in G12	
13	Test no claims discount is transferred from D24 to G13	Increment spinner to 4 years	4 years is returned in G13	

Preparing the quotes – entering the multipliers for calculating the total cost

TEST NUMBER	PURPOSE OF TEST	TEST DATA USED	EXPECTED OUTCOME	ACTUAL OUTCOME AND COMMENTS
14	Test the multipliers are looked up correctly from the worksheet named Multipliers	Select Peugeot 406	H8 should return £264	
		Enter sex male	H9 should return 1.3	
		Enter age 40-44	H10 should return 1.2	
		Select High Risk	H11 should return 2.4	
		Choose Third Party Insurance	H14 should return 0.39	
		Choose Extra driver	H12 should return 1.3	

Calculating the total cost of the quote

TEST NUMBER	PURPOSE OF TEST	TEST DATA USED	EXPECTED OUTCOME	ACTUAL OUTCOME AND COMMENTS
15	Test the formulas H16, H18 and H20 calculate bill correctly	Data for Test 14 above	Bill worked out on calculator. Total cost = £200.45	

Automating the filing of quotes

TEST NUMBER	PURPOSE OF TEST	TEST DATA USED	EXPECTED OUTCOME	ACTUAL OUTCOME AND COMMENTS
16	Test the macro 'filequote' to see if data is transferred correctly to the Customers worksheet	Routine data i.e. short name and address plus car details	On running the macro, details should appear in the customer sheet	
	Test the macro 'filequote' to see if data is transferred correctly to the Customers worksheet and within the column widths set	Routine data BUT a longer name and address plus car details	On running the macro, details should appear in the customer sheet	
	Test the macro 'filequote' when no data is entered	No data entered	A blank row should appear in the customer sheet	

Clearing the current screen to enter a new quote

TEST NUMBER	PURPOSE OF TEST	TEST DATA USED	EXPECTED OUTCOME	ACTUAL OUTCOME AND COMMENTS
17	Test macro 'clear screen' after Start up	Routine driver and car details	Screen should be clear	
	Test macro 'clear screen' after a quote has been filed	Routine driver and car details	Screen should be clear	
	Test macro 'clear screen' after it has been run once	No data	Screen should be clear	

Printing the quote

TEST NUMBER	PURPOSE OF TEST	TEST DATA USED	EXPECTED OUTCOME	ACTUAL OUTCOME AND COMMENTS
18	Test details are taken from the Quotes sheet to the Printed quote worksheet sheet	Normal driver and car details	Details display correctly on the Printed quote sheet	
		Driver with long name and address and different car details	As above	

Adding the user options

TEST NUMBER	PURPOSE OF TEST	TEST DATA USED	EXPECTED OUTCOME	ACTUAL OUTCOME AND COMMENTS
19	Test Print Quote	Test macro button for each option in test 18	Prints quote and page layout is correct	
20	Test View Quotes	Test macro button	Moves to Customers sheet	
21	Test Edit Groups	Test macro button	Moves to Groups worksheet	
22	Test Edit Multipliers	Test macro button	Moves to Multipliers sheet	
23	Test links to the other worksheets and the return options	Test the macro buttons	Be able to switch to chosen sheet and back to Quotes worksheet	

Customizing the Interface and finishing touches

TEST NUMBER	PURPOSE OF TEST	TEST DATA USED	EXPECTED OUTCOME	ACTUAL OUTCOME AND COMMENTS
24	Test the auto_open macro starts the system correctly	Start the system up	System loads and removes Excel standard features	
25	Test the auto_close macro closes down the system properly	Close the system down	System closes and restores Excel standard features	

Adding the front end and further options

TEST NUMBER	PURPOSE OF TEST	TEST DATA USED	EXPECTED OUTCOME	ACTUAL OUTCOME AND COMMENTS
26	Test again the auto_open macro	Start the system up	System loads Front End screen	
27	Test the About macro button	None, test macro button	On-screen help message given	
28	Test the Exit macro button	None, test macro button	System closes down	
29	Test the Enter macro button	None, test macro button	Quotes screen loads	

User testing

TEST NUMBER	PURPOSE OF TEST	ACTUAL OUTCOME AND COMMENTS
30	Install the system in the office at PB Insurance for a week for Paul Bryant and his assistant to see if it meets his requirements	

Testing dos	Testing don'ts
• Don't forget. The purpose of testing is to show your solution works. • To find errors you have to try and provoke failure. Try to make your solution go wrong! • Remember that you are testing whether the data is processed correctly, not just whether a button works or not. • Test the solution against the end-user requirements. Does it do what you set out to do?	• Don't forget. The purpose of testing is to find errors. Do not be afraid to report them. • Don't include many similar tests such as testing all the buttons that move between sheets. Find a way of grouping them into one test.

The **end-user**, if possible, should also be involved in testing or if there is not a real end-user get a colleague to go through your solution.

You could use a questionnaire and analyse the results.

They may comment on:
○ its ease of use;
○ consistencies of layout, fonts, buttons, colours used;
○ look and feel of the interface;
○ simple vocabulary, spelling and grammar used.

2   Implementation

This section should contain clear evidence that you have implemented each part of your project. The information presented here should reflect your specification and design plans.

Screen dumps and/or printouts need to be used to support and provide evidence of work done. Where you have used formulas include a printout or screen shot showing the formulas.

Implementation report

In setting up the solution, I have carried out the following tasks:

1 **Set up the Insurance Groups worksheet with details of cars and insurance groups**
2 Set up the Multipliers worksheet
3 **Set up the Quotes worksheet with the input controls to enter the driver details**
4 Set up the Quotes worksheet by setting up the LOOKUP functions to bring in the quote data
5 Set up the Quotes worksheet by entering the multipliers to be used in calculating the quote
6 **Calculated the total cost of the quote.**
7 Set up the Customer worksheet to store details of quotes issued
8 Automated the filing of quotes
9 **Automated clearing the current screen to enter a new quote**
10 **Designed the printed quote**
11 Added user options to the quotes screen
12 **Customized the interface and added finishing touches**
13 Added the Front End and further options.

Six of the steps are documented in this section to show the student an approach to documentation. The tasks documented are shown in bold.

Implementation dos	**Implementation don'ts**
• Be clear and concise. • Use screen dumps to support your explanation. • Describe all the steps in setting up your solution. • Describe clearly the features of the software you have used. • Describe any validation you have included. • Ensure screen dumps are readable.	• Don't undersell the work you have done and remember exam board moderators can only give credit for what they can see. • Don't submit self-generating code and claim it as work done by you! • Don't reproduce large tracts of Excel manuals.

1 Setting up the Insurance Groups worksheet with details of cars and insurance groups

I entered the makes, models and insurance groups of cars in cells A1 to D21 and the insurance group costs into cells H1 to I21. Each make of car has a number attached in column A which will later be used to look up the car details.
I named the areas A1 to E21 **Groups** and H1 to I21 **Costs** as the **Name** box shows in Figure 20.5.

Costs								
Groups	te	Model	IG	Car Name	F	G	IG	Basic Cost
2 1		Peugeot	106	3	=B2&" "&C2			1	174
3 2		Peugeot	206	3	=B3&" "&C3			2	180
4 3		Peugeot	306	4	=B4&" "&C4			3	187
5 4		Peugeot	406	10	=B5&" "&C5			4	194
6 5		Peugeot	806	10	=B6&" "&C6			5	202
7 6		Ford	Ka	2	=B7&" "&C7			6	210
8 7		Ford	Fiesta	4	=B8&" "&C8			7	222
9 8		Ford	Escort	5	=B9&" "&C9			8	235
10 9		Ford	Puma	9	=B10&" "&C10			9	248
11 10		Ford	Focus	5	=B11&" "&C11			10	264
12 11		Ford	Mondeo	8	=B12&" "&C12			11	280
13 12		Ford	Galaxy	11	=B13&" "&C13			12	300
14 13		Honda	Civic	9	=B14&" "&C14			13	324
15 14		Honda	Prelude	14	=B15&" "&C15			14	362
16 15		Honda	Accord	8	=B16&" "&C16			15	417
17 16		Reliant	Robin	6	=B17&" "&C17			16	493
18 17		Rover	100	3	=B18&" "&C18			17	600
19 18		Rover	200	6	=B19&" "&C19			18	720
20 19		Rover	400	8	=B20&" "&C20			19	838
21 20		Rover	800	12	=B21&" "&C21			20	945
22								

Figure 20.5

I want to use a combo box to list the make and model of cars. I needed to add the make to model using the Concatenate function shown in column E. In this way Peugeot in B4 would be added to 306 in C4, giving Peugeot 306 in E4.

3 Setting up the Quotes worksheet with the input controls to enter the driver details

This part of the solution deals with the part of the worksheet where the driver options are entered as in Figure 20.6.

	A	B	C	D	E
5					
6			Forename	Charles	
7			Surname	George	
8			Address 1	16 Main Street	
9			Address 2	Derby	
10			Postcode	DE45 6LU	
11				⦿ Male	
12			Sex	○ Female	1
13					
14			Car	Ford Mondeo ▼	11
15					
16			Age	50-54 ▼	8
17					
18			Area	Medium risk ▲	2
19				Low risk ▼	
20			Type	Fully comprehensive ▲	1
21				Third party, fire & theft ▼	
22			Driver	☑ Driver	TRUE
23				Years	Per cent
24			No Claims ▲	4	60%
25			▼		
26					

K ◀ ▶ ▸I \ Groups ╱ Multipliers ╲ **Quotes** ◀ | ▶ |

Figure 20.6

The customer's name and address labels were entered into cells C6-C10. Labels for Sex, Car, Age, Area and Type were entered in the cells C12-C20 as shown.

Two option boxes were placed over D11 and D12 linked to cell E12. The number returned in E12 gives the sex of the driver, 1 for male and 2 for female.

I dragged a combo box over cell D14 and linked it to cell E14. I set the input range to Groups!E2:E21. This will make the drop-down display the cars listed in column E on the **Groups** worksheet.

In the same way I dragged a combo box over cell D16 and linked it to cell E16. I set the input range to the cells B2:B11 on the **Multipliers** worksheet. The drop-down will display the age ranges for the driver.

List boxes were set up for Area and Insurance Type linked to the cells shown above. They were designed to pull in the information needed from the **Multipliers** worksheet.

22			Driver	☑ Driver	TRUE
23				Years	Per cent
24			No Claims ▲	2	40%
25			▼		
26					

K ◀ ▶ ▸I \ Groups ╱ Multipliers ╲ **Quotes** ◀ | ▶ |

Figure 20.7

In cell D22 I placed a check box linked to cell E22. It returns TRUE when checked and FALSE when not.

I set a spinner control over cell D24 linked to cell E24, setting the minimum value to 0 and maximum to 4 to allow for up to 4 years' no claims discount. See Figure 20.7.

			Years	Per cent
23				
24		No Claims		=VLOOKUP(D24,Multipliers!B25:C29,2)
25				
26				

Figure 20.8

In E24 I used a LOOKUP function to pick up the contents of cell D24 and find the no claims discount from the range of values between B25 and C29 on the Multipliers worksheet. See Figure 20.8.

The numbers returned in column E are used next to establish the details needed for the quote.

6   Calculating the total cost of the quote

The cost of the quote is calculated by multiplying the numbers in column H. The no claims discount is picked up from cell E24.

	A	B	C	D	E	F	G	H
5								
6			Forename			Make	Peugeot	
7			Surname			Model	406	
8			Address 1			IG	10	264
9			Address 2			Sex	Male	1.3
10			Postcode			Age	40-44	1.2
11				⦿ Male		Risk	High risk	2.4
12			Sex	◯ Female	1	Extra driver	Yes	1.3
13						No claims	4	
14			Car	Peugeot 406 ▼	4	Type	TP	0.39
15								
16			Age	40-44 ▼	6	Total without discount		£501.13
17								
18			Area	High risk ▲	1	No claims discount		£300.68
19				Medium risk ▼				
20			Type	Third party, fire & theft ▲	3	Total cost		£200.45
21				Third party only ▼				
22			Driver	☑ Driver	TRUE			
23					Years Per cent			
24			No Claims ▲		4 60%			
25				▼				
26								

Figure 20.9

The formulas were set up as shown in Figure 20.10.

	F	G	H
15			
16	Total without discount		=H8*H9*H10*H11*H12*H14
17			
18	No claims discount		=H16*E24
19			
20	Total cost		=H16-H18

Task 6

⏮ ◀ ▶ ⏭ \ Groups ⟨ Multipliers ⟩ **Quotes** / ◀

Figure 20.10

9   Clearing the current screen to enter a new quote

After a quote has been made I needed to clear the screen for the next quote. The areas on the screen that need clearing are cells D6-D10, E12-E22 and cell D24. See Figure 20.11.

Task 8

	A	B	C	D	E
5					
6			Forename	Charles	
7			Surname	George	
8			Address 1	16 Main Street	
9			Address 2	Derby	
10			Postcode	DE45 6LU	
11				⦿ Male	
12			Sex	◯ Female	1
13					
14			Car	Ford Mondeo ▼	11
15					
16			Age	50-54 ▼	8
17					
18			Area	Medium risk ▲	2
19				Low risk ▼	
20			Type	Fully comprehensive ▲	1
21				Third party, fire & theft ▼	
22			Driver	☑ Driver	TRUE
23				Years	Per cent
24			No Claims ▲	4	60%
25			▼		
26					

⏮ ◀ ▶ ⏭ \ Groups ⟨ Multipliers ⟩ **Quotes** ◀

Figure 20.11

I recorded a macro called Clearscreen. I highlighted in turn the areas D6-D10 and D24 and clicked Edit, Clear, All. I highlighted cells E12-E22 and clicked Edit, Clear, Contents.

I finished the macro by returning the cursor to D6 ready for the next quote.

The macro code generated is shown in Figure 20.12.

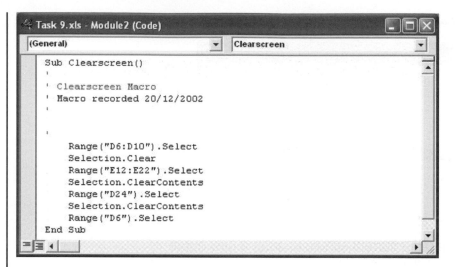

Figure 20.12

10 Designing the printed quote

I have designed the quote to look like Figure 20.13.

Date	29/12/2002

Insurance quotation for:
Roy Marshall
2 Hall Road
Derby
DE34 8PL

Make	Peugeot
Model	806
Age	30-34
Sex	Male
Extra driver	Yes
Insurance type	Fully comprehensive
Years no claims bonus	2
Quotation	£682.62
Quotation valid until	12/01/2003

Signed on behalf of PB Insurance Services Ltd

Figure 20.13

12 Customizing the interface and added finishing touches

My original interface looked like Figure 20.14.

Figure 20.14

I have customized this interface to look like this, using the drawing tools in Excel and the company logo:

Figure 20.15

Further development

The implementation section would go on to explain and illustrate how each of the other sub-tasks was implemented.

3   Testing

Results of your tests (following your test plan) should be fully documented including evidence (screen shots). If an outcome is not what was expected, explain why and document what you did to correct the error.

Label all screen dumps from your solution. Include any user testing and comments.

Examples are shown below.

(a) Test results

The Insurance Groups worksheet

TEST NUMBER	PURPOSE OF TEST	TEST DATA USED	EXPECTED OUTCOME	ACTUAL OUTCOME AND COMMENTS
1	Test the CONC function in column E combines contents of columns B and C	All makes and models in named range Groups	Make and Model combined with space in between	See Test Output 1. No problems, ensure space between speech marks

Test Output 1

	B	C	D	E	F	G	H	I
1	**Make**	**Model**	**IG**	**Car Name**			**IG**	**Basic Cost**
2	Peugeot	106	3	Peugeot 106			1	£ 174.00
3	Peugeot	206	3	Peugeot 206			2	£ 180.00
4	Peugeot	306	4	Peugeot 306			3	£ 187.00
5	Peugeot	406	10	Peugeot 406			4	£ 194.00
6	Peugeot	806	10	Peugeot 806			5	£ 202.00
7	Ford	Ka	2	Ford Ka			6	£ 210.00
8	Ford	Fiesta	4	Ford Fiesta			7	£ 222.00
9	Ford	Escort	5	Ford Escort			8	£ 235.00
10	Ford	Puma	9	Ford Puma			9	£ 248.00
11	Ford	Focus	5	Ford Focus			10	£ 264.00
12	Ford	Mondeo	8	Ford Mondeo			11	£ 280.00
13	Ford	Galaxy	11	Ford Galaxy			12	£ 300.00
14	Honda	Civic	9	Honda Civic			13	£ 324.00
15	Honda	Prelude	14	Honda Prelude			14	£ 362.00
16	Honda	Accord	8	Honda Accord			15	£ 417.00
17	Reliant	Robin	6	Reliant Robin			16	£ 493.00
18	Rover	100	3	Rover 100			17	£ 600.00
19	Rover	200	6	Rover 200			18	£ 720.00
20	Rover	400	8	Rover 400			19	£ 838.00
21	Rover	800	12	Rover 800			20	£ 945.00
22								

Groups / Multipliers / Sheet3 /

Figure 20.16

Makes and models in columns B and C combined and results in column E.

Setting up the Quotes worksheet – testing the input controls for entering the driver details

TEST NUMBER	PURPOSE OF TEST	TEST DATA USED	EXPECTED OUTCOME	ACTUAL OUTCOME AND COMMENTS
2	Test Option buttons (Sex)	Click on male/ female	Returns 1 or 2 in E12	See Test Output 2
3	Test Combo box (Car) returns correct values	Ford Ka	Returns 6 in E14	See Test Output 2
4	Test Combo box (Age) returns correct values	60-65	Returns 10 in E16	See Test Output 2
5	Test Area List box returns correct values	Low risk	Returns 3 in E18	See Test Output 2
6	Test Type List box returns correct values	Fully comprehensive	Returns 1 in E20	See Test Output 2
7	Test Check box returns TRUE/FALSE	Check the check box and uncheck it	Returns TRUE/ FALSE in E22	See Test Output 2
8	Test the Spinner control and LOOKUP returns correct discount	Increment spinner to 2 years	40% should be looked up and returned in E24	See Test Output 2. No problems to report on Test 2

Test Output 2

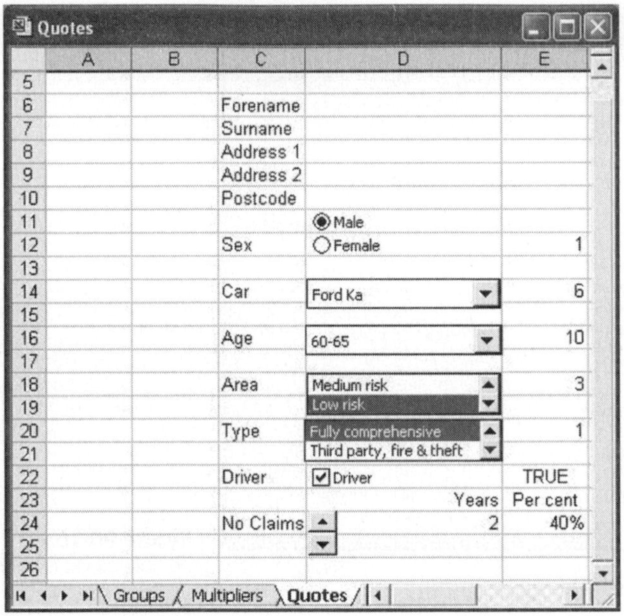

	A	B	C	D	E	
5						
6			Forename			
7			Surname			
8			Address 1			
9			Address 2			
10			Postcode			
11				⦿ Male		
12			Sex	◯ Female	1	
13						
14			Car	Ford Ka ▾	6	
15						
16			Age	60-65 ▾	10	
17						
18			Area	Medium risk ▲	3	
19				Low risk ▾		
20			Type	Fully comprehensive ▲	1	
21				Third party, fire & theft ▾		
22			Driver	☑ Driver	TRUE	
23					Years	Per cent
24			No Claims ▲		2	40%
25			▾			
26						

◄ ◄ ► ►◄ \ Groups / Multipliers \ Quotes / ◄ | ►◄

Quotes window

Figure 20.17

Calculating the total cost of the quote

TEST NUMBER	PURPOSE OF TEST	TEST DATA USED	EXPECTED OUTCOME	ACTUAL OUTCOME AND COMMENTS
15	Test the formulas H16, H18 and H20 calculate bill correctly	Peugeot 406, Male, Age 40-44, High Risk, Third Party, Extra driver, 4 years' NCB	Bill worked out on calculator. Total cost = £200.45	See Test output 5. No problems. Range of data used.

Test Output 5

The total cost was calculated correctly as shown.

	A	B	C	D	E	F	G	H
5								
6			Forename			Make	Peugeot	
7			Surname			Model	406	
8			Address 1			IG	10	264
9			Address 2			Sex	Male	1.3
10			Postcode			Age	40-44	1.2
11			◉ Male			Risk	High risk	2.4
12			Sex	○ Female	1	Extra driver	Yes	1.3
13						No claims	4	
14			Car	Peugeot 406 ▼	4	Type	TP	0.39
15								
16			Age	40-44 ▼	6	Total without discount		£501.13
17								
18			Area	High risk ▲	1	No claims discount		£300.68
19				Medium risk ▼				
20			Type	Third party, fire & theft ▲	3	Total cost		£200.45
21				Third party only ▼				
22			Driver	☑ Driver	TRUE			
23					Years Per cent			
24			No Claims ▲		4	60%		
25				▼				
26								

◄ ◄ ► ►◄ \ Groups / Multipliers \ **Quotes** /

Figure 20.18

Automating the filing of quotes

TEST NUMBER	PURPOSE OF TEST	TEST DATA USED	EXPECTED OUTCOME	ACTUAL OUTCOME AND COMMENTS
16	Test the macro 'filequote' to see if data is transferred correctly to the Customers worksheet	Routine data i.e. short name and address plus car details	On running the macro, details should appear in the Customers sheet	Details appear but in bold print. Quote not formatted to currency. See Test Output 6. **Corrective action taken**. See Test Output 7.
	Test the macro 'filequote' to see if data is transferred correctly to the Customers worksheet and within the column widths set	Routine data BUT a longer name and address plus car details	On running the macro, details should appear in the customer sheet	Problems found. Will document in user guide.
	Test the macro 'filequote' when no data is entered	No data entered	A blank row should appear in the customer sheet	Blank row appears but noughts appear in some cells. See Test Output 8. **Corrective action taken**.

Test Output 6

	A	B	C	D	E	F	G	H	I	J	K	L	M	N	O
1	Forename	Surname	Address 1	Address 2	Postcode	Make	Model	IG	Sex	Age	Risk	Extra	NCB	Type	Quote
2	**Roy**	**Marshall**	**2 Hall Road**	**Derby**	**DE34 8PL**	**Peugeo**	**806**	**10**	**Male**	**30-34**	**Medium**	**Yes**	**2**	**FC**	**682.62**
3	Alanna	Crowe	12 Fortescue Road	Derby	DE5 9PK	Ford	Ka	2	Female	30-34	High risk	No	1	FC	453.60
4	Charles	George	63 Arthur Street	Derby	DE16 6TY	Honda	Civic	9	Male	45-49	Low risk	Yes	3	TPFT	110.86
5	Horace	Bachelor	12 Main Street	Derby	DE45 6LU	Ford	Fiesta	4	Male	60-65	Low risk	Yes	4	TP	51.15

Derby — Groups / Quotes / Multipliers \ **Customers**

Figure 20.19

The new record is in bold print. Quote not in currency format. The macro was rerecorded, turning off bold. Column O was formatted to currency. The macro was then tested again.

Test Output 7

	A	B	C	D	E	F	G	H	I	J	K	L	M	N	O
1	Forename	Surname	Address 1	Address 2	Postcode	Make	Model	IG	Sex	Age	Risk	Extra	NCB	Type	Quote
2	Roy	Marshall	2 Hall Road	Derby	DE34 8PL	Peugeot	806	10	Male	30-34	Medium	Yes	2	FC	£ 682.62
3	Alanna	Crowe	12 Fortescue Road	Derby	DE5 9PK	Ford	Ka	2	Female	30-34	High risk	No	1	FC	£ 453.60
4	Charles	George	63 Arthur Street	Derby	DE16 6TY	Honda	Civic	9	Male	45-49	Low risk	Yes	3	TPFT	£ 110.86
5	Horace	Bachelor	12 Main Street	Derby	DE45 6LU	Ford	Fiesta	4	Male	60-65	Low risk	Yes	4	TP	£ 51.15

Derby — Groups / Quotes / Multipliers \ **Customers**

Figure 20.20

New record not in bold print. Quote in currency format.

Test Output 8

	A	B	C	D	E	F	G	H	I	J	K	L	M	N	O
1	Forename	Surname	Address 1	Address 2	Postcode	Make	Model	IG	Sex	Age	Risk	Extra	NCB	Type	Quote
2	0	0		0	0	0									
3	**Roy**	**Marshall**	**2 Hall Road**	**Derby**	**DE34 8PL**	**Peugeo**	**806**	**10**	**Male**	**30-34**	**Medium**	**Yes**	**2**	**FC**	**682.62**
4	Alanna	Crowe	12 Fortescue Road	Derby	DE5 9PK	Ford	Ka	2	Female	30-34	High risk	Yes	1	FC	453.60
5	Charles	George	63 Arthur Street	Derby	DE16 6TY	Honda	Civic	9	Male	45-49	Low risk	Yes	3	TPFT	110.86
6	Horace	Bachelor	12 Main Street	Derby	DE45 6LU	Ford	Fiesta	4	Male	60-65	Low risk	Yes	4	TP	51.15

Derby — Groups / Quotes / Multipliers \ **Customers**

Figure 20.21

Extra row appears. Noughts or #N/A appears in cells A2 to O2. Corrective action was taken to put instructions in the user guide on how to remove unwanted rows.

Adding the front end and further options

TEST NUMBER	PURPOSE OF TEST	TEST DATA USED	EXPECTED OUTCOME	ACTUAL OUTCOME AND COMMENTS
26	Test again the auto_open macro	Start the system up	System loads Front End screen	Front end loads when file is opened. See Test Output 9.

Test Output 9

```
PB Insurance Services Ltd                              [X]

        P.B  Insurance  Services  Ltd

              P.B Insurance Services Ltd
                    Ascot Drive
                      Derby
                    DE65  6EX
            Tel.  (01332)  583939
            Fax.  (01332)  583911




        Exit            Enter            About
```

Figure 20.22

Front end loads as expected.

(b) User testing

After Paul had used the system for a few days he made the following observations.

The system issued quotes easily and quickly which was particularly useful when dealing with phone enquiries.

Paul would have liked the system to produce carbon copies of the quote automatically as opposed to clicking Print a number of times.

He thought the system was potentially user friendly but certainly had reservations about the Start-up screen. All he wanted to do was get started and that slowed him down and eventually became irritating during the course of the day.

When entering details of the customer he wasn't sure how much space he had to enter the name and address in. He thought the printed quote would have had more of a professional feel if it had had a footer as well as the header.

He liked the interface, as did his assistant, but he found the look and feel of other screen options, e.g. the Customers, Groups completely different, far more like Excel. This was a little off-putting.

As he used the system the file of customer quotes built up very quickly, eventually going off the screen. He found he needed advice as to how to search for a particular quote.

Both Paul and his assistant were worried about how to back up the system and transfer files to the laptop for out of hours use.

4 User guide

A user guide is just that – a **guide** for the **user** or **users** of your system.

It should include details of:
- the purpose of the system;
- the minimum system requirements needed to run your system, e.g. Pentium 200 with 64Mb of memory;
- how to get started;
- the main menu options;
- how to perform each of the routine tasks that make up your system;
- common problems or error messages and possible solutions;
- security measures, backup procedures and passwords needed.

User guide to the car insurance quotation system

Introduction

The system allows the user to issue car insurance quotes both on screen and to printer. It enables the user to file away quotes and store for later reference in a user-friendly manner.

System requirements

You require a minimum of a Pentium PC with 64Mb of memory. Microsoft Office needs to be installed including the component Excel. The system will work successfully with Excel XP, Excel 2000 or Excel 97. The system uses initially 137Kb of disc space and hence the size of hard drive is not important. A laser printer is recommended to ensure fast, high quality output.

How to install the system

The system is supplied on a 1.44Mb floppy disc. It is recommended the file is installed on the computer's hard drive.

Figure 20.23

---

1   On the Desktop create a New Folder by right clicking the mouse button and clicking on **New, Folder**. Name the folder **PB Insurance**.

2   Insert the floppy disc containing the system.

3   Click on the Start button and select My Computer. Double click on **3$\frac{1}{2}$ Floppy (A:)**

4   Drag the file called Derby on to the folder PB Insurance.

Getting started

To boot up the system double click the file icon called Derby.

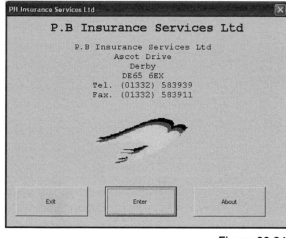

Figure 20.24

The system displays its **Start-up** screen with details of the company PB Insurance. The user is presented with three options.

1   Clicking the **Exit** button closes the system down.

2   Clicking the **Enter** button enters the system.

3   Clicking the **About** button offers further information about the system.

The user options

To enter the system click the **Enter** button on the **Start**-up screen.

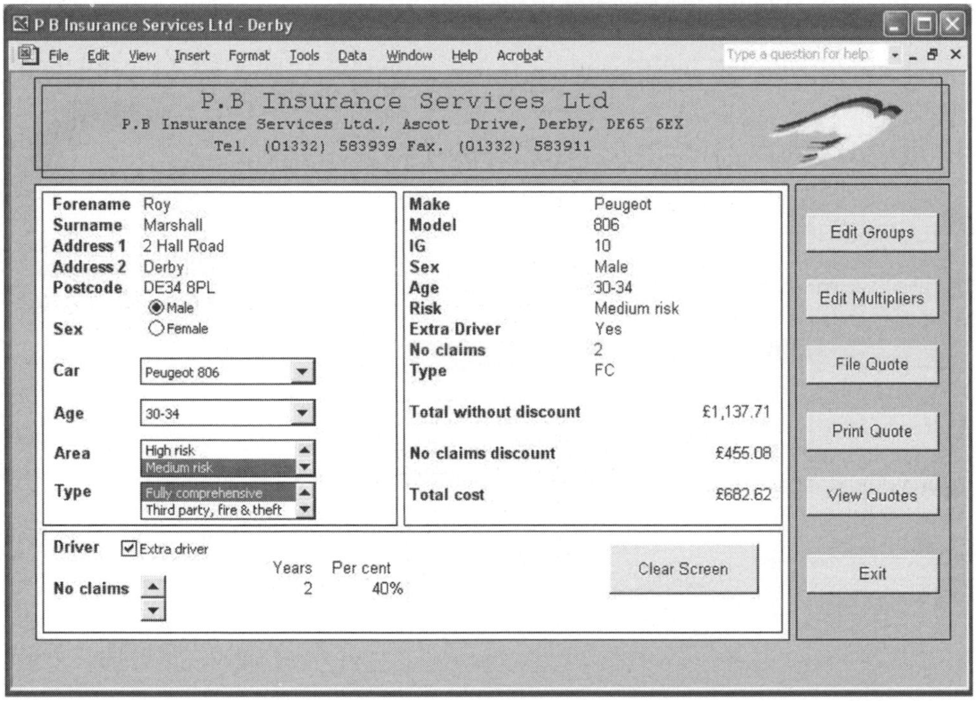

Figure 20.25

From this screen the user has access to a number of options by simply clicking the button.

- ○ Issue a quote by entering the driver details.
- ○ **Edit Groups** allows the user to change the cars and insurance ratings.
- ○ **Edit Multipliers** allows the user to edit the multiplying factors.
- ○ **File Quote** stores the quote in the system for later reference.
- ○ **Print Quote** outputs a copy of the quote to the printer.
- ○ **View Quotes** allows the user to view previously stored quotes.
- ○ **Clear Screen** removes the current quote from screen ready for a new entry.
- ○ **Exit** closes down the system.

How to issue a quote

Once the system has loaded clicking enter on the **Start-up** screen brings the user to the **Quotes** screen.

It is automatically ready to issue a quote with the cursor at Forename of driver.

If a quote is currently on screen then click the **Clear Screen** option.

Enter the name and address of the customer in the appropriate cells as shown below.

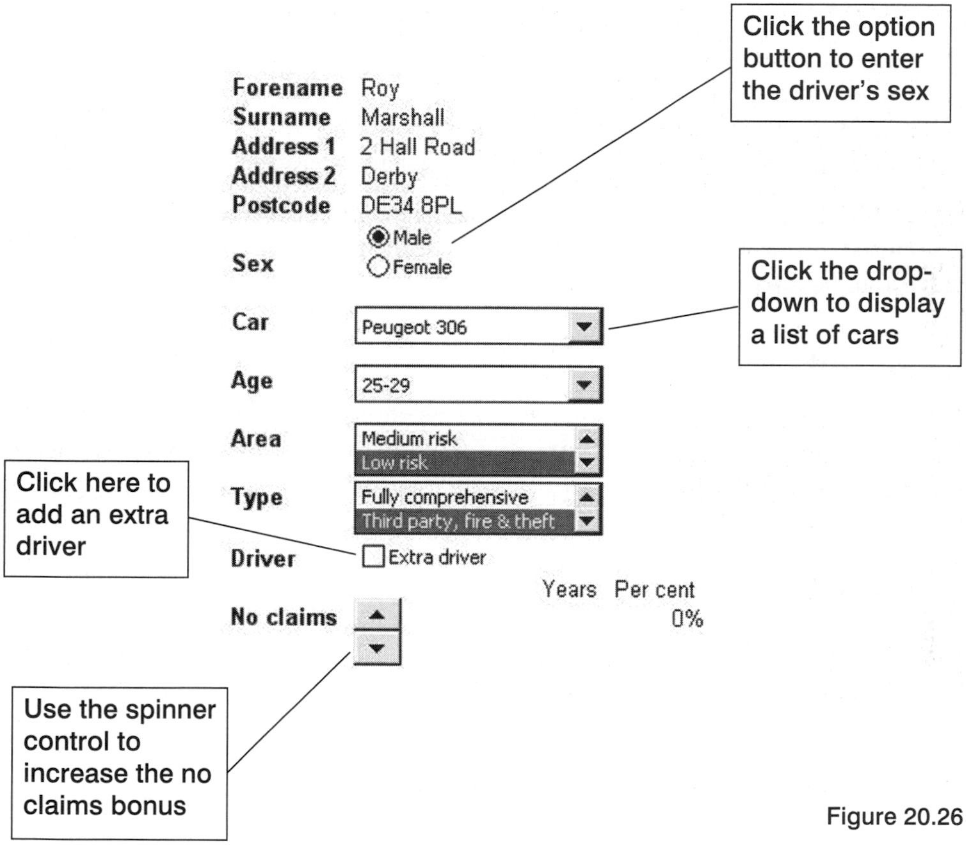

Click the option button to enter the driver's sex

Forename	Roy
Surname	Marshall
Address 1	2 Hall Road
Address 2	Derby
Postcode	DE34 8PL

Sex ◉ Male ○ Female

Car Peugeot 306 ▼

Click the drop-down to display a list of cars

Age 25-29 ▼

Area Medium risk / Low risk ▲▼

Click here to add an extra driver

Type Fully comprehensive / Third party, fire & theft ▲▼

Driver ☐ Extra driver

Years Per cent

No claims ▲ ▼ 0%

Use the spinner control to increase the no claims bonus

Figure 20.26

The driver and car details are easily entered by clicking the drop-downs and clicking your choice.

An extra driver can be added by checking the extra driver check box.

The driver's no claims discount can easily be entered by increasing or decreasing the spinner control.

When the details are complete click the **Print Quote** option for a printed quote. Click the **File Quote** option to store the quote for later reference.

Further development

It is likely that the user guide for this system would go on to include details of the other user options such as:

○ how to edit details of the cars available by using the edit groups option;
○ how to edit details of the multiplying factors;
○ instructions for filing, viewing and printing quotes;
○ instructions for backing up the system during daily operation, both when and how.

Also consideration would be given to copying the system between PC and laptop when the user needs to work away from the office. Possible problems and troubleshooting need also to be documented.

User guide dos	User guide don'ts
• It should contain simple, clear, step-by-step instructions to using your system. • It should be jargon free and well illustrated. • It might form or be part of online help built into the system.	• It should not be a guide to using the software but a guide to your system. • Don't include large tracts of text from Excel manuals and try to avoid using jargon.

5   Evaluation

This section requires the student to report on the degree of success of their solution.

Evaluation dos	Evaluation don'ts
• You should look at your original end user requirements and report on whether you have achieved what you wanted to, including successes, problems and possible solutions. • No solution is perfect. There will always be room for improvement. Outline any limitations and possible further developments.	• Don't moan about the lack of time. Time management is your responsibility. • Don't pretend it is all working when some parts are incomplete. Do not be afraid to tell the truth. • Don't report on how well you did but focus on how well your solution achieved its aims.

Evaluation report

To evaluate my solution I will look at the initial end-user requirements and also take on board comments made by the users when testing the system.

1 A solution is required to be able to give a quick quote accurately and efficiently.

The solution produced does issue quotes accurately. The solution was tested thoroughly and no errors found during the trial period with Paul Bryant. It enabled both users to deal with online phone enquiries far more quickly.

2 The solution must produce multiple copies of the quote.

At present you have to repeat the print process for however many quotes you wish to issue. I will look at automating this in the future to issue a carbon copy of the quote.

3 The solution should enable phone enquiries to be dealt with far more quickly than at present.

A test comparison was held between the old manual system and the new system. The old system took 2 minutes 14 seconds. The new system took 32 seconds to enter the details and file the quote.

4 Issued quotes need to be stored with the facility to view at a later date.

Quotes can be stored effectively but real improvements need to be made here. The database will build up very quickly and the user will need experience of Excel to be able to search and retrieve information about the quotes filed away. I need to add instructions to the user guide on how to tackle this.

5 Quotes should be issued with a professional look on letter-headed paper.

The quote itself was felt to be professionally produced but future versions will come with a footer.

6 The solution must be user friendly, yet have a professional look and feel.

The user feels the solution is user friendly but when entering customer details it is not clear how many characters are allowed for each item of data. I may investigate the use of validation checks here or simply advise the user in the user guide.

The other user screens need customizing along the lines of the quotes screen to be consistent and give a common feel to the solution.

7 The solution should be easy to transfer between the laptop and office-based PC.

The initial system uses 137Kb of disc space. Using copy and paste I added 1000 customers, which increased the file size to 375Kb. The system can be easily transferred using a floppy disc.

Limitations and possible enhancements

I might in a future version of the system remove the start-up screen by adjusting the auto_open macro so that start-up is quicker for the users.

I could customize the user interface further by running the whole system from a UserForm.

It might be easier to handle if every quote was issued with a quote reference number and a date of issue to aid searching in the future.

Over a period of time this file will get very large and the user needs to establish procedures for clearing out quotes that are not needed or are past renewal. This could be manually done in Excel but I might try to automate this feature in the future.

Both users were worried and concerned about backups and transfer of files between laptop and PC. A system needs to be implemented such that a backup is made whenever a quote is issued and procedures in place so that quotes are never issued on more than one machine. I will provide advice in the user guide.

It is unlikely that disc space will be a problem but a Zip drive may provide greater security.

Presenting your coursework documentation

Documentation should:
- be well written and presented;
- be well organized and illustrated;
- clearly show the development of the system from the initial analysis to design, through to its implementation and testing.

When your project documentation is finished you should:
- produce a front cover; your name, centre and candidate number should be clear;
- get your project in order; page numbering and the use of headers and footers is to be encouraged;
- produce a contents page which clearly cross-references to each section in the project;
- bind your project securely. Often coursework has to be sent for checking. It needs to be firmly attached but ring binders are not encouraged.

PART FOUR

Excel tricks and tips

⊕ Unit 21 50 Excel tricks and tips

Here are 50 tricks and tips that have been found to be more than useful in implementing Excel projects. Many of them have been discovered by students themselves.

1 Getting more than one line of text in a cell
2 A quick way of displaying formulas
3 Putting a tick into a cell
4 Making an entry fit the cell
5 Linking a text box to data in a cell
6 Formatting non-adjacent areas
7 Using the Drag Copy short cut
8 Using AutoFill to enter data quickly
9 What is a circular reference?
10 What is the difference between Paste and Paste Link?
11 Inserting multiple rows and columns
12 Quickly copying cell formats to other cells or cell ranges
13 Using angled text to improve your presentation
14 Switching rows of cells to columns or columns to rows
15 Putting the title across many cells (Merge and Center)
16 Displaying the date and time
17 Fixing problems with dates
18 Entering numbers as text
19 Calculating with dates
20 What day of the week is a date?
21 Hiding columns
22 Hiding the contents of a cell
23 Improving the format of a table (AutoFormat)
24 Setting how your worksheets will look at the start (Format Style)
25 Creating an automatic backup of your work
26 A quick way of closing all those open files
27 Changing the default folder for Excel to store files

1 Getting more than one line of text in a cell

Press ALT+ENTER to start a new line in the same cell.

Or, if your text is too long to fit in a cell, highlight the cells, and click on **Format, Cells**. Click on the **Alignment** tab and click on **Wrap text**. The text will be displayed on multiple lines.

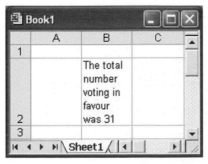

Figure 21.1

2 A quick way of displaying formulas

Hold down the CTRL **+** ` (next to 1 on the keyboard). This will switch to showing formulas. Press these keys again to return to normal mode.

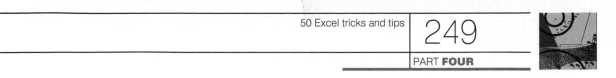

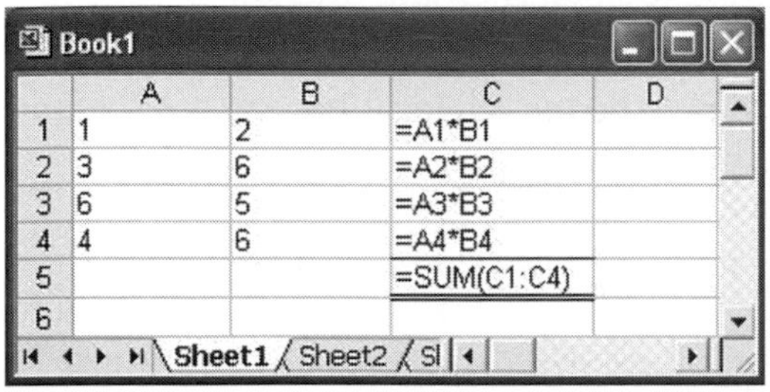

Figure 21.2

3 Putting a tick into a cell

Enter in the cell **=CHAR(252)** and set the font to **Wingdings** font.

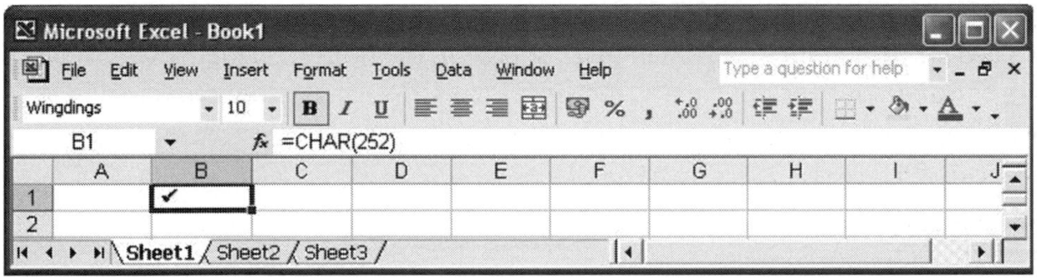

Figure 21.3

4 Making an entry fit the cell

Excel can automatically resize the text to fit into a cell if you don't want the cell to shrink or grow to accommodate an entry.

Highlight the cell(s), click on **Format, Cells, Alignment** and check the **Shrink To Fit** box.

Figure 21.4

5 Linking a text box to data in a cell

You can link a text box so that it displays the contents of a cell. To do this, follow these steps:

(a) Click on the **Text Box** icon on the **Drawing** toolbar, click and drag out a text box on the worksheet.

(b) Click in the formula bar and enter = followed by the cell location, e.g. **=A7** if you want the contents of A7 to be displayed in the text box.

6 Formatting non-adjacent areas

If you want to format groups of cells on a worksheet that are not next to each other, you need to select them. Do this by:

(a) dragging to select the first group of cells;

(b) holding CTRL down and dragging across any other groups of cells.

Use this method if you want to draw a graph of data in non-adjacent cells.

7 Using the Drag Copy short cut

When a cell is selected there is a small black square in the bottom right-hand corner. If you move the cursor over this square, it changes from the usual white cross to a hairline black cross.

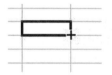

Figure 21.5

If you now drag this cross down to other cells it will copy the contents of the first cell to all the others; it will also make an intelligent guess at a sequence.

Try the operation on a word, a formula, Product 1, a day, a month in a cell.

	A	B	C	D	E
1	Good	=G1*H1	Product 1	Monday	January
2	Good	=G2*H2	Product 2	Tuesday	February
3	Good	=G3*H3	Product 3	Wednesday	March
4	Good	=G4*H4	Product 4	Thursday	April
5	Good	=G5*H5	Product 5	Friday	May

Book1 — Sheet1 / Sheet2 / Sheet3

Figure 21.6

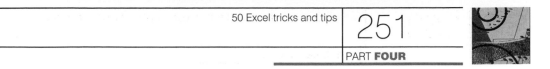

If you enter the first two numbers of a number sequence or a date sequence, highlight both cells and drag down, the sequence continues.

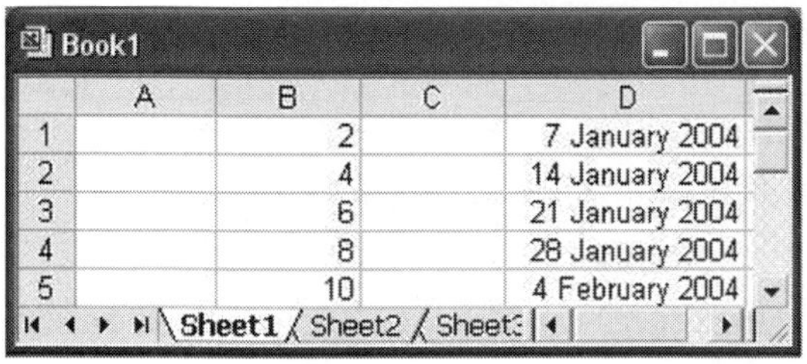

	A	B	C	D
1		2		7 January 2004
2		4		14 January 2004
3		6		21 January 2004
4		8		28 January 2004
5		10		4 February 2004

Sheet1 / Sheet2 / Sheet3

Figure 21.7

8 Using AutoFill to enter data quickly

Another way of performing the same operation is to:

(a) enter the first piece of data in the series;

(b) highlight the cells you wish to fill;

(c) click on **Edit, Fill, Series**;

(d) click on **AutoFill,** enter the **Step value** and then click on **OK.**

9 What is a circular reference?

Type $= \mathbf{A6} + \mathbf{A7}$ into A7.

You will see this error message.

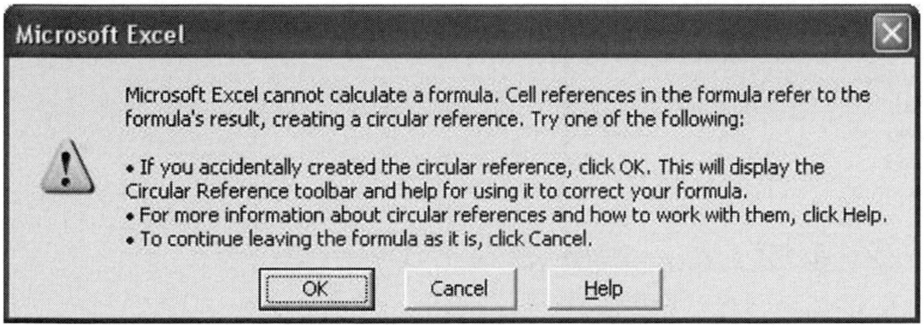

Microsoft Excel

Microsoft Excel cannot calculate a formula. Cell references in the formula refer to the formula's result, creating a circular reference. Try one of the following:

- If you accidentally created the circular reference, click OK. This will display the Circular Reference toolbar and help for using it to correct your formula.
- For more information about circular references and how to work with them, click Help.
- To continue leaving the formula as it is, click Cancel.

OK   Cancel   Help

Figure 21.8

This is because the formula in A7 refers to A7. This error is called a circular reference.

10 What is the difference between Paste and Paste Link?

When you copy data from one cell and paste it into another cell, if the first cell changes the second cell does not change.

By using **Paste Link** you can link the two cells, so that if the first cell is updated, so is the second.

(a) Click on the source cell and click on the **Copy** icon.

(b) Click on the second cell and click on **Edit, Paste Special**.

(c) Click on the **Paste Link** button.

11 Inserting multiple rows and columns

If you need to insert one row, select a row by clicking on the row number, right click and click on **Insert**.

To insert multiples (for example three rows), select three rows, right click and click on **Insert**. Three rows will be inserted. This also works for columns.

12 Quickly copying cell formats to other cells or cell ranges

(a) Click on the cell whose formatting you wish to copy.

(b) Click on **Format Painter** icon (a paintbrush picture on the **Formatting** toolbar).

(c) Click on the cell or cell range you want to copy the formatting to.

Note

To continue formatting to a number of locations double click Format Painter and click the button again when you have finished.

---

13 Using angled text to improve your presentation

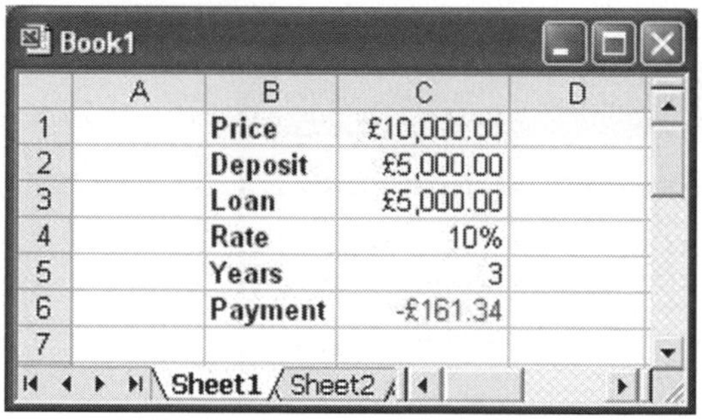

Book1

	A	B	C	D
1		Price	£10,000.00	
2		Deposit	£5,000.00	
3		Loan	£5,000.00	
4		Rate	10%	
5		Years	3	
6		Payment	-£161.34	
7				

Sheet1 / Sheet2

Figure 21.9

To put text at an angle:

(a) highlight the cells B1 to B6 and click on **Format, Cells**;

(b) click on the **Alignment** tab;

(c) enter the required angle or drag the guide-line around the 'clock face'. See Figure 21.10.

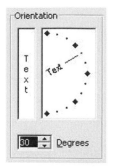

Figure 21.10

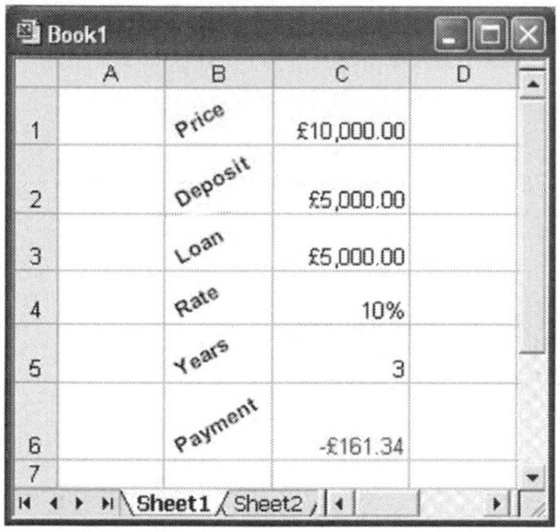

Figure 21.11

Note Angled text loses its sharpness.

14 Switching rows of cells to columns or columns to rows

How can we change from the layout in Figure 21.12 to that in Figure 21.13?

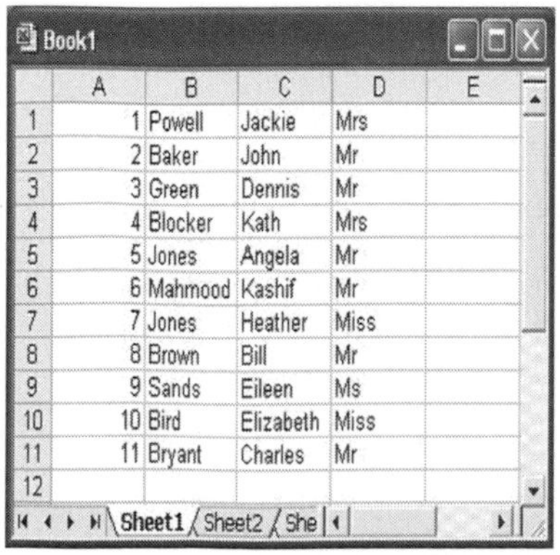

	A	B	C	D	E
1	1	Powell	Jackie	Mrs	
2	2	Baker	John	Mr	
3	3	Green	Dennis	Mr	
4	4	Blocker	Kath	Mrs	
5	5	Jones	Angela	Mr	
6	6	Mahmood	Kashif	Mr	
7	7	Jones	Heather	Miss	
8	8	Brown	Bill	Mr	
9	9	Sands	Eileen	Ms	
10	10	Bird	Elizabeth	Miss	
11	11	Bryant	Charles	Mr	
12					

Figure 21.12

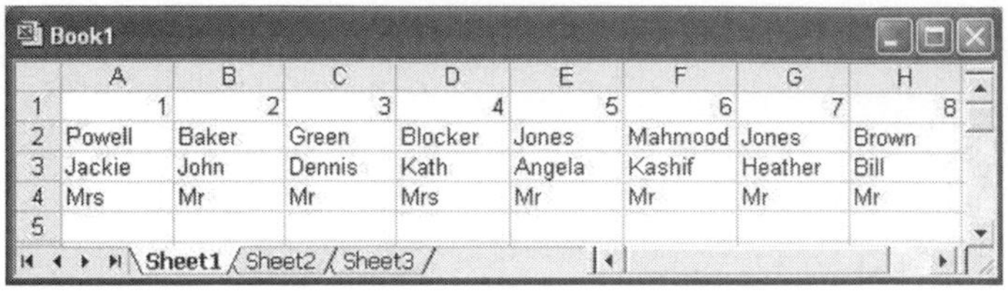

Excel tricks and tips

	A	B	C	D	E	F	G	H
1	1	2	3	4	5	6	7	8
2	Powell	Baker	Green	Blocker	Jones	Mahmood	Jones	Brown
3	Jackie	John	Dennis	Kath	Angela	Kashif	Heather	Bill
4	Mrs	Mr	Mr	Mrs	Mr	Mr	Mr	Mr
5								

Book1 — Sheet1 / Sheet2 / Sheet3

Figure 21.13

(a) Select the cells that you want to switch.

(b) Click on **Edit, Copy**.

(c) Click on the top-left cell of the paste area. The paste area must be outside the copy area. In the example shown in Figure 21.13, a new worksheet has been used.

(d) Click on **Edit, Paste Special**.

(e) Select the **Transpose** check box. Click on **OK**.

15 Putting the title across many cells (Merge and Center)

To center a heading across a range of cells, e.g. A1 to G1, use the Merge and Center icon.

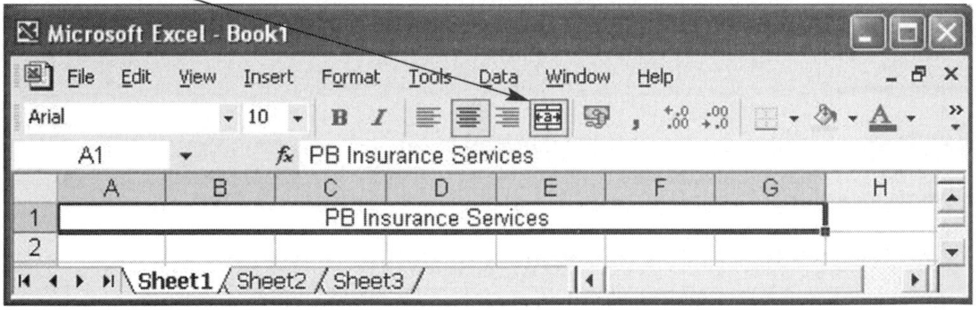

Figure 21.14

(a) Enter the heading into cell A1.

(b) Highlight the cells A1 to G1.

(c) Click on the **Merge and Center** icon.

To remove Merge and Center, click on the **Format Painter** icon and then click on the last merged cell.

16 Displaying the date and time

To enter the date and time into an Excel worksheet:

(a) Click on the required cell.

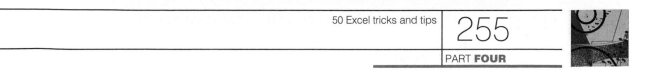

(b) Enter **=TODAY()** for today's date.

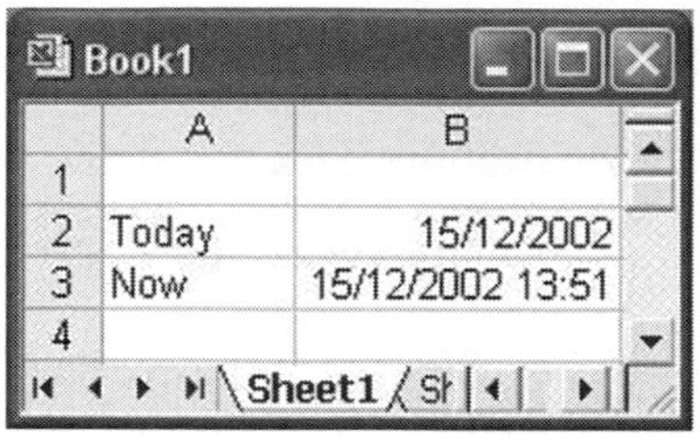

Figure 21.15

(c) Enter **=NOW()** for today's date and the current time.

The format may not be exactly how you require the date.

(d) Use **Format, Cells** to format the date or time as required using the options shown in Figure 21.16.

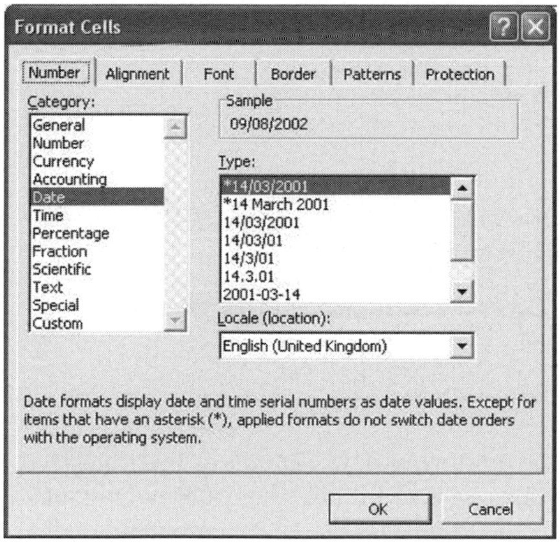

Figure 21.16

Dates and times entered using =TODAY() or =NOW() will be updated when you next open the file.

Hint

You can enter the current date or time quickly:

- ○ To enter the current date in a cell, press CTRL and ; (semi-colon).
- ○ To enter the current time in a cell, press CTRL and : (colon).

Dates and times entered using this method will *NOT* be updated when you next open the file.

Excel tricks and tips

17 Fixing problems with dates

Sometimes the date appears as a number such as 36680. This is because Excel stores dates as numbers in order starting on 1st January 1900 which is stored as 1.

For example, 3rd June 2000 is stored as 36680. To change the number back to a date, click on **Format, Cells** and select **Date**.

18 Entering numbers as text

If you wish to enter a number as a code, e.g. 000262, Excel will store it as a number and only display 262.

To enter 000262, type in an apostrophe first **'000262**. The apostrophe formats the cell to text format. 000262 is displayed and not the apostrophe.

However, the apostrophe is displayed in the formula bar as shown in Figure 21.17.

fx	000262
C	
000262	

Figure 21.17

Similarly, you might have conducted a survey and typed 1-4, 5-8 and 9-12 into three cells. Excel changes them to 1 April, 5 August and 9 December.

This is because Excel has formatted the cells as dates. To prevent this, type an apostrophe at the start of the data, e.g. **'1-4**.

19 Calculating with dates

Use the DATEDIF function to calculate the number of days, months or years between dates, for example to work out how old someone is or for how many days a book has been borrowed.

(a) Put the first date in A1.

(b) Type **=NOW()** in A2.

(c) Type **=DATEDIF(A1,A2,"y")** in A3.

You will see the difference between the two dates in full years.

Use **"m"** for the number of full months in the period and **"d"** for the number of days.

20 What day of the week is a date?

(a) Type a date in A1.

(b) Type **=WEEKDAY(A1)** in A2.

1 means Sunday, 2 means Monday and so on.

21 Hiding columns

Suppose you want to hide all of column C from the user.

(a) Select column C by clicking on the C in the column heading at the top.

(b) Right click anywhere on the column.

(c) Click on **Hide**.

To remove this feature:

(a) Highlight the two columns on either side of the hidden column (B and D).

(b) Right click anywhere on one of these columns.

(c) Click on **Unhide**.

22 Hiding the contents of a cell

(a) Select the cell(s) you wish to hide.

(b) Click on **Format, Cells** and then click on the **Number** tab.

(c) In the **Category** list click on **Custom.**

(d) In the **Type** box select the existing codes and delete.

(e) In the **Type** box enter **;;;** (three semicolons).

Note

To undo this, click on **Format, Cells, Number**. In the **Category** list click on whatever category the cell was before, e.g. General, Number, Currency, Date, etc.

23 Improving the format of a table (AutoFormat)

(a) Click on any cell in a table of data.

(b) Click on **Format, AutoFormat** to format the table.

You will be given a choice of several different formats that you may wish to use.

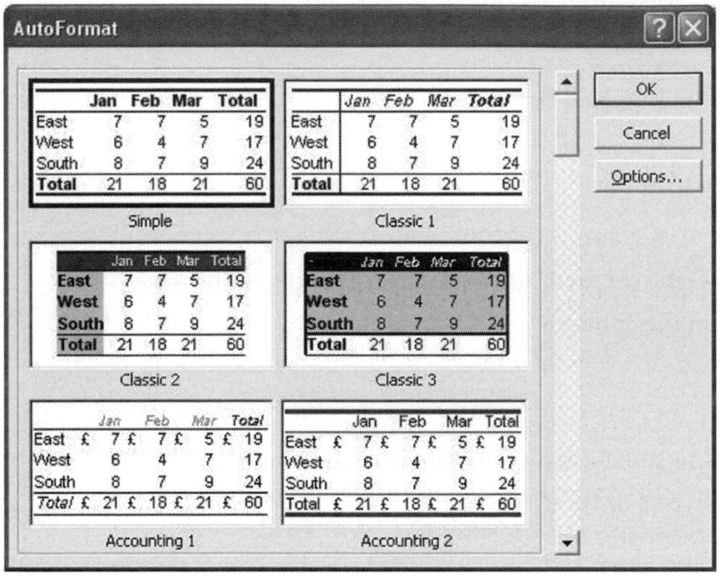

Figure 21.18

Use this function to make your tables look smarter.

24 Setting how your worksheets will look at the start (Format Style)

If you want all your worksheets to be in a different font or colour:

(a) Click on **Format, Style**.

(b) The box in Figure 21.19 appears. Click on **Modify** to change the general format of cells, such as colour of background, borders, fonts, etc.

The style will change for all worksheets in the workbook.

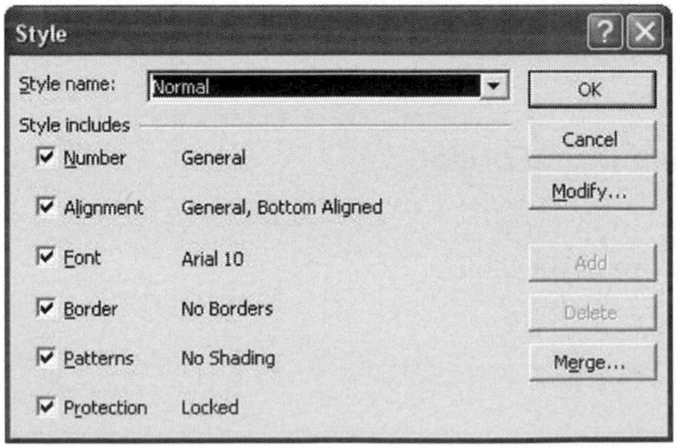

Figure 21.19

25 Creating an automatic backup of your work

Excel allows you to create an automatic backup of a file as you work, so that you cannot lose all your work if the system crashes.

In Excel XP:

(a) Click on **Tools, Options** and click on the **Save** tab.

(b) Set the AutoRecover settings to the appropriate time.

(c) Set the save location as needed.

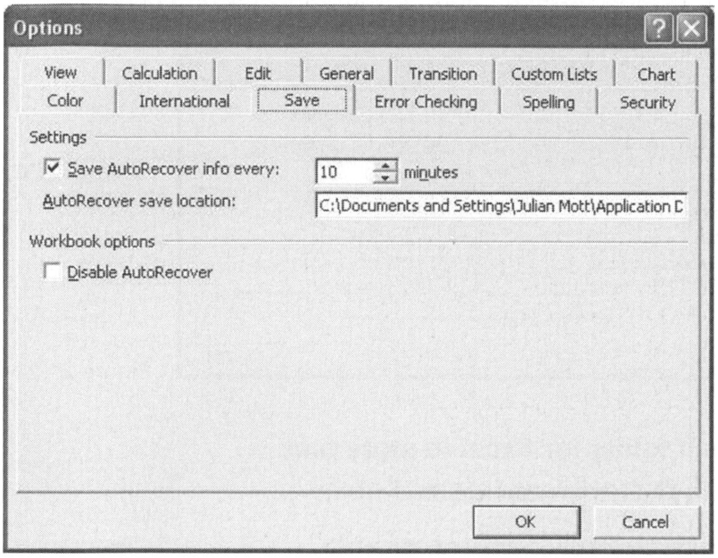

Options

| View | Calculation | Edit | General | Transition | Custom Lists | Chart |
| Color | International | Save | Error Checking | Spelling | Security |

Settings

☑ Save AutoRecover info every: 10 minutes

AutoRecover save location: C:\Documents and Settings\Julian Mott\Application D

Workbook options

☐ Disable AutoRecover

OK   Cancel

Figure 21.20

In previous versions of Excel:

(a) Click on **Tools, AutoSave**.

(b) Check the box and set the file to be saved every 5 minutes.

AutoSave

☑ Automatic Save Every 10 Minutes.   OK

Save Options   Cancel
● Save Active Workbook Only
○ Save All Open Workbooks   Help

☑ Prompt Before Saving

Figure 21.21

Note

AutoSave is an **Add-In** which is not automatically installed with Excel.

If AutoSave isn't on the Tools menu:

(a) Click on **Tools, Add-Ins**.

(b) Check the **AutoSave Add-In** box.

26 A quick way of closing all those open files

Clicking on **File, Close** only closes the active Excel file.

Close all open Excel files by holding down the SHIFT key and clicking on **File, Close All**.

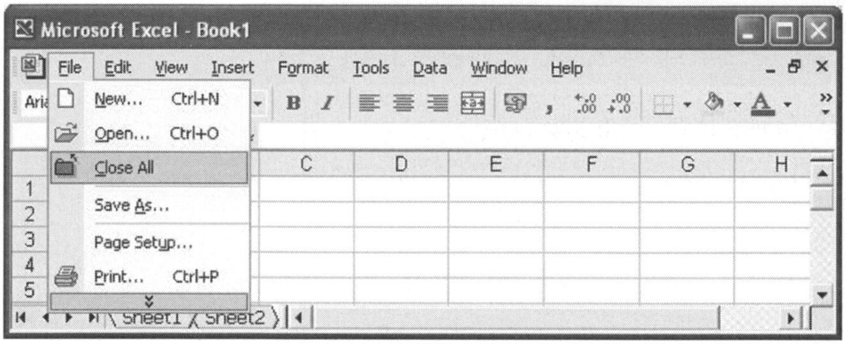

Figure 21.22

27 Changing the default folder for Excel to store files

(a) Click on **Tools, Options** and click on the **General** tab.

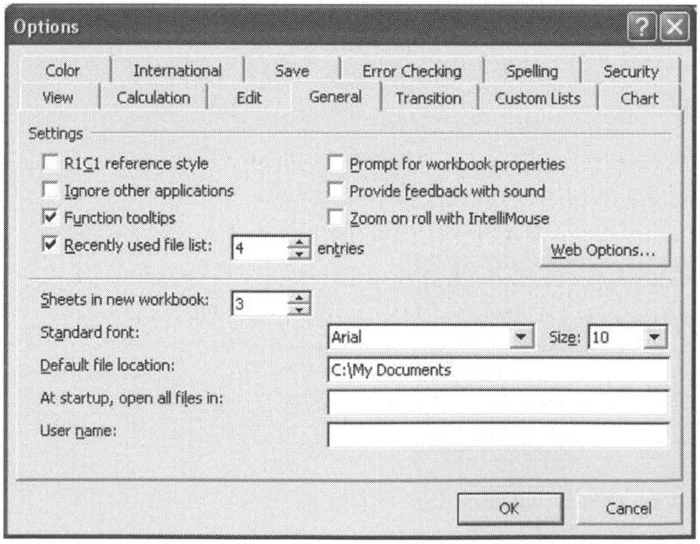

Figure 21.23

(b) Enter the path name of the folder you wish to use in the **Default file location**.

28 Increasing the number of recently used files in the File drop-down menu

(a) Click on **Tools, Options** and click on the **General** tab as in Figure 21.23.

(b) In the **Recently used file list** section, enter the required number of files that you wish to see displayed at the bottom of the file drop-down menu.

29 Adding comments to your work

A comment is a small on-screen 'Post-It' note that you can attach to a cell to tell the user some more information.

If a cell has a comment attached, there is a red triangle in the top right-hand corner of the cell. As you move the cursor over the cell, the comment appears.

	A	B	C	D	E
5		**School Play Ticket Sales**			
6	Day	Time	Adult		
7	Wednesday	evening	45	*First night. Tickets £2.50 adult £3.50 adult*	121
8	Thursday	evening	54		135
9	Friday	evening	52		172
10	Saturday	matinee	92	46	138
11	Saturday	evening	66	106	172

Book1 — Sheet1 / Sheet2

Figure 21.24

To enter a comment:

(a) Click on the cell.

(b) Click on **Insert, Comment**.

(c) Enter the comment.

To delete a comment, right click on the cell and click on **Delete Comment**.

30 Automatically correcting common typing errors (AutoCorrect)

Microsoft Excel has a useful feature called AutoCorrect. Common spelling mistakes are automatically corrected as you type. For example *recieve* would automatically be corrected to *receive*. The word *I* is automatically capitalized.

You can customize it to add your own words using **Tools, AutoCorrect**.

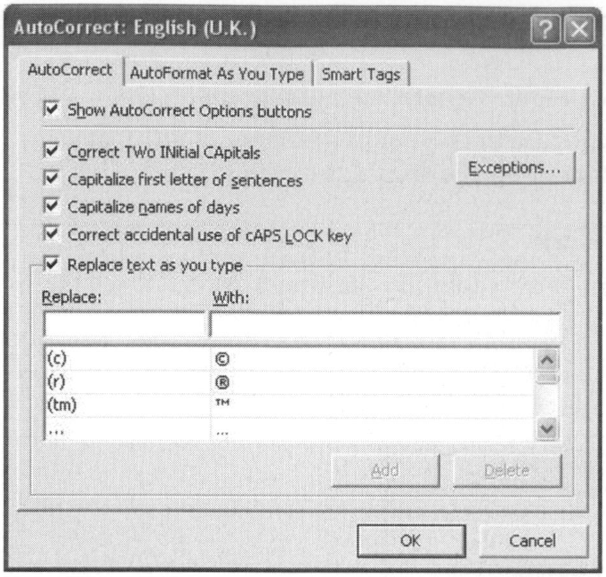

Figure 21.25

Enter the incorrect word and the correct word into the boxes.

Another useful feature of AutoCorrect is if you accidentally leave the CAPS LOCK turned on and type in a name like *sMITH* it automatically changes the word to *Smith* and turns off the CAPS LOCK.

The AutoCorrect feature also exists in Microsoft Word.

31 Switching case

If you want to turn the text in a cell to all upper case (capital letters) you can use the UPPER function, e.g. **=UPPER(D2)** will display the text from D2 in upper case.

There are similar functions called LOWER and PROPER.

LOWER, e.g. **=LOWER(D2)**, turns text into lower case (small letters).

PROPER, e.g. **=PROPER(D2)**, turns all words into proper noun form. (The first letter is in upper case and the rest in lower case.)

32 Customizing your screen output

You can customize your screen output by clicking on **Tools, Options** and clicking on the **View** tab.

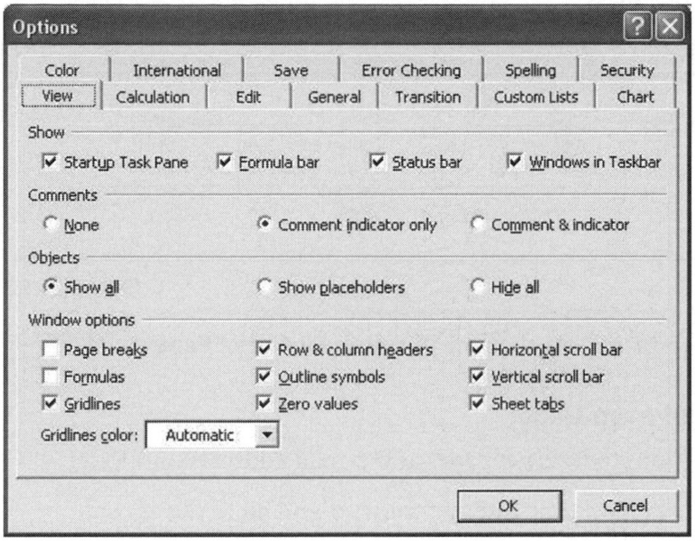

Figure 21.26

Amongst the options available are:

- zero suppression – leaving a cell blank if its value is zero;
- gridline suppression – hiding the gridlines;
- removing the tabs and scroll bars;
- removing the status bar and the formula bar;
- showing the comment all the time, only when the mouse moves over that cell or not showing it at all.

33 Stopping a header row disappearing off the screen (Freeze Panes)

A company has details of customers stored in an Excel worksheet. As they scroll down the page the top line (the header row) disappears.

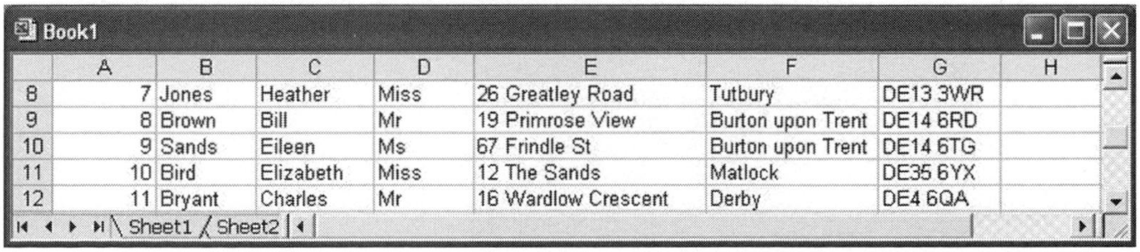

	A	B	C	D	E	F	G	H
8	7	Jones	Heather	Miss	26 Greatley Road	Tutbury	DE13 3WR	
9	8	Brown	Bill	Mr	19 Primrose View	Burton upon Trent	DE14 6RD	
10	9	Sands	Eileen	Ms	67 Frindle St	Burton upon Trent	DE14 6TG	
11	10	Bird	Elizabeth	Miss	12 The Sands	Matlock	DE35 6YX	
12	11	Bryant	Charles	Mr	16 Wardlow Crescent	Derby	DE4 6QA	

Figure 21.27

They want to keep the column headings on the screen. They can do this using **Freeze Panes.**

(a) Click on row header 2 to highlight row 2.

(b) Click on **Window, Freeze Panes**.

	A	B	C	D	E	F	G	H
1	Customer	Surname	First name	Title	Street	Area	Postcode	
9	8	Brown	Bill	Mr	19 Primrose View	Burton upon Trent	DE14 6RD	
10	9	Sands	Eileen	Ms	67 Frindle St	Burton upon Trent	DE14 6TG	
11	10	Bird	Elizabeth	Miss	12 The Sands	Matlock	DE35 6YX	
12	11	Bryant	Charles	Mr	16 Wardlow Crescent	Derby	DE4 6QA	

Book1 — Sheet1 / Sheet2

Figure 21.28

The top line is now locked. To turn it off click on **Window, Unfreeze Panes**.

34 Linking to the internet from Excel

You can include hyperlinks (links to internet pages and e-mail addresses) in Excel.

Clicking on a web page link will load your internet browser and go to the chosen address.

Clicking on an e-mail address will load your e-mail software so that you can type a message.

To enter a hyperlink in older versions of Excel:

(a) Click on **Insert Hyperlink**.

(b) Type the internet address into the top box.

Insert Hyperlink

Link to file or URL:

http://www.yahoo.co.uk   Browse...

Enter or locate the path to the document you want to link to. This can be an Internet address (URL), a document on your hard drive, or a document on your company's network.

Path: http://www.yahoo.co.uk/

Named location in file (optional):

Browse...

If you want to jump to a specific location within the document, such as a bookmark, a named range, a database object, or a slide number, enter or locate that information above.

☑ Use relative path for hyperlink

OK   Cancel

Figure 21.29

Note that the dialogue box is slightly different in Excel XP.

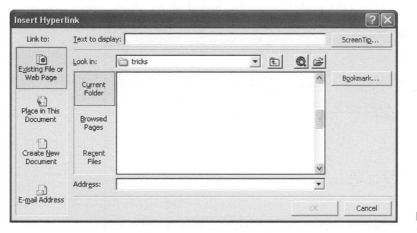

Figure 21.30

When you click on OK the link will be inserted into your spreadsheet. When you move the mouse over the link, the familiar hand appears to show that it is a link.

If you prefer to put the name of the site rather than the address:

(a) type in the site name;

(b) click on **Insert, Hyperlink;**

(c) enter the address as before.

You can choose which you prefer:

| http://www.yahoo.co.uk/ | Yahoo |

Figure 21.31

It is also possible to put in a hyperlink to another location in your file, for example to another worksheet. In Excel 97 or Excel 2000, click on the bottom **Browse** button to get this dialogue box.

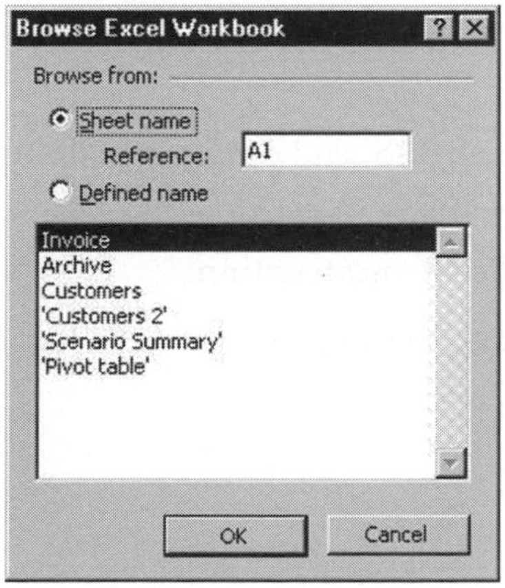

Figure 21.32

You can choose the sheet and the cell you wish to link to. In Excel XP, click on **Place in This Document** and choose the worksheet you want to link to.

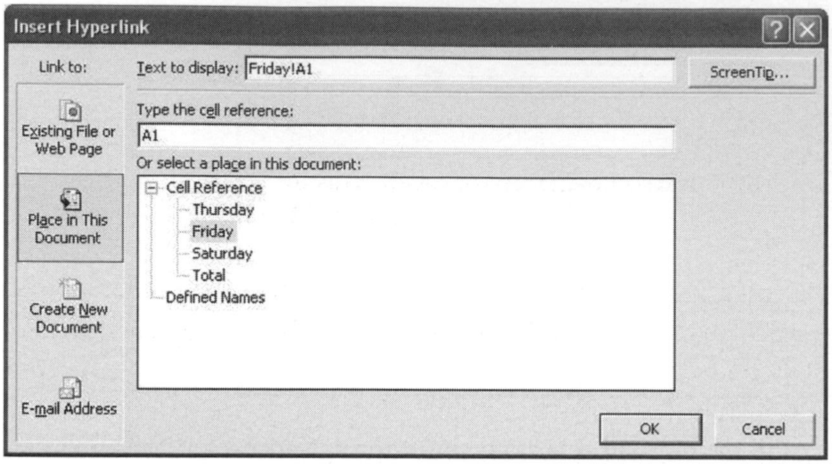

Figure 21.33

35 Combining the contents of two columns

When storing details of customers' names, it is usual to store the data in three different fields: surname, first name and title.

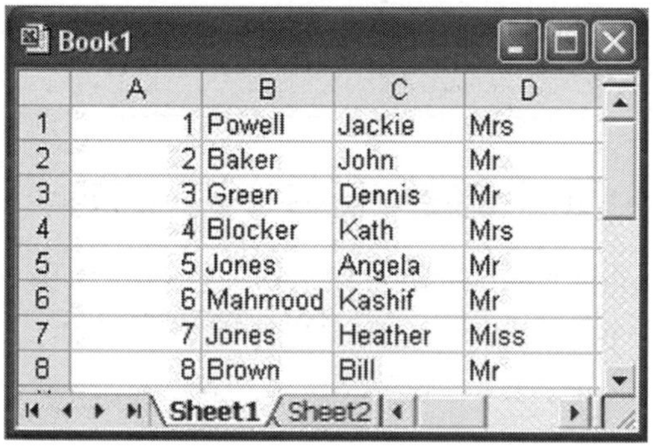

Figure 21.34

This means that we can sort into alphabetical order but can also send out personalized letters. The name on the invoice will be either Mrs Jackie Powell or Mrs J. Powell.

Joining two or more words together into one word is called **Concatenation**.

To do this in Excel use the CONCATENATE function using the ampersand key (&) as follows:

(a) Enter the data in Figure 21.34.

(b) In E1 enter the function = **D1&C1&B1**.

(c) Copy and paste the function down the column.

	A	B	C	D	E
1	1	Powell	Jackie	Mrs	MrsJackiePowell
2	2	Baker	John	Mr	MrJohnBaker
3	3	Green	Dennis	Mr	MrDennisGreen
4	4	Blocker	Kath	Mrs	MrsKathBlocker
5	5	Jones	Angela	Mr	MrAngelaJones

Sheet1 / Sheet2 / Sheet3 /

Figure 21.35

The function joins the text together. You then need to force spaces between the words.

(d) In E1 change the function to **= D1&" "&C1&" "&B1**. (There is a space between the quotation marks.)

(e) Copy and paste the function down the column.

	A	B	C	D	E
1	1	Powell	Jackie	Mrs	Mrs Jackie Powell
2	2	Baker	John	Mr	Mr John Baker
3	3	Green	Dennis	Mr	Mr Dennis Green
4	4	Blocker	Kath	Mrs	Mrs Kath Blocker
5	5	Jones	Angela	Mr	Mr Angela Jones

Sheet1 / Sheet2 / Sheet3 /

Figure 21.36

If we want the name Mrs J. Powell to appear on the invoice, we need to use the LEFT function: **=LEFT(C1,1)**.

This is the first letter of the word in C1. Join the two functions together as follows: **= D1&" "&LEFT(C1,1)&" "&B1**.

Note

There are RIGHT and MID functions as well.

For example

RIGHT(D5,3) will take the three characters at the end of the word(s) in D5.

MID(E40, 5, 8) will take 8 characters from the middle of the text in E40, starting at the 5th character.

36 A table stores names as John Smith. How do I split this into John and Smith?

Suppose you have names in cells A1 to A3 as shown in Figure 21.37.

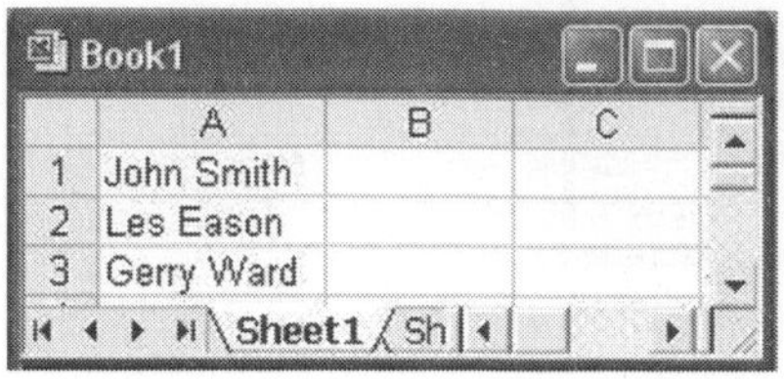

	A	B	C
1	John Smith		
2	Les Eason		
3	Gerry Ward		

Figure 21.37

(a) Highlight the cells and click on **Data, Text to Columns...**

(b) A wizard will start. Click on **Delimited** and click on **Next**.

(c) Check the **Space** box as shown in Figure 21.38.

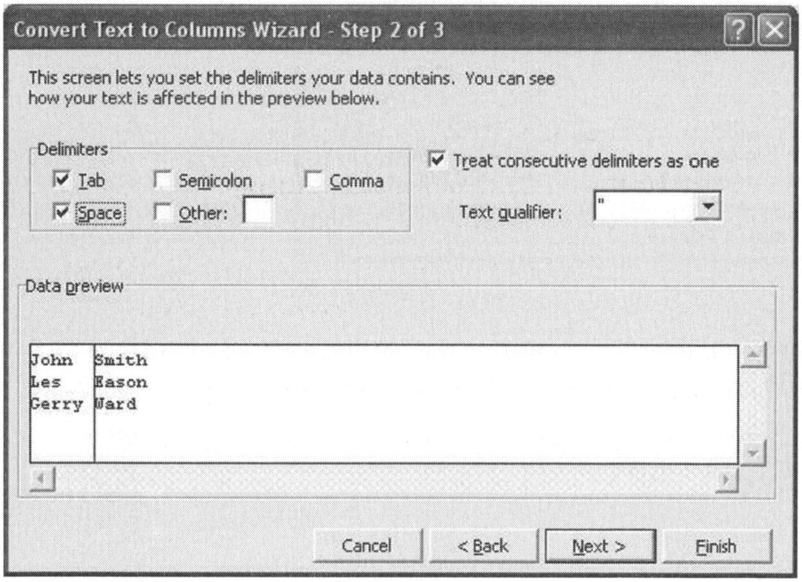

Convert Text to Columns Wizard - Step 2 of 3

This screen lets you set the delimiters your data contains. You can see how your text is affected in the preview below.

Delimiters
- ☑ Tab   ☐ Semicolon   ☐ Comma   ☑ Treat consecutive delimiters as one
- ☑ Space ☐ Other: [   ]   Text qualifier: [" ▼]

Data preview

John	Smith
Les	Eason
Gerry	Ward

[Cancel] [< Back] [Next >] [Finish]

Figure 21.38

(d) Click on **Finish**. The result is shown in Figure 21.39.

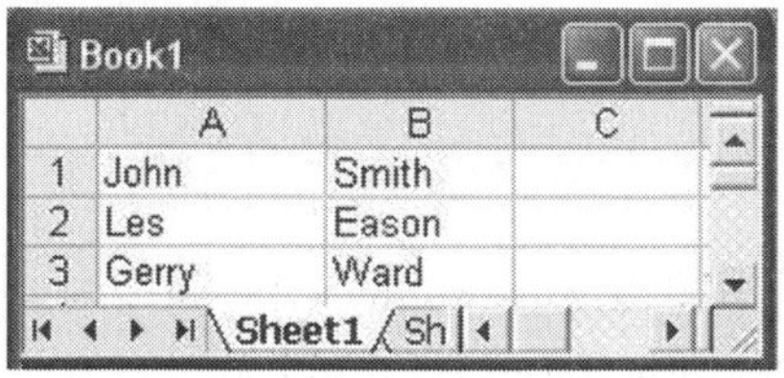

	A	B	C
1	John	Smith	
2	Les	Eason	
3	Gerry	Ward	

Figure 21.39

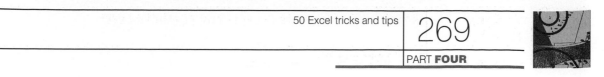

37 Password protecting your files

It is easy to add a password to an Excel file to prevent unauthorized access. When you save your file, click on **File, Save As...**

Then click on **Options**. (In Excel XP **Tools, General Options**.) If you wish to add a password, type it in the top box.

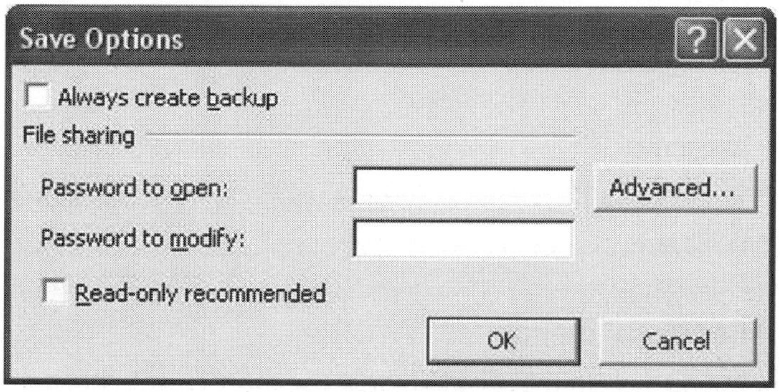

Save Options

☐ Always create backup
File sharing

Password to open: Advanced...

Password to modify:

☐ Read-only recommended

OK   Cancel

Figure 21.40

You will be asked to retype the password as verification.

Every time you load this file, you will be asked for the password. But be careful. If you forget your password, you will not be able to access your file.

If this doesn't work, there are companies that produce software to recover such files. You can download them from the internet. They are *not* free. Try sites like http://www.lostpassword.com/

This just proves that Excel passwords aren't as secure as you might expect.

Remember that passwords are case sensitive so check that CAPS LOCK is turned off.

38 Using help

Online help is available by pressing F1. Type in the keyword and search for advice.

Excel 2000 and Excel XP also have an 'Answer wizard' which enables you to type in a question and get help.

There is a separate but similar online help for Visual Basic.

39 Removing the Office Assistant

The Office Assistant is an on-screen animation in Office 2000 and Office XP that is supposed to be helpful. Many people find it annoying when it suddenly appears without any apparent reason.

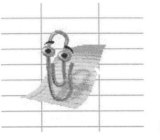

Figure 21.41

To turn off the Office Assistant when it appears:

(a) Right click on the Office Assistant.

(b) Click on **Options**.

(c) Uncheck **Use the Office Assistant**.

40 Turning on and off 'intelligent' menus

Excel 2000 has an 'intelligent' menu system that displays only the most recent choices. This can be quite annoying as the positions of items on the menus are constantly changing.

To turn off the 'intelligent' menus, click on **Tools, Customize**. Click on the **Options** tab. Uncheck the box for **Menus show recently used commands first**.

Figure 21.42

Recheck this box to turn the intelligent menu back on.

This feature has been removed in Excel XP.

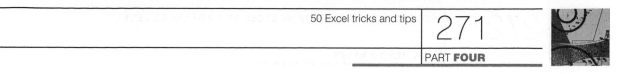

41 Using Auditing Tools for debugging (Trace)

The **Trace** command helps you with debugging as it tells you which cells will change when you change another cell. These cells are **dependent** on the first cell.

(a) Click on a cell.

(b) Click on **Tools, Auditing, Trace Dependents**.

(In Excel XP, turn on the Formula Auditing toolbar and use the Trace Dependents icon.)

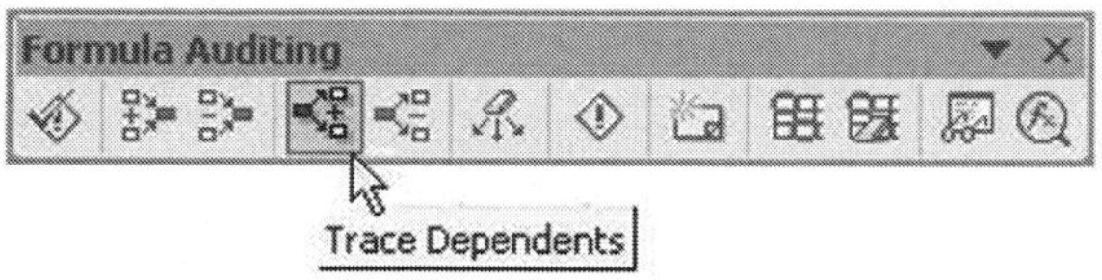

Figure 21.43

(c) A blue arrow appears pointing to the dependent cell(s). You can repeat the process for this cell to see if it too has any dependants.

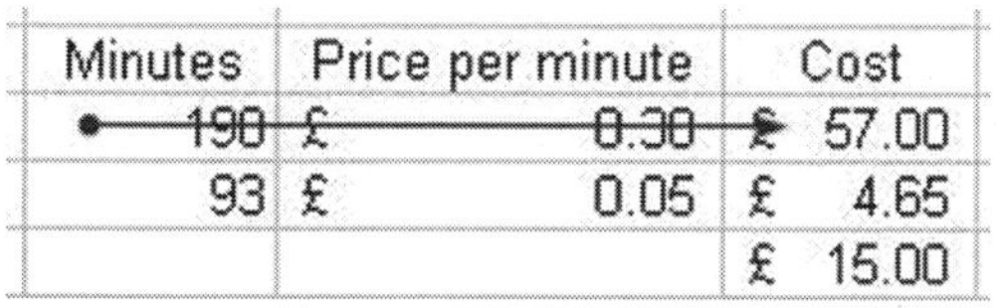

Minutes	Price per minute	Cost
190 £	0.30	£ 57.00
93 £	0.05	£ 4.65
		£ 15.00

Figure 21.44

Changing the 190 will change the amount in the cell two columns to its right.

Click on **Tools, Auditing, Trace Precedents** (or use the Trace Precedents icon) to find any cells that affect a cell containing a formula.

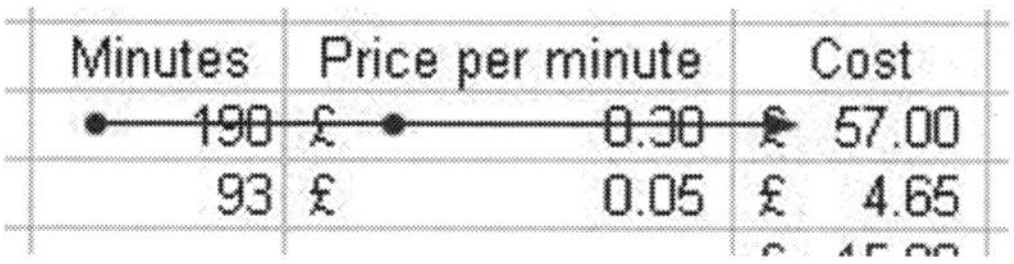

Minutes	Price per minute	Cost
190 £	0.30	£ 57.00
93 £	0.05	£ 4.65

Figure 21.45

Remove the arrows with **Tools, Auditing, Remove All Arrows**.

42 A quick way of entering the name of a range of cells (Paste name)

If you are using a named range of cells in a function such as SUM or VLOOKUP, you do not need to type in the name. Just press F3 to get a list of names available.

43 Using Go To Special

You can use Go To, Special to highlight special cells on your workbook, e.g. cells with formulas, cells with validation, cells with comments or cells with conditional formatting.

(a) Click on **Edit, Go To**.

(b) Click on the **Special** button.

(c) Select the type of cell required.

44 Highlighting changed cells

Click on **Tools, Track Changes, Highlight Changes** and check **Track changes while editing**.

Cells that are changed have a blue triangle in the top left-hand corner.

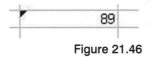

Figure 21.46

You can choose whether to accept or reject these changes by clicking on **Tools, Track Changes, Accept or Reject Changes**.

45 Splitting panes

Click on **Window, Split** to split your window into four sections. You can scroll on each section separately.

This is very useful if you want to work on two or more parts of the same worksheet that are not close to each other.

Click on **Window, Remove Split** to return to the conventional screen.

46 What is a workspace?

You can group two or more workbooks together by saving them as a workspace file.

A workspace file (*.**xlw**) saves details of all open workbooks and their locations, window sizes, and screen positions in one file. To save a workspace:

(a) Open all the workbooks you want to group together.

(b) Position the workbook windows as you want them to appear when you open them.

(c) Click on the **File, Save Workspace**.

Note   The workspace file is a very small file as it only saves details about the stored workbooks and not the contents of the workbooks themselves.

47 Useful web sites

There are many internet sites offering tips and hints in using Excel. As with all internet sites, the quality varies, good sites can be hard to find and sites are appearing and disappearing all the time.

Go to any search engine and search on *Excel Hints*. Here are just a few examples:

(a) **http://www.microsoft.com/office/** is full of information tips, tricks, and how-to articles and frequently asked questions for Microsoft Office programs like Excel.

(b) **http://support.microsoft.com/** has technical support information and self-help tools for Microsoft products and a link to the knowledge base below.

(c) **http://search.support.microsoft.com/kb/c.asp** The Microsoft knowledge base. Allows you to search Microsoft's knowledge base of information about their software.

(d) **http://www.pcworld.com/howto/index/0,00.asp** has lots of good tips from issues of *PC World* magazine. Search on Excel in the **How-To** section.

(e) At **http://www.finance-analyst.com** there is a monthly newsletter with spreadsheet tips and hints.

(f) At Alan's Excel Goodies (**http://www.barasch.com/excel/**) there is information on Excel Visual Basic for Applications with code examples, frequently asked questions and Excel links. Lots of information on formulas. Very useful.

(g) Free answers to your questions on Excel are offered by **http://www.allexperts.com/getExpert.asp?Category=1059**

(h) **http://www.aeverett.btinternet.co.uk/tips_excel.htm** Lots of tips about Excel.

(i) **http://www.excel97.com/hints_01.htm** You can download an Excel file of tips.

48 Switching between relative and absolute references

A relative reference is something like:
=SUM(C6:C10)

An absolute reference (which doesn't change when cells are copied) is something like:
=SUM($C$6:$C$9)

To switch between the two automatically and so avoid having to enter the $ signs:

(a) Enter the formula with relative references.

(b) Highlight the formula in the formula bar.

(c) Press the F4 key.

If you press F4 again, only the rows are set as absolute references:
=SUM(C$6:C$9)

Press F4 again for the columns to be set as absolute references:
=SUM($C6:$C9)

Press F4 again to return to relative references.

49 How can I change data just by clicking on it?

Is it possible to change data in a cell just by clicking on it? For example, in the school play file **Play**, can I set it up so that if I click on a cell that seat becomes sold? Then if I click again the seat becomes vacant.

We will set this up for the Thursday sheet on the Play file.

(a) Load the file **Play**.

(b) Load the Visual Basic Editor (ALT + F11).

(c) Make sure the Project Explorer window is visible. (**View, Project Explorer.**)

(d) Double click on **Sheet 1 (Thursday)**. The VB window opens as in Figure 21.47.

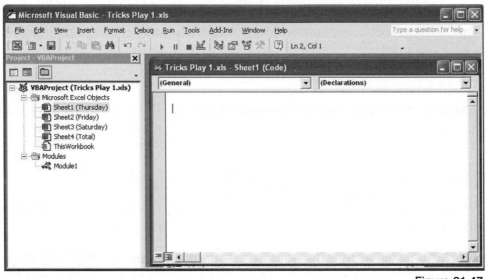

Figure 21.47

(e) Click on the first drop-down arrow and select **Worksheet**. The second drop-down box should display **SelectionChange**.

```
Private Sub Worksheet_SelectionChange(ByVal Target As Range)
On Error Resume Next
If (ActiveCell.Value = 1) Then
ActiveCell.Value = ""
Else:
If (ActiveCell.Value = "") Then
ActiveCell.Value = 1
End If
End If
End Sub
```

Figure 21.48

(f) Type these lines between the **Private Sub Worksheet** line and the **End Sub** line as shown in Figure 21.48.

```
On Error Resume Next
If (ActiveCell.Value = 1) Then
ActiveCell.Value = ""
Else:
If (ActiveCell.Value = "") Then
ActiveCell.Value = 1
End If
End If
```

> There should be two identical lines here

This coding checks if the value of the active cell is 1. If it is, it changes it to a blank. It also checks if the value is blank. If it is, it changes it to a 1.

(g) Click on the View Microsoft Excel icon to switch back to the sheet and try it out.

(h) Do the same for the Friday and Saturday worksheets.

50 Changing the status bar and caption text

Try this macro.

```
Sub display()
Application.Caption = "St Mary' s School Play"
Application.DisplayStatusBar = True
Application.StatusBar = "Project by L.J.Smith ©2003"
End Sub
```

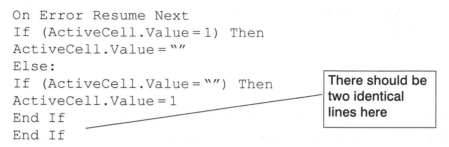

Figure 21.49

Excel displays the file name after the Caption Text, in this case **play**. Clever use of file naming can give the Caption more meaning.

PART FIVE

Appendix

⊕ Appendix

- ○ Excel glossary of terms
- ○ Excel toolbars
- ○ Keyboard shortcuts in Excel
- ○ Excel error messages
- ○ Taking screen shots
- ○ Coursework requirements of the different examination boards

---

Excel glossary of terms

Absolute reference	An **absolute reference** is one that will not change if a formula is copied to a different cell. It is of the form **$B$7**.
Active cell	The **active cell** is the one that has been selected. It is shown with a thick black border.
Advanced filter	The **advanced filter** function is a filter that enables to user to search data based on complex criteria.
AutoFilter	The **AutoFilter** is a simple filter for selected records on simple criteria.
Auto_close	The **auto_close** macro is a macro that runs automatically when a file is closed.
Auto_open	The **auto_open** macro is a macro that runs automatically when a file is opened.
AutoSum	The **AutoSum** function is used to add the contents of chosen cells.
Button	A **button** or **command button** is a small rectangle on the screen. Click on the button to run a macro.
Chart	A **chart** is a graph in Microsoft Excel.
Check box	A **check box** is a small box on the screen that can be either selected or not selected. Clicking on a check box puts a little tick in the box. This is called **checking**. Clicking again to remove the tick is called **unchecking**.

Combo box	A **combo box** offers the user a choice. Clicking on the combo box displays the choices available in a list. One of these choices can be selected. It can also be called a drop-down box.
Comment	A **comment** is a way of adding extra information about a cell. The text appears on a small 'Post-it' note called the comment box.
Dialogue box	A **dialogue box** (or in American English a dialog box) is a box on the screen that enables the user to select choices and/or enter data.
Drop-down box	See combo box.
Formula	A **formula** is an equation that performs calculations on values in your worksheet. All formulas begin with =, e.g. **= H4+H5.**
Formula bar	The **formula bar** is a box on the Excel screen, beneath the toolbars and above the column headings. The value of the selected cell or its formula appears in this box and can be edited here.
Front end	A **front end** is the name given to a user-friendly interface that appears on the screen when the file is loaded. Usually it will give the user a menu of options.
Function	A **function** is a built-in calculation in Excel, e.g. SUM, MAX, MIN and IF. A function can be used in a formula, e.g. **= SUM(H4:H5).**
Gridlines	The **gridlines** are (usually grey) lines dividing up the cells. You can choose whether or not to display and print the gridlines.
Legend	The **legend** is the key on an Excel chart.
List box	A **list box** is similar to a combo box; a list box displays the choices available in a list format. The user can scroll down to see additional choices.
Lookup	**Lookup** is an Excel function that looks up values in a table.
Macro	A **macro** is a program that stores a series of Microsoft Excel commands so that they can be executed as a single command.
Message box	A **message box** is an on-screen dialogue box, usually giving the user some information.
Named cells	It is possible to give a cell or a range of cells a name. This makes it easier to refer to these cells.
Nested IF	Including one or more IF statements inside another IF statement to give more than two choices.
Option button	An **option button** is used for choosing one from a list of options. You can select only one option button at a time. Also called a radio button.
Relative reference	A **relative reference** in a formula stores the position of a cell relative to the cell that contains the formula. When copied it will change depending on the cell it is copied to.

Scenario	A **scenario** is a set of values that are saved in a worksheet. Several different groups of values can be created and saved.
Scroll bar	The **vertical scroll bar** appears on the right-hand side of the screen, to enable the user to move up and down a worksheet. The **horizontal scroll bar** at the bottom right of the screen enables the user to move to the right or left in a worksheet. It is possible to add your own scroll bar, linked to a cell, to increase or decrease the value in the cell.
Spinner	A **spinner** consists of two arrows on the screen; one pointing up, the other down. Clicking on the up arrow increases a value in a cell, clicking the down arrow decreases it.
Start-up folder	Whenever Microsoft Excel is loaded, any files in this folder will be opened automatically.
Status bar	A horizontal bar near the bottom of the screen that displays useful information about a selected command or an operation in progress, e.g. the status bar shows whether CAPS LOCK has been pressed or if you are recording a macro.
Tabs	The names of the different worksheets in a workbook appear on **tabs** at the bottom of the screen. To move to another worksheet, click on the tab.
Template	A **template** is a special sort of workbook that is used as the basis for other workbooks. An Excel template is stored in the form *.xlt.
Text wrap	Fitting text on to multiple lines so that it fits into one cell.
Toolbar	A **toolbar** is a row of icons, usually at the top of the screen.
UserForm	A **UserForm** is a dialogue box that enables you to run macros, perform other operations and enter data. It could be used as part of an automated front end.
Visual Basic	**Microsoft Visual Basic** is Microsoft Excel's own programming language. Macros can be written in this language or recorded.
Workbook	A **workbook** is a standard Microsoft Excel file. Workbooks can contain many **worksheets**, so that related information can be stored on different worksheets in a single file. A workbook is stored in the form *.xls.
Worksheet	**Worksheets** are the main feature of Microsoft Excel. They are the documents used to store and work with data. They consist of a grid of cells in rows and columns. They are also called a **spreadsheet** or just a **sheet**. A worksheet is part of a **workbook**.

Excel toolbars

The Excel toolbars that you are most likely to use are shown below:

Standard toolbar

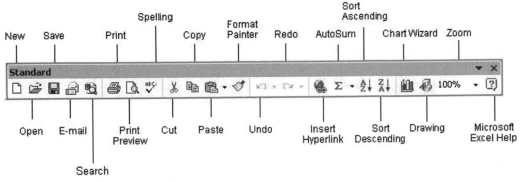

Figure 22.1

Formatting toolbar

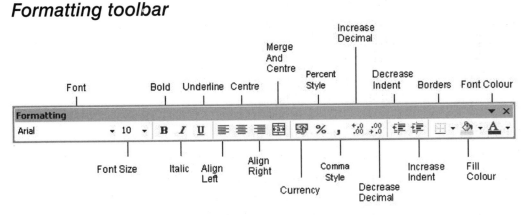

Figure 22.2

Drawing toolbar

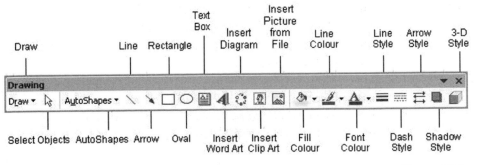

Figure 22.3

Picture toolbar

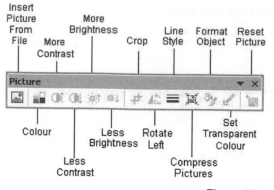

Figure 22.4

Pivot table

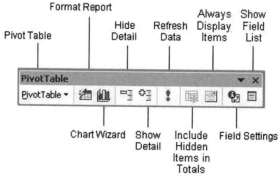

Figure 22.5

Chart

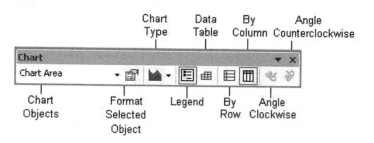

Figure 22.6

Forms

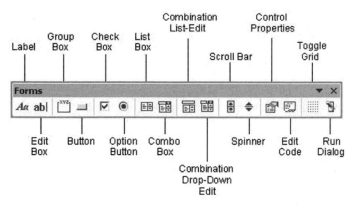

Figure 22.7

Visual Basic

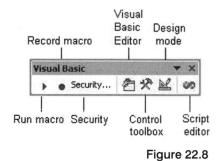

Figure 22.8

Keyboard shortcuts in Excel

There are several keyboard short cuts to help you move around the screen in Excel and perform other common tasks. Here are some of the most useful.

KEYSTROKE	ACTION
HOME	Changes active cell to column A in the same row
CTRL + HOME	Changes active cell to A1
CTRL + END	Changes active cell to the bottom right of all cells used
PAGE DOWN	Moves down one page
PAGE UP	Moves up one page
ALT + PAGE DOWN	Moves right one page

Keyboard shortcuts in Excel – *continued*

KEYSTROKE	ACTION
ALT + PAGE UP	Moves left one page
CTRL + PAGE DOWN	Moves to the next worksheet
CTRL + PAGE UP	Moves to the previous worksheet
F3	Pastes a name (of a range of cells) into a formula
F4	Repeats last action
F5	Go to. Then type in the cell required, e.g. H6
SHIFT + ENTER	Enters data and moves up one row
SHIFT + F2	Inserts a comment
SHIFT + F5	Find
SHIFT + F11	Inserts a new worksheet
SHIFT + SPACEBAR	Selects current row
CTRL + SPACEBAR	Selects current column
CTRL + A	Selects entire worksheet
CTRL + 1	Format cells
CTRL + 7	Toggle standard toolbar on and off
CTRL + Z	Undo
CTRL + X	Cut
CTRL + C	Copy
CTRL + V	Paste
CTRL + K	Insert a hyperlink
CTRL + F9	Minimize current window
CTRL + F10	Maximize current window
ALT + F1	Draw graph of selected cells
ALT + F8	Run a macro
ALT + F11	Load Visual Basic Editor
ALT + =	AutoSum. (The same as clicking the AutoSum icon)
ALT + '	Displays the Style format
ALT + ENTER	Adds another line to the cell
CTRL + ;	Enter current date
CTRL + :	Enter current time
CTRL + ` (next to 1 on keyboard)	Toggle between displaying values and displaying formulas
CTRL + SHIFT + _	Remove all borders
CTRL + SHIFT + O	Select all cells with comments

Excel error messages

ERROR MESSAGE	WHAT IT MEANS
#####	The column is not wide enough to display the number stored. Make your column wider.
#VALUE!	A cell contains text when it is expected to contain a number. This cell is probably in a formula that cannot be calculated. Check the formula.
#DIV/0!	A formula involves division by zero or a blank cell. Check the formula.
#NAME?	The formula refers to a named range of cells that does not exist. Check the formula.
#N/A	A formula refers to a cell that does not contain the required information, for example in a LOOKUP. Check the formula.
#REF!	This occurs when a cell reference in a formula is not valid. Possibly caused by reference to a cell that has been deleted.
#NUM!	A problem has occurred with a number in a formula, for example the number may be too large or too small.
#NULL!	A formula refers to an incorrect cell reference. Probably caused by typing errors in entering the reference.

Taking screen shots

Screen shots of your system in action are vital both to prove that the system is working properly and to include in the user guide and technical instructions.

Using Windows Paint

To get a screen shot in Windows, press the **Print Screen** key on the keyboard. This puts the whole screen into the Windows clipboard.

You can then use **Edit, Paste** to paste the screen shot into your work.

The steps are:

1   Press the **Print Screen key** to capture the screen shot.

2   Switch to **Windows Paint.**

3   Click on **Edit, Paste.**

4   You may be told your image is too big and asked if you would like to expand the image. Click on **Yes.**

5   Save the image. (In *Windows 98* or later, you can save the image as a much smaller file by saving it as a **jpg** or a **gif**.)

6   Insert this image in your document.

If you only need to display part of a screen shot you will need to **crop** it. Cropping means cutting unwanted parts from the top, bottom or sides of a picture. Cropped pictures are smaller and so use less disk space.

Using Paint Shop Pro

Image manipulation software like *Paint Shop Pro* is ideal for screen shots, offering different options such as easy cropping of images and reducing the number of colours in an image to 16 or 256 to reduce the file size.

Paint Shop Pro also offers a screen capture function, enabling you to capture the whole screen or part of the screen and include the cursor if needed.

1   Before capturing the image, you must set your preferences using the Capture Setup dialogue box shown in Figure 22.9. Click on **File, Import, Screen Capture, Setup**. (In older versions of Paint Shop Pro click on **Capture, Setup**.)

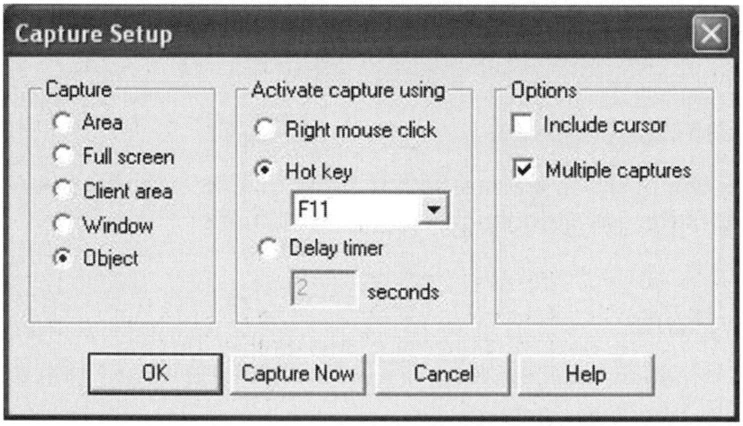

Figure 22.9

2   Click on the required **Capture** type. The capture type determines which area of the screen will be copied.

Area	Select a rectangular portion of the screen
Full Screen	Copy the entire screen
Client Area	Copy the input area of the active window
Window	Copy the entire active window
Object	Copy a window feature or group of features

3   Click on the way you want the screen capture to operate. Captures can be activated by using
- o the right mouse button;
- o a hot key;
- o a timer delay.

There is an option to include the cursor or not. If you choose to include the cursor make sure it is in the correct position before activating the capture.

4   Click on the **OK** Button to close the dialogue box and save the capture set-up settings.

5   To activate the screen capture, click on **File, Import, Screen Capture, Start**, press SHIFT + C, or click on the **Start Capture** icon.

(In older versions of Paint Shop Pro click on **Capture, Start**.)

Paint Shop Pro minimizes and its button appears in the taskbar.

6   Open the image or feature to be captured.

7   Right click or press the hot key that you chose during the set-up.

8   If you chose **Area**, you will need to drag over the required part of the screen.

Paint Shop Pro will reopen with the screen capture.

Coursework requirements of the different examination boards

Introduction

The following section offers guidance on these issues:

- o structure of the AS, A2 and VCE qualifications;
- o pointers to the examination board modules/units supported in this book;
- o assessment criteria currently used by the different examination boards.

Course structure for AS and A2

All three examining boards, AQA, OCR and Edexcel, offer Advanced Subsidiary (AS) and Advanced (A) Level qualifications in Information and Communications Technology (ICT).

The AS level is a qualification in its own right or can be the first half of the A level. With all the boards, the AS course consists of 3 units, two are examined by written papers and the third unit is a coursework submission.

The full A level is made up of the AS units plus three more units called A2. The first two A2 units are again examined by written papers and the third unit is again coursework.

The information in this book can be used to support the following coursework units where students are required to provide an ICT solution based on the use of **appropriate applications software**.

AQA

Module 3 (AS) ✓

This module counts for 40% of the AS level mark and 20% of the A level mark. Candidates are expected to tackle a task-related problem using the facilities of one piece of **generic software**.

Module 6 (A2) ✓

Candidates are required to research a realistic problem for which there must be a *real end-user*. The solution may be provided by **generic application software**. This module is 20% of the A level mark.

OCR

Unit 2513 (AS) ✓

This unit consists of structured practical ICT tasks set by the board. Candidates are required to base a solution on the use of an **appropriate applications package**. This unit of assessment counts for 40% of the AS level mark and 20% of the A level mark.

Unit 2516 (A2) ✓

This unit requires candidates to identify a well-defined problem, involving a third party user and to generate a solution using **applications software** as chosen by the candidate. This module is 20% of the A level mark.

Edexcel

Unit 3 (AS) consists of two coursework tasks worth 40% of the AS assessment.

Task 1 (16%) ✗ is a written report/study of an ICT administration process.

Task 2 (24%) ✓ requires the student to produce and document an ICT solution to a significant problem using a standard **commercial application generator**.

Unit 6 (A2) consists of two coursework tasks worth 40% of the A2 assessment.

Task 3 ✗ is a written report on ICT issues.

Task 4 ✗ requires the student to produce and document an ICT solution using event-driven object-based programming.

Course structure for VCE

All three examining boards, AQA, OCR and Edexcel, offer Advanced Subsidiary (AS) and Advanced Vocational Certificate of Education (VCE) qualifications in Information and Communications Technology (ICT).

For Advanced Subsidiary VCE candidates must take the following units:

Unit 1: Presenting Information
Unit 2: ICT Serving Organizations
Unit 3: **Spreadsheet Design** ✓

In Unit 3 candidates are expected to design and test spreadsheet solutions to specified problems. The requirements will require the use of some of the more complex spreadsheet facilities. The unit is assessed through portfolio work.

For Advanced VCE, candidates must take the same Advanced Subsidiary units plus 3 others.

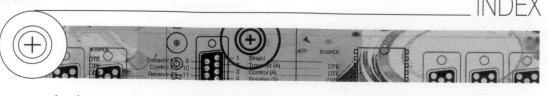

Index to *Spreadsheet* Projects